DO YOU DREAM?

DO
YOU
DREAM?

TONY CRISP

A Dutton **dep** *Paperback*

NEW YORK
E. P. DUTTON & CO., INC.
1972

'In this age brothers, we are almost through the veil that has hid us from ourselves. Come, let us break through!'

'But where is The Guru who will teach us? Where will we find God and the ancient mysteries; and how may we find our ageless one who knows all life?'

'Brothers, they are as close to you as your dreams, and as available as your own sleep. Let us venture in.'

Without the grace of THAT this book
could not have been written.

TO

L.R.C.

The unborn son of my dream.

First published 1972 by E. P. Dutton & Co., Inc.
All rights reserved. Printed in the U.S.A.

FIRST EDITION

Copyright © 1971 by Tony Crisp

SBN 0-525-47326-2

CONTENTS

ONE

What did you dream last night?

'I was in a large, old house. It was pleasant, and interesting, being like an old "folly". It had passages leading off all over the place that one could explore. I was being led up the stairs by a very wilful child. It wanted to explore the house, and was dragging me with it. As we went up the stairs, a man came out of a door and walked down past us. He looked at me as if to say, "Don't go up"; or, "If you go up, be prepared." He looked like a caretaker, but was very indistinct and shadowy.

'The child led me on up however into what was like a loft where I had never been before. It was attached to, yet somehow distinct from the rest of the house. Also it was very light and filled with ancient books and objects. I looked at them and felt that there was something oriental and mysterious about them. Somehow they seemed like a treasure, all dusty, but full of wisdom about life.

'Then the child went to a door that was split in two halves, a higher and lower. It could not get through the lower, but went out the top half.'

Yes, of course, it is only an account of a dream. An experience in that strange inner world we travel in sleep. A wandering along what at first sight appears as a senseless footpath of thoughts and feelings. Some people are certain they never dream, but experiments on sleeping people prove that everyone dreams. Even if we do dream, however, what is the point? Again, painstaking research has come to our aid in answering that question. All dreaming is accompanied by eye movements. Having discovered this, researchers were able to wake those being tested each time they began to dream. The result was that within a few days, the non-dreamers showed signs of mental illness and breakdown.

So, in some way, dreaming is necessary to maintain psychological and physical health; exactly how is not yet quite understood. But what of the dream itself? Can this tell us anything? Taking the dream already mentioned, although it is not as fantastic or wild an account as dreams go, it still appears senseless at face value, but let us look beyond its surface.

The person who told me the dream is a young married woman in her twenties, whom I will call Ann. Ann was a student teacher until events led to marriage. An early child took her from college to the new discipline of parenthood and homemaking. This she enjoyed a great deal, but she also missed her other, college life, with its promise of a career.

In the dream, Ann sees herself in an 'old folly'. Could this be the 'folly' of her sudden marriage due to pregnancy, and the inner struggle it led to? However, the old house is not oppressive, it has many passages and rooms possible of exploration, which in itself is an excellent description pictorially of Ann herself. At college Ann found her interests running here and there, exploring this, tasting that, building odd bits of information in any old way as her interest led her. So behind the image of the house we find a shrewd summing up of Ann.

Coming to the next part of the dream, we see that Ann is being led, or pulled along by a 'wilful child'. When we first spoke of this dream, neither Ann nor I could understand even a part of it. As we talked, however, first of all the house, then the meaning of the child became clear. Just prior to the dream, Ann had become deeply immersed in an evening class dealing with the works of T. S. Eliot. The study had taken such a hold on her, that for some weeks she could think of nothing else but exploring the meaning of his poetry. She had literally been dragged along by her interest, and through it had discovered a new world of understanding about life and one's relationship to it.

At the time she had rather wondered where it was all leading to, but the dream clearly and distinctly outlines its possibilities. Her interest in Eliot is shown as a child, youthful urges that had previously not satisfied themselves in her other interests. These urges show her a part of herself (the house) she had never seen before. The books and objects clearly depict the mystery about life and religion she found in her understanding of Eliot. While the man is seen as the more down to earth part of her, worrying lest she is swept away by her interest in 'higher' things. But it was only in this way that the child, her impetuous desire to explore and so 'discover' herself, found release. It could not get out of a lower door through interests in household pursuits, only through the higher door of self understanding.

Of course, when it is all written down, with all the meanings neatly explained, it looks so easy. It becomes obvious in the wider knowledge of Ann, and her inner feelings, what the dream is all about. In fact, it would now be difficult not to understand the dream. Yet it took Ann and I a good hour of conversation to unravel it. Of such are the mysteries of dreams made.

Why is it then that most of our dreams, or even all of them, appear to be ridiculous or devoid of any meaning? Is it perhaps simply because we do not have the key to unlock the sense in them? Let me put it this way; if a political cartoonist draws a fat man sitting upon a tiny thin man; at first sight, if we are not following or knowledgeable upon world events at the time, it may be quite meaningless; but if we know that a very large country has, through its tariffs, immobilised the exports of another country, we easily see meaning in the cartoon. A dream is very much like a cartoon. If we do not follow the politics of our own hopes and fears, our own best interests, the dream will be meaningless. Once we understand the symbols, however, it is often difficult *not* to understand. Not that all dreams will become open books to us, because we are not usually that well up on the politics of our own inner world. But many dreams will become crystal clear when approached correctly. In fact you will understand them as easily as you have understood my use of pictorial analogies in the above sentences, in the words 'open books'—'well up'—'crystal clear'.

Looking at what has been said about Ann's dream, we can see that it has several important results. First of all the image of the house brought a clearer summing up of herself. So a dream can bring *self understanding*. In the child we see that the need to explore one's own mental and emotional possibilities is often as urgent and compelling, and as important as one's sexual life or career. This part of her had remained a child due to never having found release. So a dream clarifies our *inner politics*, what is going on within.

The books and objects, which were only glanced at in the dream, show Ann the wealth of inner wisdom that awaits investigation. So a dream can give us *new information*, and *confidence in ourselves*.

In fact, depending upon our interests, dreams can open to us a wealth of new ideas, energies and information. It is well known, for instance, that Robert Louis Stevenson wrote Dr Jekyll and Mr Hyde from the plot of a dream, but it is not usually realised that many of his stories also had their basis in dreams. Stevenson said, '... What shall I say they are but my Brownies, God bless them! who do one half my work for me while I am fast asleep.' 'When the bank begins to send letters and the butcher to linger at the back gate, he (Stevenson) sets to belabouring his brain after a story, for that is his readiest money-winner; and behold! at once the little people begin to bestir themselves in the same quest, and labour all night long, and all night long set before him truncheons of tales upon their lighted theatre.'

Mary, the wife of Shelley, dreamt the plot of Frankenstein; while in the world of philosophy, Descartes had, as the basis of much that he wrote, a series of dreams. Dante and Bunyan alike claim a dream as the inspiration of their greatest works. More recently, John Oxenham, best known for his religious poetry in 'Bees in Amber', wrote his most inspirational message on life after death through a dream experience.

At one time, in the Middle East, great temples were set up as centres for dreams of healing. Thousands upon thousands visited these Temples of Aesculapius, and many were cured by a release of healing forces within a dream.

Even science has not been left untouched by the world of dreams. Dr Otto Loewi, who discovered the chemical theory for the transmission of the nervous impulse in a body, claims that the crucial experiment to prove the theory came to him while asleep. Fredrich Kekule, who discovered the arrangement of atoms within a molecule of benzene, also arrived at the idea in sleep.

Such events are only touched on here, however, as this book is designed not to argue the validity of dreams, but to explain a method of using them, and discovering for oneself whether such validity exists.

But let us return to the point—do apparently senseless dreams hold meanings for us? Let us look at a few more dreams to find out.

In his book *Psychology In Service of the Soul* Dr Leslie Weatherhead mentions one of his experiences in regard to dreams. A woman under severe emotional stress was sent to him by her medical doctor. An accompanying letter said that the doctor could find nothing wrong with her physically, and could only prescribe sedatives and a holiday. These he felt would not really effect a cure. Even during the interview with Dr Weatherhead, the woman was very disturbed, crying and shaking, making it difficult to arrive at the cause of her trouble. The difficulty was solved, however, when she told of a dream she had experienced. In the dream a great storm was raging. The woman was standing under the cover of her porch, but her brother was in the middle of the road getting drenched. Eventually the dreamer ran out to her brother, threw her coat over him, and took him into her house. Having made a study of dreams, Dr Weatherhead was able to read the fairly obvious symbolism of the dream, and asked the woman to make up her quarrel with her brother. She was amazed that he should know of such a quarrel, but agreed to write to her brother, inviting him to visit her. In doing so she was cured. Her problem being her feelings of guilt over her self-righteous attitude, that had left her brother to face his problems alone.

In dreams storms usually represent emotional turbulence, hatred, fears, etc., and in this dream we see that a way out of her ill-health is shown by the dream. From this, one can gain a little understanding of how health or healing could be regained in the Temples of Aesculapius.

Taking the dream of a young man, we can see how dreams can also show the possible outcome of a particular attitude of mind. In the dream the young man saw himself walking up a dimly-lit cobbled street. The street was going up a hill, and on the left was a pub with two young men standing outside. They were holding pint jugs of bitter. As the dreamer drew near them, one turned to the other, looking at his bitter, and said, 'Shall I let him have it?' Being encouraged, he threw the bitter over the dreamer. Naturally he was very annoyed, and tried to brush it off his overcoat. He wanted to retaliate, but felt himself no match for these two, who walked back into the pub. Someone with the dreamer said that there was a policeman at the top of the hill, why not tell him. So climbing the rest of the hill, and turning to the right, he found the policeman and told him. The policeman very officiously took out his notebook and asked whether there were any witnesses. There were, but the policeman maintained his air of doing only what he was forced to do by law, which upset the dreamer and he walked away.

Looking at the symbolism, this 'young man' begins to take shape before us, for we see him through his dream. To climb a hill in real life is not only to expend energy, to face a difficulty, but also, if successful, to benefit by seeing the view from the top. A hill, in fact, gives us a wider view of things. So to climb a hill is to face the energetic task of widening our opinions, rising above narrow limited views, growing up. In fact, the dreamer was going through a period of finding new ideas and outlooks. The pub and young men, on the left, are symbols for the pleasure loving, down to earth, rough and ready side of himself. Something on the left of us in a dream often means that it is unknown, or little used (i.e. the left hand is usually the one we are least conscious of, and use the least). The dream is saying these parts of him are not expressed much in life. This is quite true, as the man was a quiet, serious person, religious and somewhat introverted. The dream shows that his pleasure loving, outgoing side, due to their repression, are drinking the bitters of life, and in fact, this stifled side of his nature causes him to be bitter himself. He tries to 'brush this bitterness off', rather like one might say, 'I feel depressed, but I'll soon overcome it.' Due to his retiring temperament, he does not feel he can face these other parts of himself. In a similar way, a person who inwardly wished to be noticed, might through shyness, not even be able to converse. Thus two parts of oneself may war against each other. The dream goes on to show the dreamer's present, conscious efforts to deal with the conflict leading to bitterness. The policeman is on the right, representing his more conscious attitudes. The policeman usually represents our sense of right and wrong, conscience and lawgiving. So the dreamer, in his efforts to deal with his attack of bitterness, tries to use his morals, his sense of right and wrong. But this side of himself is shown as unsympathetic, only really worried about the rules, and the dreamer realises he will not be helped by that attitude.

This particular dream only outlines the problem, and how one is trying to deal with it. It does not, as the previous dream, show a positive method of dealing with the situation.

When we see how clearly such dreams explain and fit the

dreamer's everyday life, it is difficult to understand why dreams are not more generally understood. When one hears the parables of Jesus, such as that of the Talents, one immediately sees behind the story to its symbolical meaning. *Aesop's Fables* have amused and educated children and adults for centuries. We can see ourselves in the frog who tried to gain respect by believing he was bigger and greater than he was. We can see that in a parable or fable, the outer story hides an inner truth, yet for hundreds of years in the West, dreams have been looked upon as nonsense. Even with the coming of Freud, only a limited interpretation of these nighttime parables was broached. Now, through the work of more liberal thinkers, the dream has at last come into its own again.

In the three dreams that follow, we can see, not only this parable making ability of one's own mind, but also its concentration on particular problems, and its sense of continuity through several dreams. The dreams are all by one woman, whom we will call June. They were all dreamed within a period of three weeks, during a time of financial insecurity. June's husband had been on social security, but was now working. He was not due to receive any wages until the work was complete however. So the problem was one of surviving for many weeks on next to no money.

Here are the dreams. 'I dreamt that I was sitting in my bedroom and Bill was with me (friend of husband). I had two children by him, and one by Alan (husband). Suddenly Bill turned into Alan and had a parcel that Richard (next door neighbour) was expecting containing drugs. He opened it and started smoking "pot" (hashish). As he smoked he changed rapidly into a hard, depraved sort of man, careless of others. Sue (Bill's wife) came into the room at this point, sorrowful at what had happened between myself and Bill. I told her that this wasn't important. What was important were the changes taking place in Bill-Alan. At that moment the police came and rounded up all those who were smoking pot. As I expected, they betrayed Alan to the police, and denial was useless because his entire state gave him away. They took him, and I didn't know what would happen now. His picture was on the front page of the newspaper; it would finish off our business. Even as I thought this a customer came, and I thought that when she knew, she wouldn't want to do business with us.'

2ND DREAM

'I had a huge pile of coloured washing to do, but the machine wasn't working properly. I put the washing in anyway and stood back. A tall, unknown male figure was beside me all the time. He gave me the impression of being a priest or teacher of some kind, with arms folded into wide hanging sleeves of a long robe. As we stood back a small explosion occurred and I could see a small fire had started beneath the machine. As I looked there appeared to be a huge pit under the machine, filled with a great glowing fire. A person stood in the midst of the fire supporting the machine, and as the fire burned so the machine began to be powered, and the clothes were washed. Both figure and machine remained unharmed by the flames, and I was reminded of Daniel in the lion's den.'

3RD DREAM

'I was with a group of people who had found a very small tunnel in a hillside. I knew that we all had to go through it; although it was so small and dark that it seemed impossible. There was barely room to even wriggle through, and a woman declined to go. Once we were in the tunnel I was surprised to find how short it was in length. It was so short it could hardly be called a tunnel. One of the others then went back to fetch the woman who had stayed behind.'

At first sight, these dreams appear to have little or nothing in common with each other. Also, the size of the first one, and its complexity, make it difficult for a simple explanation. Starting with this one but sticking to the main features, the theme soon begins to appear, however, so we find in June's associations that Bill is an idealistic, youthful and impetuous person, who seeks to leave a mark on the world. This represents June's own idealism and desire to leave something of herself in the world. This part of her nature has given her two children—that is, has developed two traits in her. The Bill within her never really came to the fore until her marriage, and thus these parts of her are still growing. They are her interest in the mysteries of life and death, and her practice of

14

self analysis. The self analysis was *born of* her desire to express in life, due to the fact that in trying to be herself, she found inner problems.

Her husband, Alan, is like Bill in many ways, but more mature, more ready to accept things as they are. The dream child from this part of her represents her growing ability to face the difficulties of life, to face her own inner problems.

However, due to her financial situation, or at least, the worries arising from it, Alan takes pot, which for June symbolises a fear of not having what it takes to meet the problems of life, or to face her own fears courageously. Pot is an avoidance, a running away from difficulties for her. This represents the breaking down of her strength to cope with her own inner fears and doubts concerning the outer situation. This gives rise to feelings of cutting off all sympathetic links with other people and the world. Such links of sympathy are painful to her diminished faith in life. Then June's sense of rightness (police) comes along to make her realise the social, inner, danger of these attitudes of mind. In fact, such feelings of unsympathy, of giving up, fear of not meeting one's problems, threaten to break down her ability to support herself in the workaday world symbolised by the business.

That first dream outlined her problem, which is quite complex, as it shows various parts of her implicated and threatened by her fears. The next dream deals with how to find a way through these difficulties. The huge pile of coloured washing is the pile of feelings and emotions that need cleaning. But the machine, which in real life is an automatic Bendix, is not working properly. In other words, usually she simply thinks to herself, 'Things will take care of themselves. Just be patient and my worries will disperse.' This attitude of mind, that usually *automatically* clears her worries, is now not working.

Meanwhile, in her dream there is the figure standing slightly to one side and behind her. This represents her innermost feelings, her deepest intuitions. In the dream she feels the man is encouraging her to put the washing in the machine despite the fact it does not seem to be working. Previous to this particular period of financial difficulty, June used her attitude of carrying on despite troubles automatically. But this time she had begun to wonder whether such an attitude was right. Was she hiding behind it just to let things slide from bad to worse? Was her faith really an excuse to avoid life? (We see even clearer here the inferences of taking pot in the first dream.) It is because of this doubt that the automatic washing machine is not working. The dream, through the figure of the teacher, points out very clearly that she is not wrong here, but to use the machine again. In doing so, which is a direct act of faith in her deepest feelings (in other words, through deciding to let events and the financial situation work itself out), an explosion occurs, new energy is released, and she sees her faith as a male, creative figure, engulfed in flames, yet not hurt. Faith is a state of mind constantly threatened, yet not destroyed; but through the very flames, gaining energy to drive the machine that cleanses us of unnecessary worries and fears.

The third dream confirms this, and suggests that the 'tight squeeze' through the darkness of her own fears and difficulties, will not be nearly as long as she expected. The symbolism, with its tunnel also suggests a birth into a different type of experience altogether. Even her fearful part, is eventually brought through the darkness.

In the above review of a few dreams, the possibility of finding an understanding of them becomes evident. Although what has been said so far may raise a host of sympathetic, information seeking, or critical questions; as already explained, this book does not attempt to justify the methods used in any detail. But there are a host of other books that will occupy the critical mind. Meanwhile, our quick look at dreams has revealed but a fraction of their possibilities. So, let us hasten on!

TWO

What is a dream?

From the earliest ages in mankind's shrouded history, dreams have been a source of wonder and speculation, inspiration and fear. This chapter deals with some of the explanations men have given for why and how one dreams. It must be understood, however, that these various accounts are put here, not because they are necessarily correct accounts of dreaming, but simply to give a 'background' of information on the dream.

The most ancient peoples, whether separated by seas, geographical barriers, or culture, usually had in common an enormous respect for dreams. Many early societies had a very dualistic philosophy regarding life. That is, they believed that their life was divided into two distinct aspects. One aspect was their everyday physical world, the world of the body. The other was the world of sleep, dreams, visions and death. In sleep, early man believed that one's soul, or consciousness left one's body, and travelled the sleep world, the world of dreams. This dream world was very real to them, so real in fact that many felt that the dream world was more real than the physical world. For instance, if a man dreamt that his wife had slept with another man, it was not simply shrugged off as 'only a dream' but was taken very seriously.

J. A. Hadfield, in his book *Dreams and Nightmares* humorously says the 'modern instance is that of a young wife who dreamt that her husband was making love to a blonde and was furious. Being reminded that it was only a dream, she replied, "Yes! But if he does that sort of thing in *my* dream, what will he do in his own?" '

In the dream world of early man, it was stated that one's soul could travel to distant places in the real world—could experience or know one's innermost feelings—could contact and converse with the dead—or meet the gods and spirits, or see God. We cannot simply dismiss these beliefs as valueless, because modern research and investigation is now concerning itself with a serious inquiry into all these possibilities.

In these early societies, where such beliefs were a part of life itself, youths of both sexes were helped to establish their maturity by initiations which often used or sought dreams. At such times, the young girl or boy would go to some lonely spot where they would fast and await a sign, by dream or vision (i.e. waking dream) that gave them a clue to their direction in life. To give an actual case, written down by Father Lalemant, a Jesuit: at the age of about sixteen, a youth went alone to a place where he fasted for sixteen days. At the end of this time he suddenly heard a voice in the sky saying, 'Take care of this man, and let him end his fast.' Then he saw an old man of great beauty come down from the sky. The old man came to him, looking at him kindly, and said, 'Have courage, I will take care of thy life. It is a fortunate thing for thee to have taken me for thy master. None of the demons who haunt these countries will have any power to harm thee. One day thou wilt see thine hair as white as mine. Thou wilt have four children, the first two and last will be males, and the third will be a girl, after that thy wife will hold the relation of a sister to thee.' As he finished speaking the old man offered him a raw piece of human flesh to eat. When the boy turned his head away in horror, the old man then offered him a piece of bear's fat, saying, 'Eat this then.' After eating it, the old man disappeared, but came again at crucial periods in the person's life. At manhood he did have four children, as described. After the fourth, 'a certain infirmity compelled him to continence. He also lived to an old age, thus having white hair, and as the eating of bear fat symbolised, became a gifted hunter with a second sight for finding game. The man himself felt that had he eaten the human flesh in the vision, he would have been a warrior instead.

So we see that such initiatory dreams fulfilled many functions. Not only did they affirm the dreamer of a 'spirit' protector, giving him confidence to leave the physical protection of his mother and father, but also gave his most fitting employment as hunter, and the main events of his life. With such knowledge, he could approach life more confidently.

An even more complete idea of how early societies related to their dreams is given by M. L. von Franz in his article *The process of Individuation—Man and His Symbols*—by Carl G. Jung. Writing about the 'self' as the inner centre to all our experience, he says,

'This inner centre is realised in exceptionally pure unspoiled form by the Naskapi Indians, who still exist in the forests of the Labrador peninsula. These simple people are hunters who live in isolated family groups, so far from one another that they have not been able to evolve tribal customs or collective religious beliefs and ceremonies. In his lifelong solitude the Naskapi hunter has to rely on his own inner voices and unconscious revelations; he has no religious teachers who tell him what he should believe, no rituals, festivals or customs to help him along. In his basic view of life, the soul of man is simply an 'Inner companion', whom he calls 'My friend' or 'Mista peo', meaning 'Great Man'. Mista peo dwells in the heart and is immortal; in the moment of death, or just before, he leaves the individual, and later reincarnates himself in another being.

'Those Naskapi who pay attention to their dreams and who try to find their meaning and test their truth can enter into a greater connection with the Great Man. He favours such people and sends them more and better dreams. Thus the major obligation of an individual Naskapi is to follow the instructions given by his dreams, and then to give permanent form to their contents in art. Lies and dishonesty drive the Great Man away from one's inner realm, whereas generosity and love of one's neighbours and of animals attract him and give him life. Dreams give the Naskapi complete ability to find his way in life, not only in the inner world but also in the outer world of nature. They help him to foretell the weather and give him invaluable guidance in his hunting, upon which his life depends. . . . Just as the Naskapi have noticed that a person who is receptive to the Great Man gets better and more helpful dreams, we could add that the inborn Great Man becomes more real within the receptive person than in those who neglect him. Such a person also becomes a more complete human being.'

Although possibly not as unspoilt as the Naskapi beliefs, those of the Seneca Indians are worthy of note. The Jesuits began preaching to these Indians in 1668. Father Fremin wrote much about their ideas, although in a slightly critical vein, saying, 'The Iroquois have, properly speaking, only a single Divinity—the dream. . . . The Tsonnontonens (Seneca) are more attached to this superstition than to any other.'

Father Ragueneau, in 1649, described the beliefs behind their so-called superstition as follows. 'In addition to the desires which we generally have that are free, or at least voluntary in us, and which arise from a previous knowledge of some goodness that we imagine to exist in the thing desired, the Hurons believe that our souls have other desires, which are, as it were, inborn and concealed. These, they say, come from the depths of the soul, not through any knowledge.

'Now they believe that our soul makes these desires known by means of dreams, which are its language. Accordingly, when these desires are accomplished, it is satisfied; but, on the contrary, if it be not granted what it desires, it becomes angry ... often it revolts against the body, causing various diseases, and even death....'

The Indian tribes mentioned often had a sort of social psychiatry in which dreamers were allowed to live out their hidden (unconscious) desires that were threatening health and well being. Thus a dreamer would be allowed sexual freedoms with others; unlawful actions; objects desired; or feasts, etc; although these peoples as a society were usually modest and shy, and chastity and marital fidelity were public ideals.

Thus we see in the beliefs of the 'backward' Indians, ideas that took our civilised societies three hundred years longer to arrive at. Admittedly, our psychiatrist's couch and enormous mental institutions take the place of the more public 'acting out' of hidden desires. Nevertheless, mentally or emotionally induced illnesses were recognised and treated. So we see that early man recognised conscious and unconscious parts of self. They realised that dreams expressed these 'hidden' desires, often in a symbolic form, enabling us to deal with them before they produced sickness.

Turning to more recent sources of dream beliefs, it is distressing to see how less, instead of more, understanding is expressed. Most of the ancient world, including the Far East, believed that dreams were sent by gods or spirits, but do not seem to have worked out such a clear conception as the North American Indians, and later became very intellectually speculative. Aristotle, for instance, writes on the idea that dreams arise from movements in the body, saying, 'The conclusion to be drawn from all these facts is that the dream is a sort of image and that it is produced during sleep, for the appearances manifest themselves when our senses are free. But not every image that manifests itself in sleep is a dream. For, sometimes, certain persons perceive in a certain manner in their sleep both sounds and light, both savours and contacts, but faintly and as if from afar. In fact, people who have seen in their sleep what was, according to them, the light of a lamp, realised immediately after waking that it was the light of a lamp; and people who have heard cocks crowing, or dogs barking, have recognised them clearly on waking.... But the images that come from the movement of sensible impressions, when one is sound asleep, that is a dream.'

In the Aesculapius dream temples, the dreams were said to be invoked by the god, whose symbol was also a serpent. Thus a childless woman, going to the temple to secure fertility, dreamt that the god approached her followed by a snake. The snake then entered her sexually. After the dream, and within the year, she had two sons. Sometimes the person would dream that they had been made well and would awake to find the dream accomplished. The rooms in which patients slept were occupied by snakes of a harmless variety also. This, along with the necessary rites and purifications, set the patient in the right frame of mind and emotion, to receive a healing dream.

Such dream induction by a particular setting and rites is very similar to the more ancient practices of fasting and waiting for the initiating dream. Similar, that is, in the sense of seeking a particular type of dream at a particular time and place.

Islamic traditions also have a rite called Istiqara, where the participant repeats a particular prayer, said to have been given by Mohammed, enabling one to dream the answer to a problem. This was used in recent years by Dr Mossadegh. The resulting dream was of a being who told Dr Mossadegh to make all haste in efforts to nationalise Iranian Oil. As Dr Mossadegh was convalescing from illness, this was difficult. Also the political climate at that time regarding the nationalisation of oil seemed hopeless. Some months later, however, due to Dr Mossadegh's continued efforts, Iranian Oil was in fact nationalised.

In the Bible, there are many references to dreams. The history changing dreams of Pharoah about the fat and thin kine, along with New Testament dreams, are taken to be given by God, or angels. In the dream of Peter, where the unclean animals are let down in a sheet, and Pharoah's dream, we see clearly symbolic dreams, the meaning of which is arrived at through interpretation.

At other places, we find mention of God's intervention in our dream life. Thus in Genesis 20:3, we read, 'But God came to Abimelech in a dream by night, and said to him, Behold, thou art but a dead man, for the woman which thou hast taken; for she is a man's wife.' Later, in Job 33:15, it says, 'In a dream, in a vision of the night, when deep sleep falleth upon men, in slumberings upon the bed, then he (God) openeth the ears of men, and sealeth their instruction, that he may withdraw a man from his purpose, and hide pride from man.'

In the Indian Yoga teachings, they mention four states of consciousness, that is, waking—dreaming—dreamless sleep—superconsciousness. Although, as in Patanjalis' *Aphorism's* mention is made of dreams as a subject for meditation, Yoga practitioners seek to become aware at the dreamless and superconscious levels. That is, they seek to get behind the images of dreams to that which is conscious of them, i.e. the Self, the basic part of our being. In the Tibetan *Book of the Dead* one sees a detailed commentary on how to become liberated from inner images analogous to dreams. This too, we must consider as one of the aims of a modern dream investigator.

Turning to more modern concepts of dreams and dreaming, one finds, largely, a slide into a materialistic attitude. For instance there was for long the opinion that dreams were caused by a late, heavy meal, or eating highly stimulating foods. One could call this the 'indigestion' theory.

Some experimentation was also undertaken in the realm of dreams produced by outside influences. Thus, a number of people have slept and been exposed to drops of water, tickling, sounds, scents, bells, electrical brain stimuli and even hypnotic suggestion. All of these produced dreams in some way explanative of the stimulus. For instance, Alexandre Arnoux writes how, when in a rest camp, he dreamt that the Germans had sent over a poisonous gas smelling of quinces. He awoke gasping for breath, only to see that his friend had just entered the room eating a quince. Another writer, Massey, on having water dropped on his face, dreamt he was in Italy, drinkink wine and perspiring heavily. In the case of the electrical probe to the brain, particular memories were evoked, clear and distinct.

Another popular theory is that dreams are the uncontrolled wanderings of the sleeping mind. This theory sees the images of

dreams as occurring due to the natural psychological law of association of ideas. Thus, as we drift into sleep, we may be entertaining
the idea of a bicycle. The idea bicycle associates with journey,
journey with someone we wish to see, this with fear of their not
being there to welcome us, which links with our walking alone, etc.

J. A. Hadfield, in his excellent book *Dreams and Nightmares*, lists
all these ideas and more. He points out that each of these ideas is
true as far as it goes, but none of them explain all factors about
dreams. Recent experiments have shown that even outside stimulus
does not *produce* the dream, it merely enters into its images. Nor
is a dream merely past memories, as a dream often uses images in
unique formation, and we have to ask ourselves what has reshaped
the images of our memory. In the dream of Arnoux, for instance,
the smell of quince definitely enters into the dream, but if we are
honest, we have to admit that an interior fear and terror is also
expressive in the dream, and can thus be used as a means of self
analysis.

The internally produced dream theory of Aristotle has proved
itself, however, at least partially true. Observations of dreams has
shown a number of times how a person may dream of a particular
part of his body due to sickness in that area. Armaud de Villeneuve,
for instance, dreamt that a dog bit his leg. A few days later a
cancerous growth became visible on the same spot. A Swiss poet,
Gessner, dreamt that a snake bit him in the left side, and shortly
afterwards developed a malignant tumour there. The great many
experiences of this nature are explained on the grounds that during
sleep we are more sensitive to inner disturbances than in waking.
As with dreams woven around outside stimuli, the inner irritations
of developing sickness can announce themselves in the images of
our dreams. However, due to the claims of mystics, and the present
tentative findings of parapsychology concerning the possibility
that human consciousness exists outside of the body, or for one
person to know or receive the thoughts and feelings of another, it
seems likely that it is not only subtle sensations in the *body* that
may stimulate dream images. We can therefore say that some of
the causes may be physical sensations from within or outside the
body—moods, fears, desires or pressures, etc., existing in the personality of the sleeper—unconscious realisation of ideas, levels of
being and new states of mind—and stimuli from other minds.

Before we progress to the great dream authorities of the twentieth century it will be illuminating to quickly look at the ideas expressed by an American of the nineteenth century. I use the word illuminating, as here is a man who expressed the idea of evolution to the world some years before Darwin published his works. This man was Dr Andrew Jackson Davis, born in 1826. In 1850 (nine years before Darwin's work) he wrote and published *The Great Harmonia*, in which we read:

> The progressive development of the animal kingdom up to man may be traced from its very beginnings, when—as the result of a marriage between the highest forms and essences in the vegetable kingdom—there arose the first form of animal life—the inferior order of radiata. At a later era the pisces was followed by that of the birds. The marsupial was next, and then the mammalian. The primary change from this last into inferior types of human organism is so easy that the anatomical and physiological transformation is scarcely perceptible.*

Excuse my enthusiasm in quoting something that seemingly has nothing to do with dreams. I feel, however, that 'dream historians' have overlooked a great mind in A. J. Davis, and the quote is a reference to his qualifications, this being felt necessary as his source of information is psychic rather than scientific. That is, through his unique ability, he was able to explore the interior of his own being—consciously. So his remarks on evolution arose from information he obtained from what might be called a dream state. Davis called it 'The Superior Condition'. However, here are his remarks and theory on sleep and dreams.

> Sleep is that mode by which the fatigued soul withdraws partially from the physical organism and gathers inwardly for purposes of recuperation. At the same time it remains sufficiently within them to inspire the involuntary systems with constant motion, that they may fulfil their respective functions. The place into which it (soul-consciousness) retires is the most interior portions of the viscera and the deepest recesses of the

* Not that evolution is unique to our culture. Jalaludin Rumi, a thirteenth-century mystic, clearly wrote of it.

sensorium. The superior brain or cerebrum yields up its powers to the cerebellum and this resigns in turn to the medulla spinalis. During the period of natural rest the cerebellum never sleeps, and in the waking hours the cerebrum is in constant activity, guiding and controlling the organisation. The spirit (energising principle), when (we are) asleep, moves with the greatest precision through the whole organic domain, but especially the inner chambers the sensorium and the ganglionic and lymphatic batteries of the visceral system.

The phenomena of dreams are controlled by established laws which may be applied to education and the development of mind. Properly speaking there is no such condition as absolute suspension of consciousness, only of external powers of memory. When the mind passes into a coma, the spirit* takes up the thread of previous interior experiences. The mind has two memories, one of the body and the world without, the other a more inward scroll, on the deepest folds of which are registered those experiences which the soul has obtained from the world within. The significance of dreams depends upon their nature and derivation.... Even in prophetic warnings, the soul does its own work almost invariably, by extending its sensiferous faculties towards the future, and thus perceiving those events which laws of cause and effect are certain to develop.

... Owing to wrong living and intemperance (in amount and quality of food), no one enjoys perfect slumber except for exceedingly brief periods; but when experienced in its fullness, and when the soul is resigned to the will of God through recognition of Nature's laws, the individual is then on the confines of the other life. True sleep is a temporary death of the body and a rest of the soul. It is distinguished from imperfect slumber by the absence of all ordinary dreaming.

Davis also gives very practical hints, although general, in understanding dreams.

It follows that dreaming deserves investigation as a precursor

* One might also think of spirit as life energy.

and accompaniment of disease. Lively dreams are in general a sign of attenuated excitement of the nervous system. Soft or vapourish dreams denote slight cerebral irritation, or alternatively, a favourable crisis in nervous fevers. Frightful dreams betoken a determination of arterial blood to the head. Dreams about blood and red objects, houses and ships on fire, imps, demons, etc., indicate an inflammatory condition of the semi-intellectual and perceptive faculties of the cerebrum. Dreams about water, rain, floods, deluges often characterise diseased mucous membranes and dropsy. Dreams in which a person sees any portion of his own body, especially in a suffering state, point to disturbances in that area. So also dreams of food, feasts and so forth are usually traceable to impaired digestive functions. This explanation of a certain class of dream does not pose as a solution of all such mental phenomena.

He goes on to say that such interpretation is only dealing with physical relationships. His main theme, however, is how to obtain 'great' or 'spiritual' dreams.

In those (dreams) which emanate from the world of spirits, it is a fact that spiritual dreams only occur in a state of perfect slumber. The will and faculties of thought must be in a state of complete quiescence.... Such influences cannot enter when the front brain (intellect, will) is at all positive. Perfect slumber is nigh unto death. The higher departments of mind are not occupied by thought, the holy elements of feeling are stilled; the front brain or cerebrum is a tranquil domain; there is no sentinel at the gate of the brain but the vigilant cerebellum. The mind is then ready for a high order of dream.

Leaving the Poughkeepsie Seer, as Davis was called, we turn to another more recent seer, Edgar Cayce of Virginia Beach. As early as 1925 Edgar Cayce was already interpreting dreams from a viewpoint free of fixed sexual or intellectually psychological attitudes. He must rate, along with leaders of this more open attitude such as J. A. Hadfield, and Leslie Weatherhead, as one of those who brought the dream 'home' to the public. Some of his pupils would like to claim him as the beginner of such attitudes, but J. A.

Hadfield, from the point of psychology, and Weatherhead from a Christian viewpoint, had already given long years of public service before 1925. Nevertheless, the work of Cayce has directed the attention of thousands to their dream life. The groups organised to work on their dreams, in their collective numbers, probably out-weigh the work of the others.

Possibly Cayce's attitude to dreams may be summed up by this statement he made from a deep sleep state:

> These (dreams), as we see, may be used to the edification of the entity into that of how spiritual laws are manifested in the physical world.

All such statements about dreams, and the countless other sub-jects he mentioned, were spoken from a trance or sleep state similar to that of Davis. This is rather like listening in to what the unconscious mind says about itself. In another such statement, he says that through a study of dreams, a person,

> May gain the more perfect understanding and knowledge of those forces that go to make up the real existence—what it's all about—and what it's good for—if the entity would but com-prehend the conditions being manifested.

Cayce taught, like others, that dreams reflect activities in the body, in the emotions, mind and general attitudes of a person. But his main point was that the dream helps the individual understand his relationship with the whole—with Life or God. He said, in 1923,

> Forget not that it has been said correctly that the Creator, the Gods and the God of the Universe, speak to man through his individual self. Man approaches the more intimate conditions of that field of the inner self when the conscious self is at rest in sleep or slumber, at which time more of the inner forces are taken into consideration and studied by the individual, not someone else. It is each individual's job, if he will study to show himself approved by God, to understand his individual con-dition, his individual position in relation to others, his individual

manifestation, through his individual receiving of messages from the higher forces themselves, through dreams.

Shane Miller in his article 'Working With Dreams as Recommended by the Cayce Readings', says:

The Cayce premise states in effect that anyone, whether psychically gifted or not, who will record his dreams in an attitude of prayerful persistence can, in time, bring about a complete restoration of the dream faculty. (The dream faculty at present seems to be the remains of a long disused and discredited function of the higher mind.) ... any dream which has a certain story content or mood, particularly if it is in colour, should be studied; and that is the complete premise which, if *faithfully* followed can bring about a new dimension into the experience of anyone who will keep everlastingly at it!

In this sense a dream can be a message from the Highest, expressed in the symbolic language of the unconscious. So in looking at a dream, we may be reading a letter from God. That is, a correspondence between the universal forces that have formed us, and the individual that in being formed calls itself 'I'. A conversation then, between God and I.

Obviously, the word 'God' for many has repugnant religious undertones from which they shy away. They may therefore miss some of the important ideas Cayce has presented. Possibly this other theory, which is a synthesis of several liberal ideas on dreams will be more attractive.

Consciousness is the result of various energies combining as our being. Yet consciousness, if studied carefully does not, in a peculiar way, rely upon the factors that give it expression. For instance, we are shown in modern brain operations, that only when the small area of the brain, the thalamus, is removed, does one lose consciousness. The other large areas can be cut off or damaged without the person 'losing' consciousness. This seems to suggest that consciousness is due to the thalamus, allied to the body. But from the information in other experiments, this seems to give a false idea. It would be better to say that the thalamus *enables consciousness to express*. In the same way, an electric fire allows electricity to express some of its potential. If one removes the thalamus, or the fire from the circuit, it has *not* removed consciousness or electricity, merely takes away their vehicle of expression.

From this viewpoint we can think of consciousness as always existing, but not necessarily expressing all of its potential. This would give us an entirely new concept of sleep. For sleep would be the partial withdrawing of consciousness from the organs of its expression, and a sinking into its most basic levels of existence. Thus the individual, in sleep, would sink into the primordial level of being that existed even prior to his or her birth. For if consciousness is what I think it is, it, like the electricity, is a principle of nature, and pre-exists the apparatus through which it realises itself in the physical world. Thus, a dream may well be the reaction expressed in images, of the conscious aspect of self meeting its primordial and eternal aspect in nature. The dream would then remind us of the spark between two electrical charges of different potential as they touch and become balanced. A dream would express the 'difference' between the individual and his source. From it one may understand how he relates to the whole.

The words of Nietzsche add yet another dimension to this attitude. *In Human, all too Human,* he wrote,

I hold that as man now still reasons in dreams, so men reasoned also when awake through thousands of years.... This ancient element in human nature still manifests itself in our dreams, for it is the foundation upon which the higher reason has developed and still develops in every individual; the dream carries us back into remote conditions of human culture, and provides a ready means of understanding them.

As already mentioned, J. A. Hadfield has done much through his life work and books, to bring understanding of inner experience to the ordinary person. His own view on dreams is summed up as follows:

According to what we shall call the Biological Theory of dreams, the function of dreams is that by means of reproducing the unsolved experiences of life, they work towards a solution of these problems.

Firstly,

Dreams stand in the place of experience. Thus by making us relive the experiences and difficulties of the day in imagination they relieve us of the necessity of going through the actual experience by trial and error and thus save us many a disaster. ... It is obvious, therefore, that dreams serve the same purpose as ideational processes, much as we exercise in normal thought in waking life.

Also,

Every individual has potentialities in his nature, all of which are not merely seeking their own individual ends, but each and all of which subserve the functions of the personality as a whole. But in the course of life many of these potentialities become repressed. In analytic treatment we attempt to release these repressed emotions, and direct them to the uses of life for which they were intended—and so make the personality *whole.* But dreams were attempting the same thing long before analytic treatment was thought of, and therefore dreams also, by releasing repressed experiences and emotions, are striving to solve these problems and to restore the personality to efficient functioning as a whole.

Turning at last to Freud and Jung, an attempt will be made to synthesise their particular standpoint regarding dreams. Starting with Freud, we cannot properly understand his statements without an understanding of *Libido.* To take an image from an earlier statement, we can think of libido as the energy behind our living process. If we think of the body as an efficient machine, then perhaps libido could be thought of as the electricity or power that works the machine. Not only does this energy emerge as motion and function, but it also lies behind our instincts, emotions, sexual drive, desire for social standing and recognition, our intellectual curiosity, and all the other aspects of life. Thinking of libido as a *stream* of energy, flowing out via our sexual, intellectual, emotional and other activities, we see, in the full expression of this energy, psychological health. However, if some of this energy, on entering our sexual activity is not released, it causes inner pressures we call neuroses, or a complex. (For the energy may be expressed morbidly or in an unacceptable manner as in homosexuality.)

For Freud, the dream is a wish fulfilment of these hidden desires which he maintained were usually of a sexual nature. The dream in this sense, is a method of making conscious unacceptable desires. Thus, if one wished to be rid of one's father, or to sleep with one's mother, but could not express either of these even in speech, because of the forbiddeness of such, one could do so in a dream. However, due to the fact that such desires arouse deep guilt feelings, we may not wish to openly express them even in a dream. Thus the dream both expresses and disguises the desires all at once. For instance, Freud considered that to dream of having sexual intercourse with an old woman, was a disguised dream concerning one's mother. Or putting a key in a lock symbolises sexual intercourse.

So far we see that the Seneca Indians held much the same views. Similarly they believed dreams had a latent and manifest content; that is, a hidden, or difficult to understand meaning behind the obvious events in the dream. Also, Freud maintained that all dreams are potentially understandable. They all arise from some cause, and if understood this cause becomes revealed. That is not to say, of course, that all dreams *are* understood.

Originally, Freud maintained that dreams were all wish fulfilments of hidden urges relating to our sexual nature. Later this was widened to include wish fulfilments of repressed aggressiveness.

Jung, following upon Freud and Adler's work, maintained that the 'dream shows in what direction the unconscious is leading' the dreamer. Also, he says, 'In dream interpretation we ask what conscious attitude does the dream compensate.' Thus, dreams for Jung, point to the fact that the processes in man's consciousness that he is unaware of, attempt to fulfil or realise themselves in a particular direction. A plant for instance, has hidden within it the possibility of stem, leaves, flower and seeds. These it attempts to produce. Similarly, a man has the possibility of further extensions of consciousness, of realisation, of abilities and desires which may be held back by conscious attitudes. For instance, a man may have latent artistic abilities which are held back from 'flowering' due to his conscious insistence on purely logical and money-making activities.

In this case, the dream may portray the man doing irrational things, because it *compensates* for his 'Oh so logical' conscious attitude. Also Jung began the direction of looking to dreams as a search for one's wholeness—not only sexually, but in all functions. Our sexual drives, our urge for power and social position, our intellectual curiosity, our innate desire to understand ourselves, and relate harmoniously to others and life around us, are all dealt with in dreams.

In *Man and His Symbols*, Jung talks of God in a way not found in other branches of psychiatry.

Christians often ask why God does not speak to them, as he is believed to have done in former days. When I hear such questions I always think of the rabbi who was asked how it could be that God often showed himself to people in the olden days while nowadays nobody ever sees him. The rabbi replied: 'Nowadays there is no longer anybody who can bow low enough.'

This answer hits the nail on the head. We are so captivated by and entangled in our subjective consciousness that we have forgotten the age-old fact that God speaks chiefly through dreams and visions. The Buddhist discards the world of the unconscious fantasies as useless illusions; the Christian puts his Church and his Bible between himself and his unconscious; and the rational intellectual does not yet know that his consciousness is not yet his total psyche (self).

Perhaps in the end, we can see that none of these views need be discarded. As one writer has remarked, several men all looking at the same landscape may all describe, and even 'sense' it differently. A geologist would see it differently to an artist, who in turn would feel about it differently to a farmer, and so on. In sleep, we may approach some inner landscape that represents our wholeness— the latent qualities of our own being. The wonderful thing is that our dream is our own. It uses our own symbols, our own emotions, our own understanding, our own possibilities. With these it paints a truly personal wonder we call a dream. Surely this is worth understanding?

THREE

Getting to grips with the dream

I can imagine a reader, having read this far, saying, 'Possibly dreams do have something in them that we can learn. The only thing is, I never dream!'

Of course, before one can start dealing with a dream, one has to remember it. So many people cannot recall having dreamt, that the act of remembering becomes a necessary prelude in our technique. Fortunately, one can be assured that the attempt to remember is not a waste of time. In other words, there *is* something to remember. In laboratory experiments up to the present time, no person has been found who does not dream. These experiments have been conducted in many countries, with various aims in view. Groups consisting of people who claim they have never dreamt, all have been found to dream. This has been done by fixing electrodes just above the eyelids. These are sensitive to eye movements, which always occur during dreaming. Thus, when these 'non-dreamers' exhibited the eye movements they were woken, and realised they had been dreaming. Such tests were also carried out on those who claimed total insomnia. It was found that although these people slept less than normal, they did sleep and dream; which was proved by their eye movements, and the recorded patterns of brain activity that change during sleep. However, these people would exclaim the next morning, 'There, you see, I never slept a wink.' Their recorded responses, and the watch kept upon them, proved otherwise.

It was found by Shapiro and Goodenough, that particular psychological mechanisms may underlie such dream forgetfulness. Testing groups of those who did and did not remember their dreams, they found that the non-rememberers took much longer to awaken when roused. In each bedroom was an electric bell and microphone. When a sleeper began the rapid eye movements typical of dreaming, the bell was sounded, and the person asked if they had dreamt. The non-dreamers, to recall their dreams had to be woken suddenly by a greater bell volume, otherwise the dream was lost to recall. Many years previous to such experiments, Freud had said that, 'The forgetting of dreams depends far more on the resistance (to the dream elements) than on the mutually alien character of the waking and sleeping states.' Shapiro also felt, from the experiments, that the person who does not remember dreams, may be one who deals with his problems by denying (forgetting) them. For during the delay in waking experienced by the 'non-dreamers', the mechanism of their forgetfulness erased remembrance of dream portrayed emotions and desires they may not wish to be conscious of.

Due to the information such research has uncovered, it would be reasonably easy for a 'non-dreamer' to prove that in fact, he or she dreamt. For instance, apart from showing that everyone dreams, it was also discovered that one's dreams occur in regular cycles. During a period of seven hours sleep, it was found that *every person tested*, went through the same cycle of five periods of dreaming. As Edwin Diamond has said in his book *The Science of Dreams*, 'This nightly pattern is as universal as sleep and as regular as the motions of the heavenly bodies.'

The dream periods run as follows: sixty to seventy minutes after falling asleep, we dream for approximately nine minutes. After a further ninety minutes or so, one dreams for about nineteen minutes. Then after another ninety minutes one dreams for about twenty-four minutes. After the next ninety minutes the dreaming period increases to twenty-eight minutes, and the last stage, after a further ninety minutes, one dreams more or less until waking.

So to 'catch a dream', the 'non-dreamer' could set an alarm to go off after about six hours of sleep. This should catch them well into the fourth dream of the night. Realising that such cycles begin only from the time one went to sleep, this would have to be accounted for. Also, the alarm would have to rouse the person suddenly, due to their mechanism of forgetfulness. If this did not work first time, then the alarm could be set below or above the six hours. One would naturally have to make some record of the dream, as a further period of sleep could easily obliterate the hard won memory.

Fortunately, this ambush type technique to catch a dream may not be necessary. It has been noticed time and time again by those working on dreams, that once a sincere interest in dreams has been aroused, one usually begins to remember them. While you are reading this book for instance, you are undoubtedly unaware of your big toe. However, now that your big toe is mentioned, you begin to become aware of the sensations of its form, clothing upon it, position in relationship to the rest of your body, etc. Similarly, when one's interest is aroused regarding dreams, one begins to become far more aware of them. If one subsequently writes them down and tries to understand them, then such remembrance becomes even easier. Therefore, allowing one's interest and enthusiasm full rein, will in itself usually pierce the veil of forgetfulness. In fact, you will probably remember a dream tonight!

There are also a number of ways in which we can further and extend such remembering. Realising what was said concerning the mechanism of forgetting, we can use these same principles for remembering. It was said, for instance, that one may forget because there is an unconscious wish not to face the symbolised emotions, desires and fears of the dream. Therefore, if we change our attitude, release it, so to speak, we may find dream memory more forthcoming. To do this we have to realise that the main aspects of our being can be summed up as instinct and sex drives—feelings and emotions—thoughts, principles, philosophy—and the unknown parts of ourselves. Do we, for example, hold rigidly on to particular ideas, unwilling to explore new thoughts, other religious codes, extensions of learning? Do we limit ourselves to only a particular set of emotions and sensations, preferring not to explore the ranges of our feelings? Do we deal with our instincts by denying any such part of our being? And what of the unknown? Is it disclaimed; denied? Or are we willing to tread carefully into it?

Asking oneself such questions, as sincerely as possible, may help one to discover whether or not there is a strong unconscious desire to 'forget' anything outside of one's present experience. These parts of ourselves might be summed up by the words, Sensuality—Sexuality—Sympathy—Empathy—Insight—Understanding—Transcendance. If we are shutting any of these forces or factors out of our experience, we may be missing some element of ourselves necessary for completeness. Admitting the possibility of such incompleteness, is an important step in remembering dreams.

Obviously, the putting aside of emotional or mental attitudes is important in *any* type of remembering. This includes memory of real events just as much as dreams. Therefore, to understand the workings of our everyday ability to remember might also be helpful. This is because we can use it as a technique to 'call up' dreams.

If we take the trouble to analyse carefully any act of memory, we see that a very special state of mind is necessary. This becomes more obvious when we remember the times of not being able to recall ordinary memories that usually are so available. Supposing there has been an accident for instance, and I am telephoning for an ambulance. If I know the injured person well, and am asked to give their name and address, because of the emotion of the moment it might easily happen that I am flustered by the question and find it difficult to answer. Or else, if in a situation such as an exam, where questions need a speedy reply, and a great deal rests upon being able to answer, one might very well find known information beyond recall due to one's fear of forgetting, or over-active attempt to remember. One other typical situation is the attempt to remember somebody's name, which somehow seems 'on the tip of one's tongue', yet never emerges. When analysed, this is often due to feeding into our memory system a wrong re-call stimuli. Or, put more simply, we may feel sure the name begins with 'B' and are searching through the 'Bs'; while in fact the name is Miller, and thus should have been called up under 'M'. So holding the 'B' in mind has actually blocked the memory. Then, as soon as we drop the search, and thus drop the blockage, up pops the right name.

From this very quick résumé of memory tactics, we can build a method of recalling dreams that will work if used correctly. It is obvious from the examples used that strong desires to remember are as blocking as the fear of failure. Particular emotional or mental biases are also causes for blocking. So also is the search conditioned by information that is thought to be right, such as our search through the 'Bs'.

As for the actual method, it is this. As soon after waking as possible, ask the question 'What has been dreamt?' Having formed the question, one now has to realise that as one has never been conscious of the answer, one is looking for information one has never known. Therefore, all attempts to *search* for the answer must be avoided, as one does not know where or how this information is filed. The question must be held steadily without even a hope of response, or fear of failure.

Also, as we have no idea of the subjects or images of the dream, we have to leave ourselves wide open to all images and ideas. I can only describe this as standing in a stream of images and ideas, letting them all drift past without interference until the right one comes. When the *actual* memory comes, there will be an immediate realisation that this was a dream, despite all the other images. Why this is so I cannot explain. But just as, when the *right* name is remembered, there is a feeling of sureness, fitting the name to the face; so there is immediate sureness fitting the memory to the question. Such a technique has many other uses, but is excellent for bringing dreams to consciousness, and with practice, one begins to feel one's way around in the technique. If all this seems rather technical, then the simple expedient of trying to recall dreams as soon as one awakes, will work wonders.

RECORDING THE DREAM

If remembering the dream is the first step, recording the dream is definitely the second step in dream interpretation. The importance of this lies not simply in having a record of the dream. Having already mentioned the tricks memory can play with dreams, we can see that the recording of the dream is also to guard against such vagaries. One should therefore attempt to write down the dream as soon as possible. All relevant details should also be included. The following example of a dream record shows two possibilities of recording the same dream.

'I dreamt that a short slightly glowing bolt had entered into my side, and I knew in that moment I had become pregnant with *my* child. I turned and told my husband, but as he did not seem to hear I did not repeat it. It seemed only to matter to myself.'

If we analyse the feelings in the dream closely, however, the description of the dream might enlarge as follows: 'I dreamt that a short, slightly glowing bolt had entered my side. I felt great excitement at this, as if I had long awaited it, and was now fulfilled in my waiting. In the dream I knew that the bolt was something divine that had now entered my being. I also knew in that moment that I had become pregnant with *my* child, and it would change my life. I told my husband about this, but it was as if he couldn't hear because I was speaking on a different wavelength or something. Then I realised that this should be kept to myself. That I was to give myself over to the child within, that it would grow strong.'

These little additions are so important in correct dream analysis. If they are lost much relevant information arising from them in interpretation is lost also. If we are earnestly working with our dreams, such a record should be made of *every* dream. Even those that seem inconsequential should be noted down. Why this is so will be explained in later chapters. Therefore, even such a small scrap of a dream as this next one is important : 'Dreamt that the vision in my left eye was distorted at times, making me see things out of focus or as one would see the reflections in water after a stone is flung in.'

To anyone who has worked on dream interpretation the meaning is very obvious, and also reveals helpful advice to the dreamer. If you cannot yet see its meaning, come back to it after reading the next few chapters. In this way you will see that an apparently unimportant fragment should be recorded.

A large, stout notebook is best for recording, as in this way all one's dreams are kept together for easy reference. Possibly a looseleaf notebook is most adequate, as interpretations and further comments can then be added. But if one cannot find time to *write* one's interpretations, at least write down the dreams and *date* them.

There are also other methods of recording the dream, such as drawing or painting it. Writing it in story or poetry form also is excellent. These methods are more fully dealt with under the chapters on 'Interpretation'. Although it is not necessary to use these other forms, they do have a very real place in dream analysis; and where the dreamer feels an inclination towards them, should be indulged in. I have only mentioned writing, painting and drawing, but any art form can be used to express and give concrete form to the dream content. Always record it as a straight description first, and then express it in art form, if inclined, later.

Such methods of recording the dream are by no means new. In our mention of the Naskapi Indians, it was said that the individual Naskapi tried to follow the instructions of his dreams, 'and then to give permanent form to their contents in art'.

Many dreams have thus been the basis of *plays* and religious *rituals*. In this way, whole groups could take part in the dramatisation and experiencing of the emotional, instructive and transforming influence of a dream. If it is wondered what point there is in this, we have to remember that as individuals and as a society, we face certain difficulties. We may have terrible depressions that block our normal activity in life, or it might be eruptions of anger, aggressiveness, or sexual drives, that we find difficult to deal with. In other people or races, lethargy, intellectual inertia or fear may prevent a balanced life. Dreams sometimes portray to us an antidote to such states of being. This is usually done in the dream by the release or expression of a new realisation, a new emotion, a new symbol, or a new energy. But the dream happens in the subconscious. So the task is to bring this 'antidote' to our everyday life. To 'bring it home' to oneself and others, a permanent record of the dream's content in art form or drama is tremendously effective.

In recording our dream, our temperament can be given free rein. Basically, however, it is sufficient to write it down in full.

FOUR

Seeking to understand

We have already said that the dream can be likened to a cartoon, which expresses or comments upon a situation by symbols. The dream can also be likened to a strange language, which we have to translate to arrive at its meaning. As Nietzsche suggested, it may be that the dream is our own archaic language, which at one time was the universal thinking process of man. To some extent we can easily see the possible truth of this by a simple experiment. The experiment also helps us in understanding the language of dreams, and thus begins the process of interpretation.

The experiment is simply this—try to think without the use of words! To be more specific, imagine that you wish to tell some-one that: 'What most people call prophecy, if looked at rationally, is usually an unconscious analysis of present events, and our projection of their consequences into the future.'

I have purposely given a rather difficult idea to use in the experiment, and it should be done now before reading on. Then one finds, that without words, one is thrown back upon the use of images, symbols, dramatisation and depiction of various emotions. It would be interesting to know exactly how the reader has been able, if at all, to express the given idea about prophecy. But here is how a dream has done it. 'I was looking into a crystal ball, when suddenly I could see a whole file of men walking along some railway lines. I called John (the dreamer's husband), and said "Look, there is a picture in the crystal!" He looked, but then pointed behind me, and I could see that what I saw in the crystal was only a reflection of what was actually going on in the street behind me.'

This experiment of expressing ourselves without words, is very important. It demonstrates a number of things necessary in dream interpretation. Firstly, it shows that the dream may be our heritage from the past. It could be the method of thought used prior to man's use of words. If so, it suggests that man's consciousness is stratified, and our present type of consciousness is built over and developed from the older level. It also clearly shows how we link up ideas such as 'prophecy' with an object such as a 'crystal'. The complex idea of the future being a reflection of the present is dealt with by the clever positioning of several images in the dream. The difference between speculative and logical thinking is also expressed by the man and woman.

If we explore this idea a little further, we will quickly be able to see how a dream might be able to use common objects and events in our everyday life. Just as we have seen how a crystal expresses the idea of the future, or prophecy, our favourite armchair could express comfort or our sense of relaxation. To understand such things we have to be careful to investigate just exactly what we *do* feel or think about such things. For instance, our car is something we use to get from one place to another. It is a *vehicle*. In a sense, a school is also a vehicle, it transports us from ignorance to knowledge. But if we always feel ashamed when in our car, because it is shabby; then the car used in the dream represents our shame, our desire for better things.

Therefore we have to carefully note what our relationship with the dream symbols is. Our dream may not use *our* car, but just *a* car; when it becomes just a means of transport, about which we have no feelings. Similarly, if friends or acquaintances are pictured in dreams, then they are used because of the ideas and emotions we associate with them. Therefore, a friend who is always miserable and unsure of himself, represents our own feelings of uncertainty and misery. The warm emotional friend likewise is a symbol of our own feelings.

Sometimes dreams play on words and symbols together. Thus, if we dream of finding an old leather bag which did not belong to us, unlocking it with a key, only to find rotten and evil smelling food inside, this would be a very caustic comment on our sexual relationships. In effect it is saying, I picked up an 'old bag', had sexual intercourse with her, but found it unsatisfying and in the end, distasteful.

Although we have said that the dream may be a pre-language thinking, now that words have been added to our experience, the dream will naturally use them. In fact the dream uses any available material quite without our conscious sense of appropriateness. Thus, colours, words, images and feelings will all be collected to express the dream. In most cases, however, we can arrive at the meaning of the symbols through our own associations with them. Of course, many symbols, like the crystal, would be almost universal, but they are only universal because enormous numbers of people have the same, or very similar, associated ideas concerning them. If one's mother had used a crystal ball to hit one on the head as a child, it would no longer associate with prophecy, but punishment. A look at advertisements shows us how often such symbols are used to quickly convey a message without words. Thus a *doctor* or *nurse* expresses healing or sickness—a *lightning flash* is energy, speed and power—a *policeman*, law, protection or conscience—a *shapely girl*, sexual or emotional pleasures—and so on.

Very often, the dream picks up a theme from the day's experiences, and uses it to illustrate some inner condition. The following dream is an example of this. 'I was looking everywhere for some green stuff to eat. I saw a field of cabbages, but, as they were not mine, could not eat the leaves.' A couple of days before, the dreamer had prepared a salad for dinner, as it was winter, and the family were getting few 'living' foods. So we see that the conscious concern over 'living' foods has been used as a symbol in the dream. Thus the search for green leaves represents a search for something of her own that is *living*. The woman had been wondering what her own personal capabilities in life were. As the dream shows, she will not be satisfied or feel happy by simply taking or copying what others have done, or eating the rewards of their labours.

One last thing about the use of symbols and our attempts to interpret. Some symbols may be used a number of times in different dreams. In such cases, or in analysis generally, we have to realise that a symbol is influenced by the symbols it is grouped with, and the way it is used. To understand this, if we realise that words are symbols of thoughts in daily life, we will see clearly what is meant. As a demonstration of how one symbol (word) can alter its meaning due to context, I do not think I can better the efforts of Leslie Weatherhead when he wrote:

For instance, in Mesopotamia you might have an officer who had *blue* blood in his veins and who at Oxford had been a *blue*.

Rarely would he be a *blue* after dark when the whiskey went round, unless of course he went out on the *blue* on some stunt or other. Then he might be in a *blue* funk, and the air would be *blue* with his language. But in time he would recover from his fit of the *blues*, get his leave and pay, and *blue* the whole of the latter in a single day of the former, and he wouldn't spend it on *blue* stockings either.'

So when interpreting, although we have to understand each individual symbol, we also have to see that symbol in context with the rest of the dream. Only in this way can we understand it properly.

LISTING OF SYMBOLS

If we are working on our own dreams, we cannot simply lie on a couch and let somebody else ask us all the searching questions. We have to be the one asking the right questions, and the one on the couch finding the answers. In other words, we have to know what questions to ask ourselves, and also be able to relax and let spontaneous associations and replies come up. Now that something has been said about dreams in the earlier chapters, and the idea behind association of ideas dealt with, we can actually get down to the dream analysis.

So, we have had our dream, remembered it, and written it out fully. Our next step is to start the interpretation. To begin with, one of the best ways to do this is by listing the symbols. I will use a dream to demonstrate this that is fairly simple. Here is the dream: 'I was lying in the bed that I slept in whilst on holiday. There were a lot of people round me and I had had a baby. Everybody seemed to be certain that I was going to die, and the child or children I had given birth to had been taken away. I thought that I would die (if I was going to die) when I expelled the afterbirth, but I didn't seem to mind.' The dreamer added the comment, 'I had this dream during a fit of depression.'

'Holiday bed' is our first symbol. When this is written down, one must now ask oneself what this idea suggests. Some of the ideas that arose around this symbol are that one talks of 'making

43

one's bed, and lying on it'. So a bed can stand for some condition that has been created, that we now have to face. This is suggested by the dream showing that it is the 'holiday' bed, pointing to some condition that occurred on holiday. This brought up the fact that just before going on holiday, the woman had received a letter from a friend she was deeply attached to. Part of the letter had so hurt her felings that she had felt depressed all during the holiday. Here we have the 'bed' that was slept in on holiday. The dream is, in fact, pointing to the 'fit of depression'.

Turning to the next symbol, we can call it 'a lot of people'. This is associated with two things. It is all the parts of the dreamer's life that are implicated in her depression. Also, all of those about her, who are likewise influenced. Other parts of one's life are obviously involved in depression. One might usually be active and creative, writing letters to people, cooking extra treats for the family, etc., all of which are left undone during such feelings of unhappiness. Or at least, not done with the same spirit.

Then we come to 'the baby'. In real life a baby is a blending of mother and father, and all they represent. A baby is a new thing that has been 'born' out of us and the circumstances we are involved in. The dreamer said that due to the pain caused by the letter, a new attitude had arisen to the person who had written it. We can definitely associate this with the baby. It had likewise been 'born' out of her present self, and her relationship with her friend. In fact, mystics have always spoken of their pupils as 'spiritual children'. This usually referred to the relationship between the teacher and pupil. But we can see that the dream suggests a much deeper inter-relationship. When we enter the receptive or sensitive part of another human being, we often leave a seed there that develops into a new baby, a new attitude, an offspring of the relationship between us.

'Death' or 'Dying' is the next symbol, and in the light of what has already been said is not hard to understand. For with the birth of the 'new attitude' to her friend, she certainly begins to feel that her old feelings for the friend are dying. As she still associates herself strongly with these feelings, it is as if *she* is dying. If on the other hand, she could see that the old feelings are not worth holding on to because they were so susceptible to being hurt, her dream might have shown them as the death of an old friend. The dream ends with the symbol of 'the afterbirth'. The placenta is that which links our established body to the new growth. The new always develops out of the old—always builds itself out of the elements, nourishment, provided by the old. In this sense, the after-birth can be seen as the in-between condition within the woman. She could not have given birth to a new attitude unless she was near to reaching those conclusions. It also suggests those parts of the affair that 'hang on' within one, even when the affair is over. Not until these have dropped away will the old die, and the new, more vigorous attitude come into its own.

Therefore, our list of symbols will look something like this:

HOLIDAY BED—when one makes one's bed, one lies in it. The bed is my depression I felt on holiday. The dream is saying this is my bed. In other words, maybe I made this depression and had to experience it because of my own attitudes.

A LOT OF PEOPLE—All the parts of my nature involved through my feelings of depression, and the outer consequences of this.

THE BABY—The new attitude that has sprung from my pain.

THE AFTERBIRTH—All the feelings that are still hanging on con-cerning my hurt.

DEATH—The disappearance or death of my old attitude.

From all that, we emerge with a very comprehensive message and analysis of the situation. Although not a long and complex dream, nevertheless, an enormous amount can be gathered from it. If we think of it as a letter to ourselves from our Self, we might write it out thus:

The letter from P. hurt a great deal. But I could not have felt that hurt if I had not entertained the feelings about him I did. In a sense, I made 'my own bed' by thinking about him in that way. It followed that as soon as he did something that did not fit those feelings, they would be hurt.

Yet the hurt has been a positive thing, as it has 'given birth' to a new attitude that may help me see P. as he is, instead of as I wanted him to be. Obviously I am still hanging on to the old attitude, but there seems the promise that it will drop away from me. Then all the old attitude, along with its possibility of being so badly hurt, will die.'

Not all dreams are as straight forward to interpret as that one. Some dreams will be only half understood. Others always remain a mystery. The next dream is an example of a more difficult type. Where so many events and objects come into the dream instead of remaining closely bound in the one scene like the bedroom dream, it usually signifies a more complex dream.

In the dream, 'A girl had been captured by a dwarf—she'd been in hospital previous to this. He was painting and made her help him, but took all her clothes. He made her help him climb on to a big platform. While he was painting someone came up through a trap door almost underneath her, and was shocked to find her there naked and frightened. He took her away, and he and his wife gave her some clothes—bundled her into them. They kept telling her the best way to get to London; but she didn't really want to go there and kept protesting. They didn't listen, thinking they were doing the right thing. They took her to the bus terminus and left her there, having told her several routes to London and suggested she either got a bus or a lift. She wandered around hoping no one would recognise her. All the buses seemed to be going to Blackheath. She went to a refreshment stand; the girl in front of her in the queue had orange squash, and asked "Would chips be very expensive?" She had orange squash and it cost 10d. A shop beside the stall was headed, "Christmas cards *not* decorations". She went to a cafe—they were selling peas and brussels sprouts or rolls.'

It should be explained that the dreamer had not been appearing in her dreams. Therefore we see it all occurring to 'a girl'. The dreamer also made only these comments on the dream: 'I suppose the girl represents me, or more likely some part or aspect of me. The dwarf seems to stand for ugliness, cruelty—the outside world? But I am obliged to help it. Rescue comes from below—my rescuer finds this part of me helpless and vulnerable—clothes it, but in the wrong things; helps it, but in the wrong way. From this I conclude that

46

help for this part of me will not come from below. The rescuer offers ways but none of these is the right (acceptable?) way, and this part of me is not even sure it wanted to go on a journey—it only wants to keep itself hidden. I have no direct associations with "Black-heath"—except that it reminds me of Shakespeare's "blasted heath" and just sounds a rather unpleasant place to go.'

With its lack of outer associations, and length, the dream looks like a formidable problem to unravel, although this should not put one off attempting it. Even if only part of it is revealed, it is worth the effort.

Let us start with THE GIRL. In dealing with a dream like this, lacking associations, we have to let the dream itself do much of the explaining. For instance, if one saw a man's hand holding a beautiful bunch of red roses, with a note attached saying, 'With love', would it *need* associations? In the dream 'the girl' is not the dreamer. She has also recently been in hospital. So immediately the images tell us that the dreamer has submitted to a healing regime recently, and also that she does not like to see herself mixed up with the things of her dream. For one usually only disguises oneself or appears incognito, if one does not wish to be 'associated' with the situation. In outer life the dreamer had just become really interested in her dreams, and we might tentatively associate this with the hospital or healing.

THE DWARF can also be dealt with by looking at it as it appears in the dream. The dreamer's associations are not satisfactory because they do not explain the dwarf in this dream context. That is stunted growth—painting—undressing the girl—making her help him to a high(er) platform. Taking the image as it is, it becomes self explanatory. It is a part of her that is faced as soon as she submits to the healing regime. It is stunted growth of creative masculine abilities that need her help to lift it to a higher level of expression. In contacting it, however, it unveils her helplessness; it strips away the clothing of pretence and delusion she had swathed herself in, and makes her see how she relates to it—in fear and trembling.

Put in words of a more understandable nature; each of us, man or woman, has something of the opposite sex in us. The logical, cool, constructive male, underneath has a world of emotions, irrational hopes, intuitions and softness usually only associated with women. On the other hand, an emotional, motherly, illogical woman, yet has within her constructive, logical, creative male characteristics. Joan of Arc is an extreme example of the strength and masculine power a woman can wield when her male qualities blend with her female self. While perhaps Schweitzer, with his gentleness, long suffering, and lovingness, is an example of the male female union. In the dreamer, however, this male creative part of her is stunted in growth. (In psychology this male aspect of a woman is called her animus. The female aspect of a man, anima.) This part of her seeks expression in art, in creativity, but has to force her co-operation by stripping off ideas, hopes, etc. This taking away of her orthodox attitudes frightens her; just as it might any person who, settled in a career that offers regular pay and security, suddenly feels a power-ful urge to leave all this and take up some less 'sensible' job. Most people are 'rescued' from this frightening situation by similar means to the dreamer. Their 'common sense' saves them.

Moving on to the MAN AND WOMAN, we see that they fit this role of common sense, mum and dad, figures. They seem to be the easily shocked parents who try to do their inadequate best for the child. They represent orthodoxy, possibly gained from her parents. But such orthodoxy ill suits her. The clothing fits poorly; the direc-tions are not aligned with the dreamer's inner desires. That such help arises from below, further suggests that these are orthodox habits of relationship acquired in childhood from home and school. Habits are notably motivated from the unconscious—we do such things unconsciously—without thinking.

LONDON offers a more difficult symbol. It is, in the dream, recom-mended by the man and woman, so we can gain a little insight by aligning it with their possible attitudes. The orthodox usually prefer the accepted, the safe, known way of doing things. Therefore, if we think of London as a symbol of the centre of commerce, of worldly pleasure; the direction in which most people go when they wish to 'make a name' for themselves. Thus the dream begins to resolve into a representation of an inner conflict between two urges in the dreamer's life. One is her own creative urge which frightens her because it tends to be unorthodox. This she has held back in growth due to her fear. The other urge is that of the orthodox desire to seek a more 'sensible' commercial career or at least, to be more concerned with outer life. As can be seen, this is a difficult decision to make due to the inner circumstances surrounding her own creative or inner nature. We can also see that the dream is concerned with very real problems in life, and with practical affairs. For if the dreamer chooses wrongly, she may remain unsatisfied for a very long time. As the dreamer says, 'This part of me is not even sure it wanted to go on a journey—it only wants to keep itself hidden.' This shows how we may prefer not to know about our real inner feelings because of the torment of decision they will require.

That the BUSES going to BLACKHEATH follow this, is very explanatory of what the dreamer senses the consequence will be. All the buses are going to Blackheath, or 'blasted heath'. This could be taken two ways, one being that any move to commerce or acceptance of outer instead of inner values would be a journey to a very black situation, or that consciousness of the decision cannot help but lead to a period of black despair. Possibly they are both true.

In regard to the last part of the dream, she says she 'can make no sense'. I must admit I find this difficult also, made worse by not having been able to talk it over in length with the dreamer. Generally speaking, however, any search for food is a search for nourishment. Food and drink 'sustain' us, 'feed' us. Thus arose the saying, 'Feed my lambs', which in its religious setting means to sustain, to keep strong, the spiritual life of the flock. However, our dream does not have a religious setting. The episode of the refreshment stand follows upon the image of Blackheath and the dreamer's 'wandering around'. The feelings that arise from such images, if we place ourselves in them, is that of being lost, not knowing what to do, hopelessness. Certainly in such circumstances we would need sustaining, strengthening. If we ask ourselves how we sustain ourselves in such situations we see that some people use an effort of will, some reason about the situation, some pray, some visit a friend who cheers them up, some withdraw or hide the feelings by entertainment or outer activity. Without the dreamer's comments on this, we do not know what she did, but the dream suggests that she feels the price may be too high, and buys only the least expensive of sustenance.

The next image in the dream is CHRISTMAS CARDS not DECORATIONS. Again we can only speculate on this due to the lack of associations. The fact that it follows the concern over the cost, may help; for Christmas cards are things we give and receive, unlike decorations which simply belong to us as adornment. So the dream image seems to suggest that if we are to receive help we must not count the cost. It is a matter of giving and receiving, of being willing to part with things, that life and events will bring its own reward. We send a Christmas card because we wish a friend to know we remember him. It is a self expression, not a concern over personal adornment, a making of our house, our self, more decorative. Then the decorations, of other people's cards come naturally. So in applying this to the conflict, it says that in expressing what is in us, instead of simply worrying about seeing we are 'decorated' with security, things naturally come to us.

PEAS—SPROUTS AND ROLLS seem even more bizarre until we see that they all have something in common. They are all round objects. Quite simply, a round thing suggests completeness, the full circle, the whole horizon, an 'all round' person. So through give and take we arrive at the condition where we can partake of a more complete, whole sustenance, which will, because of its completeness, help us through the decision. This interpretation may seem far fetched until we see, from analysis of many dreams, that a spherical shape often refers to completeness, integration or wholeness.

However, the interpretation of the dream is far less satisfying than the previous dream. This is because it lacks the comments of the dreamer in saying whether or not these interpretations really apply. It also lacks details about the dreamer's life that would confirm or deny the conclusions. Nevertheless, it is a good example of how we can get at the possible meaning of the dream symbols if we fail to find helpful associations.

FIVE

The dream mystery explored

The method of interpretation dealt with in the last chapter is basic to all dream analysis as currently known. It can be summed up as remembering the dream; recording of dream; listing of symbols; and association of ideas. It was also seen that symbols must be interpreted in their right context, or can even be understood because of that context; which is rather like arriving at the meaning of an unknown word because of the way it is used in a sentence. Several other things were mentioned or hinted at while the dreams were being analysed. Some of these are so important or helpful, that they will now be further explained.

MAIN PHASES OF DREAM

If we look at the structure of the last dream analysed, we see that it can be split into four main phases. These are (1) episode with the dwarf, (2) being saved by the couple and directed to London, (3) wandering, (4) the search for refreshment. In any long and difficult dream, especially where little or no associations or information have been forthcoming, it is worth breaking the dream into its phases. When this has been done, instead of associating ideas with the symbols, see whether the phases have any meaning. In the case of the last dream, we would have something like this:

(1) *Episode with Dwarf* I am captured and stripped. Do I feel imprisoned or restrained by anything? What has frightened me or uncovered phases of my life I wasn't aware of or had kept covered or hidden before?

(2) *Being saved by the couple and directed to London* If I can find any sense of being imprisoned or captured, how did I deal with it? How did I 'save' myself from it? Having dealt

with my restraint, what did the ideas or emotions I had used indicate I should do?

(3) *Wandering* Presumably, I could not accept this direction, and was left in a quandary, fearful of a possible blackness—depression. Is there any indication of this? Has there been a wandering or dithering over some decision?

(4) *Search for Refreshment* This suggests a need for some refreshing experience. A thirst for something—a hunger—but a doubt about the cost in effort. Has there been a desire for a 'refreshing' change—a hunger for something to satisfy my feelings? Is there a doubt about what we will have to sacrifice or give up in exchange?

It can be seen that dealing with the dream in this way is an enormous help in asking oneself the right questions. As previously suggested, when dealing with our own dreams, we have to be both patient and analyst. But not all dreams are as easily broken into the different parts. Some dreams cannot be segmented in this way, while others have far less phases. The next dream is an example of the latter.

'I had gone to Sheila's and Uncle Frank's house at Spearing Road. They had promised I could have a room there, but I found all the rooms occupied and people were sleeping on the floor instead of in beds. Seeing there was no room I turned away and the next thing I knew I was in a train; it had rather luxurious blue leather seats but again was almost full. It contained, as far as I could see, all ladies, and I explained to them that I had been promised sleeping accommodation. Even while I was explaining this and expecting to occupy a length of three seats, I could see they had as much right there as I, and I took the single seat offered still protesting that we were promised sleeping room.'

This dream can only be broken into two, or at the most, three parts. That is, *the house, the train* and possibly, accepting the seat. If this is set out as was the previous dream, we have a clearer idea what the dream is about.

The House Searching for living space in a chilhood setting.

52

Found 'no room'. What have I been looking for in childhood attitudes? Was the 'promise' of childhood unfulfilled?

The Train Exorbitant expectations, annoyance at the fact that these high expectations cannot be fulfilled. This in a setting of getting somewhere—train. Have my expectations in getting somewhere not been as great as hoped for?

The Single Seat Grudging acceptance of practical offer. Can I see anything of this in real life?

The whole idea of using this method is to take the general events, implications and settings of a dream, and use these as a reference for asking oneself questions.

THE DREAM SEQUENCE

One of the things that is often overlooked in dreams is what we might call the *'because'* factor. This factor is fairly noticeable when once pointed out, but difficult to see until much dream interpretation has been done. The *because* factor also applies in our everyday life, and can be seen when we say, 'I was waiting for a bus and began to talk to a stranger who was also waiting. Our conversation became so interesting, that after a few minutes we went and sat in a restaurant, letting the bus go, *because* we had so much in common. Before he went he gave me his card *because* he wanted me to contact him again. I could see from what we had spoken about, that he was thinking of offering me a job in his firm. But I never followed it up *because* I didn't think I could fill the post.'

If we look into this, we see that important events occur, directions followed, decisions taken, all *because*. The word 'because' in fact hides all our background, our feelings, our predisposing urges and thoughts. The word 'disposition' can in fact be used to sum up what lurks behind the *because* factor. A little thought will show that history is made up of this 'disposition', acting through the *because* factor.

I hope this doesn't sound mysterious or complicated. This is such an important thing to understand. Our whole life, the events and outcome of it, rest upon it. Our life is what it is because of what we are—our disposition. We take an offer or reject it *because* of this. We succeed or fail in life *because* of the same factor—ourselves. 'The fault, dear Brutus, lies not in the stars/But in ourselves, that we be underlings.' When understood, we can see that every move we make in life is conditioned by subtle feelings of fear or pleasure, pride or love. At every decision we are directed by intangible hopes, despairs, conflicts and ideals. So, dreams also, arise out of the *because* factor.

Two dreams illustrate this. 'I was waiting for a visitor. Suddenly the man I had been expecting came round to the back window and peeped in. I didn't see him clearly, but took an immediate aversion to him and refused to let him in.'

Here we see that something 'waited' for by the dreamer, when it actually arrives, is not admitted due to feelings of aversion. It is not admitted *because* of aversion.

A clearer example is this. 'I was surrounded by a thick wall of briars, beyond which were wild animals. I was trapped and couldn't get out. I wondered what to do. Suddenly I noticed a hole in the ground. I looked in and saw it was a tunnel. I was just about to explore it as a way of escape, when I saw a dirty animal-like man looking up at me. I drew back from the tunnel in disgust and woke up.'

Here we see that the dreamer is trapped by his own tangle of problems, and destructive instinctive urges. A possible way out is shown in the tunnel of unconscious exploration (i.e. discovering one's hidden contents), but the dreamer, on looking within, sees an undeveloped and repulsive part of himself which disgusts him. It is *because* of this disgust that he cannot get out through the tunnel. The whole dream revolves around that point. It is also *because* of this inability to explore further due to disgust, that the dream ends. The dream is showing that it is the feelings of disgust that are keeping him trapped in his unpromising situation. In real life, he is stuck in the middle of painful experiences *because* of his own feelings of disgust about a part of his nature. Thus, the because factor in dreams is very important, and is the central point in numerous dreams.

DREAM SERIES

If we fail to understand an individual dream, light can often be thrown upon its meaning by looking at the dreams that precede and follow it. In this way one sees that the symbols are used in a gradually evolving manner. A dream series of evolving symbols is also one of the most striking proofs that dreams are not mere non-sense. The dreams that follow were all dreamt within about a month.

(1) 'Visit to M. Very nice house, high on the cliffs overlooking the sea. M. and others their usual welcoming selves. Met other pleasant friendly people, but we had to go down the hill to meet them and then some of them pointed out another way up the hill to another beautiful view, and came along to show us the way, which M. actually knew, but didn't want to spoil their pleasure in showing me. A few of those in M.'s house were not quite as nice as I had believed from M.'s description, but I liked them anyway.'

Here we start off with a house overlooking the sea—a state of looking over one's hidden contents, one's unconscious. Or we might say the dreamer is 'overlooking' certain things about herself. These things she has overlooked begin to become known in the people, parts of herself, that were not quite as nice as she had believed.

(2) 'Met uncle George. Then he and I and a few relatives and friends went on to a small boat and began a journey. I didn't know where we were going but others did, and it was such a new and pleasant experience for me that I didn't bother to ask. As it grew dusk a strange but pleasant and friendly woman, who was obviously familiar with the boat, came and closed the curtains and put the light on, so that we could be comfortable during the night.'

Just previous to dream number one, the dreamer had begun, with the help of a friend who knew a little about interpretation, to analyse her own dreams. So we see that from 'overlooking' the sea she has quickly gone on a sea voyage. The dream sums up her situation wonderfully, 'I didn't know where we were going, but others did.' She didn't at the time realise where the interpretations and dreams would lead her. Also, the sea is now much closer, and night is coming. That is, darkness and the unconscious are already making themselves felt, for the night sea journey is a classical dream of the exploration of one's unconscious contents, as with Jonah and the whale.

(3) 'Found myself in a place where I could go swimming every morning.'
Already she is beginning to enter the water, or her inner life.

(4) 'Went into a church with someone who pointed out that I was facing the wrong way. I turned round and saw a bigger and lighter altar at the other end.'
Having begun to contact her inner life via swimming, immersing in it, she sees that her attitude to religion or her own innermost feelings had been wrong. This she corrects.

(5) 'I was involved in a revolution. Everything around was collapsing, but I don't remember being frightened.'
All her old ideas are being either revolutionised, or are collapsing.

(6) 'I found myself being led in a particular direction by friendly pleasant people, who yet knew that on arrival I was to be executed. I had an immature woman of about twenty-five with me, and the same fate awaited her. I took her hand and tried to convey love and courage and to protect her from all her fears by behaving in a light-hearted manner.'
As her old ideas collapse, her old self is to die. Also the immature twenty-five-year-old part that still lives on in her is to die.

(7) 'I found myself entering a tunnel where I encountered a rather frightening little animal, but we passed each other as he went out and I went in. Then I met a larger animal with the same results. Later I met a third, a real monster, rather like a 60-ft caterpillar with a lion's head and fore feet. I did not like the encounter as I continued to walk on the left side of the tunnel, into ever deepening darkness, and he passed me on the way out. Somehow I felt that Doctor (a friend and adviser) would not have been in the least afraid, and I borrowed his courage, and woke about half-way along this monster.'

Having been ready to die to her old way of life, she can begin the descent into her unconscious contents in earnest. The two frightening animals are two fears that come up and out. The third one is too big a fear to completely pass by at this time; and its shape shows its possible sexual nature.

Here, in just seven dreams, with very inadequate comments, can be seen how the symbols evolve as the dreamer discovers her real inner nature. The 'overlooked' sea becomes travelled upon. The coming darkness on the boat develops into the 'deepening darkness' of the tunnel; while each dream shows a development on the inward journey the dreamer was undertaking. Such a series need not be about the inward journey, however, but about commercial undertakings, health, ambitions, or even answers to intellectual queries.

These seven dreams were taken from about twice that many, dreamed during the period. The selection being based on how one can understand past dreams by seeing them in context with others occurring. The important point being that one might dream of looking at the sea for years, but never enter it. Then, with a change of 'disposition', a series of swimming and diving dreams take place. In interpreting our dreams in this way, we have to watch for similar symbols in changed conditions. The sea and darkness are obvious in the series. Also the crowd of people leading her, representative of her own desires to understand herself. The interpretation is arrived at by analysing the situations the dreamer finds herself in, and how the symbols change. Thus a seed seen in one dream, and a plant just growing in another suggest growth and development. A person scorned in one dream, and loved in another, would be a change of attitude and relationship.

These three methods, the Main Phase—the Because Factor, and the Series method, all help us to see the underlying meaning of the dream through looking at the dream as a whole. Particular symbols are not worked on in the same way as in the associated ideas method. It is the relationships the dream suggests that arouse questions. In turn, these questions themselves clarify the dream for us, and help us analyse our experience to see if the dream explains or explores it. As we advance in ability to deal with our dreams, these various methods are called upon and used as required.

SIX

The creative dreamer

In a sense, no dream in itself is creative. By this I mean that even though a dream may present an entirely new idea, or new energy, it rests upon the person who dreams as to whether they will take up and use the dream contents. Because of this we can liken dreams to the gauges and dials on the instrument panel of a car or aircraft. Despite what the instruments say, the driver can choose to ignore them. While the other extreme is to become so bound up with them, that freedom of will, the sense of experiment or daring is impaired. For if dreams are like the instrument panel, and picture what is going on throughout the machine, and what its relationship with the environment is (altitude, inside and outside temperature, speed, and so on), then each activity by the pilot also changes the instrument readings. The truth of this is easily seen in dreams. Any changes we make through a conscious decision, often entirely change the dream contents and their tone. In other words, the change has not come through doing what dreams have suggested, but following some conscious direction. This is especially true where the outer change influences our feelings, or deals with the basic patterns of our behaviour. Sometimes it is contact with a new friend that triggers this change, or discovery of new ideas in books; or a change forced through the pressure of outer events. For someone who had recorded their dreams but never worked on them, then read and used the ideas in this book, definite dream changes could occur.

Possibly this can be seen in two dreams quoted by G. Heyer in his book *Organism of the Mind*. The first dream is of a man who was naturally sociable and outgoing. His interests were in events and outside things. A friend had talked him into practising meditation, however, and he began to look inwards. Here is his dream: 'I was standing in my house looking out of the window. I saw a garden I had never seen before, and decided to go out and cultivate it. I took fork and pick, and began digging the garden, which was all over-grown. I worked like a navvy. Suddenly I began to unearth live grenades and bombs. I was terrified that these would explode, and hastily went back into the house.'

This is clear enough. The garden he has never seen before represents his own inner feelings and experience. It is overgrown because he has never 'cultivated' that part of his life. He finds that to do so requires a great deal of effort. Also, as the work continues, he becomes conscious of possibly dangerous and frightening emotions within himself that make him wish to give up meditation. This is not a criticism of meditation, merely a description of what we should expect to find and deal with as we progress with inner cultivation. After all, bombs can be de-fused, and grenades let off where they will do no damage.

The other dream is that of a young girl quite opposite to the man. She is shy and introverted. Her life has been much spent in the garden he had never seen—her own inner feelings. She decided that she must make a change in her life, and become a bit more sociable and outgoing. She took a holiday at a big hotel, danced every evening, and chatted in the bar. Then she dreamt, 'I was in the hotel room looking out of the window. As I looked I noticed that the scenery was slowly moving past in a circle. This began to speed up, and I realised it was not the scenery going round and round but the hotel. I became terrified and felt I must get out. I ran down to the entrance, and saw that the hotel was like a huge tree. It was turning round and round being twisted off its roots. I jumped to the ground just before it fell.'

The circling hotel reminds us of the gay whirl of events the girl is now in. It is the merry-go-round, the new 'circle' of friends. But this is twisting her off of her roots, her basic character anchorage, her basic self.

These are both dreams critical of the new change or, at least, warning of the stresses it brings. Some outer changes bring the inner self out of the rut it has got into however. A person may be in a constant pessimistic state, which is reflected by dreary dreams. Unexpected outer events like sudden acclaim for their work, or offer of a new job, may make them decide to throw off the pessimism, and their dreams correspondingly change.

From what has been said, and from the analogy between the pilot and his instruments, we can see what the most creative relationship is with our dreams. They are guiding principles; a panel of information about ourselves. This self knowledge can be used constructively or ignored. If it is ignored we must face the consequences, social and internal. For if our speedo shows we are breaking the law, we mustn't jibe if we get caught. Or if we are out of fuel (energy) we can stop, rest and refuel, or if it is an emergency, press on as far as possible until the car stops. These are decisions the driver has to make. But he can make them a lot more capably and shrewdly if he is watching the instruments.

Therefore, a dream only becomes creative when we take note of it and use its information. The creativity lies in blending our conscious functions of will, decision, focused intelligence, and attention, with the suggestibility, diffused and intuitive intelligence of the unconscious. It is only when the merging of our conscious and unconscious interests take place, that the real creative fire is sparked off. Only the marriage of these two produces the magical infant, or divine child. The dream is only a needle on the instrument panel, reflecting hidden events in ourselves. Will we see them? It is always how we use information that fulfils or dulls us.

Thousands of men had seen oyster shells upon the hills. But it took Leonardo Da Vinci to realise that they showed the land had once been under the sea. The creative spark only comes when consciousness wrestles, struggles perplexes itself with what it sees of the unknown, the hidden, the resistant. It is not enough merely to see. One must also ponder, experiment, suffer confusion. Then the known and unknown mingle and mate, and produce a child. For this very reason, as Blake says, 'Eternity is in love with the productions of time', for time reveals the hidden contents of the eternal.

FAIRY STORIES AND MYTHS

Any attempt and success at interpretation or understanding of dreams is a creative act. I have likened it to the mating of the conscious and unconscious, the known and the unknown. In dreams it is often actually portrayed as a marriage. Sometimes one of the partners is black or dark skinned representing the darkness of the

60

unknown; while the other is white, showing the light of consciousness and the known. Even if we *do* not do anything with the
understanding, the interpretation has yet been creative. The mating
has produced a child. In other words, we have become more aware
of ourselves through the interpretation. Thus the child is consciousness—we have become more conscious—we have grown in awareness! The thing that we now know, did not previously exist as it
now does. It was not *known* in the unconscious. Neither was it
known in the conscious. The dream held it in embryo, but consciousness worked on it and brought it into being. The instrument
panel is a record of events. They remain meaningless unless the pilot
looks at them and interprets them in the light of his knowledge and
circumstance. The blending produces more awareness of the situation and how it can be dealt with.

This blending is different to either of the previous factors. Using
this knowledge to help us interpret our dreams, we can look around
us and see that since the beginning of awareness as an individual,
mankind has been attempting to understand dreams. But here I use
the word dreams in its widest possible significance. I mean not only
experiences of the night, but all the fragrant, half sensed, stumbles
towards knowledge; all the hopes, feelings, misunderstood stirrings
and urges man has struggled to clarify. All the great religions, all
the myths and legends, the scientific enquiries, the classical literature
of the world, are all men's interpretations of their dreams. Music
and the arts, poetry, social struggles, are all an attempted understanding of man's real nature. For we constantly struggle to be and
know what we are. If we wish to fully understand our dreams, then
we must see that many of the symbols appearing in our dreams
also appear in the religions of the world. They appear in art and
literature of all times and all nations. And what is so striking is that
when we review Hercules' labours, or Jason's quest, or Mithras'
slaying of the bull, or Christ's baptism, or Shiva's relationship with
Shakti, we see that the heroes are struggling with things of our own
dreams. The only difference is that in the great legends, myths and
religions, the hero has arrived at a conclusion. Hercules procures the
golden apples; Jason brings home the golden fleece; Christ
reaches eternal life, and so on. While in our own dream series, we
are still struggling with serpents, or unable to face the lion-headed
giant caterpillar, or get past the disgusting man. It is therefore ob-

vious that we can learn how these other heroes (for we are the heroes of our own dreams) have won through. What have they done to pass through their own social and inner difficulties as symbolized by the monsters and trials of their adventure?

The important thing about these religions and legends is that they are dreams plus consciousness. In other words they are the creative expression that arises from dealing with the unconscious or unknown in the right way. The reason I have gone to great lengths in explaining all this, however, is because through proper study of them our own dreams become more understandable. Also, in seeing how difficulties have been met, we find possible means of dealing with our own problems, outer and inner. This is why religions and legends have stood the test of time, much to the consternation and plain disbelief of the purely intellectual, who knows nothing of his own inner processes.

To give two brief examples of what can be gained from such sources, two well known parts of our heritage will be explained from this point of view.

Generally speaking, outside of the Catholic faith, the image of the Virgin Mary is smiled upon. Even where critics point out that many older religions also had virgin deities who gave birth to a holy child, they still often fail to see its significance as far as mankind is concerned. This does not mean, however, that a few with understanding have not openly pointed out that the Virgin Mary represents an active principle in every person. Literally, every person can turn to the Virgin Mary for help. But let me explain. Seen as dream symbols, the members of the holy family keep their historical religious significance, but they also gain a personal, inner significance to the man outside any religious beliefs. Mary is said to have conceived from the Holy Ghost and given birth to Jesus, son of God. Joseph is said to have originally doubted and questioned this, but in a dream was assured of its truth. Now, let us look at this just as we do a dream, and see what results.

MARY She is said to talk directly to angels, and to be a virgin. From this we can see that Mary represents the intuitive, receptive part of our own nature. Our feelings, our own virgin nature (i.e. that part of us not interfered with by thoughts, doubts, fixed opinions, biases and pre-conceived ideas) is open to new ideas, new opinions, new feelings. The Holy Ghost is invisible yet expressive of God. That is, it is an unknown part of us, that yet expresses the energy of our whole nature, or the energies that brought us into being. So Mary conceiving from the Holy Ghost means that our own state of receptivity, of freedom from bias and prejudice, of *'pre-conceived'* ideas, can receive parts of our nature that are as yet unknown. This is really only common sense. No new idea comes to any man with a closed mind and heart. No discovery is ever made by a person who believes they already know it all. To receive the new, we have to have at least a part of our mind 'virginal'.

JOSEPH He questions and doubts. So Joseph represents that part of ourself that always questions and doubts the new, the seemingly irrational, the intuitive side of us. He has to sleep and dream (become unconscious) to contact angelic—intuitive wisdom. Therefore we can say Joseph represents intellect, fixed opinions, revealed knowledge. He is a builder or carpenter. This signifies that he uses 'dead' or visible—that is, known ideas and facts—to build his opinions with. When men believed it was a fact the world was flat, and united this with the idea of sailing to the West, the result was the opinion that the ship would topple over the edge of the world. Even today we have to admit our knowledge of things is only partial. Therefore we have to beware of *only* building with the known. We must also be sympathetic to Mary, the receptive and intuitive, that 'gives birth' to the unknown and invisible.

JESUS He is not the son of Joseph, the intellect, but of God, the inner Self, the thing behind all creation. He is the creative being who arises from a union between the conscious and the unconscious. He is the Redeemer. That is, the unity between our Source, and our Consciousness, can lead to a *consciousness of our source*. The energies that make us a breathing thinking being, although changed at death, nevertheless still exist. As science has shown, no energy is ever lost, only changed. The symbol of Jesus suggests that through the union of conscious and unconscious, the products lead us back to an awareness of our source. As this source is eternal, our awareness of it means that we are not lost in death, but our consciousness has now gone beyond the outer, changeable part of our nature. Christ is therefore a redeemer because it is inherent in his nature, as a son of one's Source and conscious life, to redeem the limited awareness of self into a realisation of one's eternal basic nature.

Christianity is for many a huge confusing organisation, to which one outwardly either gives, or does not give, allegiance. I hope it is plain from what has been said above, that as far as our unconscious is concerned, and whether outwardly pledged to a church or not, each one of us has the Holy Family within us.

Turning to a non-sectarian type of reference, however, we see that a similar theme is followed. It is hoped that the story of Sleeping Beauty is known well enough not to need retelling here. To shorten what would be a very long commentary the story will only be dealt with from the time of the Princess's sleep. Taken as a dream, we see that due to events, a beautiful and sensitive part of us has gone to sleep, or become unconscious. As this part, like memories of early childhood, dropped into unconsciousness, all its attendant faculties, symbolised by the court, are also lost to our conscious knowledge and direction. Being young, beautiful and virginal, the Princess is a similar figure to the Virgin Mary. But in the story she does not conceive from the invisible, but falls asleep due to a self-centred, evil, plotting, malicious attitude represented by the witch. Therefore she has to be interpreted differently due to story content. We see her then, as the beautiful, loving and happy side of our own soul or inner self. If we have had a reasonably happy childhood, and have been lost in the feelings of timelessness, wonder and intimate participation of simple events that children experience, we see the Princess as representative of this part of us. We also see that this beauty went to sleep when we were about sixteen (or even as early as nine in the face of contemporary cities and standards). Then we could no longer live in timelessness, or see the wonder of a leaf blowing down the road, or enter completely into a stickleback in a stream. All the attendant faculties of this part of us also slept—are sleeping. Thus the interminable hundred years pass—the great length of time, of living in the world of time, passes, before the Prince hears a legend of the Sleeping Beauty. But what is this legend, and who is the Prince?

If, in reading this book, you have for the first time discovered the ideas relating to an unconscious, hidden part of you, with its promise of greater love, wisdom and beauty, then you have just heard the legend. But you have not heard the legend unless feelings have stirred in you telling you there is a 'sleeping beauty' to discover. The legend is the dim, subtle, difficult-to-prove feelings and hopes within us, that suggest a greater beauty sleeps and can be found. The legend is those hopes that tell us there is *more* in life if we would only search for it. It is a legend because most people believe there is no truth in it; a story fit only for children. While the prince is our conscious mind, our intellect and worldly experience, that feels incomplete, that knows a longing for this 'other half'. He is more than just our 'conscious mind' however. He is a particular state of consciousness; for he dares to search for a Myth. His longing, his incompleteness makes him brave, ready to test the truth or falsity of the Legend. He is certainly not an indifferent consciousness, who stumbles accidentally on the Beloved. He has to cut his way through the terrible briars and thorns surrounding the hidden castle. In these brambles others have been lost and died, for they are all the confusion, pain and ignorance that surround and hide our own 'Sleeping Beauty'. To reach her we have to face, to experience, to cut through this hedge of ignorance, fear and cynicism that has grown around our own happiness and completeness.

But the Prince breaks through, and stands in amazement at the sleeping court. Then, finding the Beloved of his quest, he kisses her awake, and the court wakes also. So, when we dare to face the attitudes of mind, the events, the pains and fears that have cut us off from wholeness, then we enter our innermost self and find how much of us has remained alive yet asleep; in us yet unconscious. Kissing with our consciousness that which slept and was unknown, it comes into our awareness and awakens in us. Then they marry and live happily ever after. For when consciousness unites with its source, it finds completeness and happiness, and eternal life.

This interpretation may give a slightly false impression unless a further comment is added. Namely, it would appear that the Princess *has* to go to sleep in us so that the critical intellect can develop. When this development has taken place, then the two aspects of self, the rational and irrational can marry.

It may not be immediately apparent how helpful the information hidden in fairy stories and myths is. As one faces the elements of oneself through dream interpretation however, such information is of enormous value. An attempt to understand something of the symbolism of the Greek Myths—The Gospels—Fairly stories such as Beauty and the Beast—Snow White and the Seven Dwarfs, and the other classics, can be of enormous benefit. But it is possible that they only begin to make sense when we face similar issues in ourselves.

Some dreams are rather like fairly tales, also, possibly because both arise from the same source. But a fairy tale is usually a 'worked on' or 'interpreted' dream. A dream seldom carries its issue to such a well worked conclusion as a fairy tale. That is why fairy tales can often help us to see what possible issues our dreams are leading to.

CREATING OUT OF THE DREAM

Once we realise that fairy stories, myths and religion are 'worked on' dreams. we can create our own Legend and our own Religion!

Possibly this needs some explanation to avoid misunderstanding. If we accept Jesus or Mohammed or Buddha as historical person- alities, their uniqueness rests upon the fact that they demonstrated in their everyday lives what they saw within themselves as truth. They lived and were true to their deepest feelings. As far as dream analysis is concerned, they had completely come to terms with the outer world, and their own world of instincts, feelings, sexual drives and so on. If we think of life as a creative act, like painting, then we see that what a great artist expresses on canvas, these men expressed in everyday living. Their life was their canvas. The heaven that they had found was expressed in their daily life.

What I am trying to say is that what we find and understand in our dreams, we can express outwardly in acts, or in art. This aspect of dream interpretation has already been mentioned, but not in detail. As it is so very helpful, a little more explanation will be given.

Therefore, let us take as a starting point the act of writing our dream. Then let us see how, once we have spent time on interpreta- tion the dream can now be re-written. In the first place it is a product of the unconscious. In the second version it becomes a unity of conscious and unconscious. Here is the dream:

'It was Christmas morning when I had this dream. I had actually woken up and wondered if I ought to get up and see if the children had got their presents. Then I must have fallen asleep and had this dream. I dreamt I woke up. The light was on in the bedroom, and I looked towards the bedroom door, which was ajar. It was dark out there, but a shaft of light went out from the room through the open door. In this half light I thought I saw a movement. This caught my attention and I stared intently. The door was now open wider and it was no longer dark outside the bedroom. I could now see that it was a small white mouse that moved. It was walking towards the children's bedroom. We were all staying in a friend's seaside holiday cottage at the time. I asked my wife what a white mouse was doing in the house, and thought maybe it had been a pet left by a previous holidaying family. Wanting to catch the mouse I got out of bed and went towards it. As I did so I saw that it was not just white, but shining, very beautifully. It also seemed to grow larger. First to the size of a rat, then to that of a cat. I was now close to it and it looked enormous; shining with an inner light, white and radiant. It was a thing of beauty. Its eyes especially struck me; pink but also shining.

'Turning round to tell my wife about it, I suddenly realised that it was not the mouse that had increased in size, but I who had got smaller. I also saw what at first I thought was my wife, also diminished in size to that of a large doll, sitting on the end of the bed. I waved to her. It was not my wife, but a tiny girl, very lovely with long curly brown hair to her shoulders. She waved back and I woke up.'

Without trying to interpret this dream ourselves, we will follow the course of thoughts taken by the man who dreamt it, that led up to his re-writing it. First of all he could not understand any of its symbolism. Yet it was so impressive, almost visionary in impact, that he kept trying to understand. Not getting any ready-made answers he tried association of ideas on the symbols. This led him to realise that the waking up meant that he was 'Waking up' to something. What he was waking up to was presumably symbolised by the lighted bedroom and the obscure movement. Something was moving in the house—in himself. At first it was only a hint of movement. Was something stirring in himself? He wasn't sure. The fact that it was a mouse, and shining, he could not interpret at all. His relationship with his wife was changing, maybe it had something to do with that, he couldn't tell; and that was as far as he got for some weeks. He still persisted in thinking about it, however, and suddenly he saw the meaning of his decrease in size and apparent hugeness of the mouse. He had been pondering it and remembered that Alice in Wonderland had also shrunk. This did not explain anything until suddenly he saw that in his dream the mouse had remained the same size. It had only *appeared* huge because of his *changed relationship* with it. He then saw that anything within him could remain unnoticeably small unless he approached it in the right way. Then, what had seemed unimportant could become huge. For instance, one might have feelings of love for one's wife, but not think them very 'great'. If she died, however, these seemingly small feelings could assume giant proportions. So he saw that through a different attitude of mind to things within himself, they could be made very big. He had often, for instance, turned away from his own ideas and experiences, preferring to trust 'greater authorities' than himself. He now saw that these greater authorities originally had no more experience of things than he had. But each new idea, each new thought or concept they had received had been treated as great or possibly valuable. They had thus expressed their ideas and become accepted, while his own ideas were treated as little inconsequential things.

Again, this was as far as he got with the dream until he talked with his friend Velta Wilson about the symbolism of the shining mouse. She said that a mouse in fairy tales and mythology often represents the soul, or inner feelings. While anything that shines with an inner light symbolised the innermost self, the energy behind our life, the spirit or eternal part of our being. This opened up a whole new world of meaning for him. A mouse is something that often lives in a house unknown. It symbolises a part of himself only glimpsed before. It was tame, not wild, and it connected him with his central being, or spirit. It had been 'lost' by a previous 'holidaymaker'. When one is on holiday, one 'relaxes' and 'lets go' of the many demands that press upon one. At such times we often glimpse parts of our nature, of desires and hopes, that were previously hidden and pressed back. Very often, we do not wish to return to the workaday world, because it is really something we force ourselves to do. We probably do not really like our work. Or else we do not like it under the pressure with which it is forced upon us. So we glimpse or see other parts of our nature, that on returning to work are lost or forced away. The dream is saying that a previous holidaymaker, or period of relaxation, brought the mouse and lost or left it. He saw a new part of himself that linked with his innermost being, and lost it. Now it is glimpsed again, and refound. What the mouse represented to the dreamer is difficult to explain outside of his own words in the following story. But possibly we can call it a non-grasping attitude to life. Also a realisation that with all our thinking and striving, does this tell us who we are? In attempting to put it all into words, however, in a meaningful way, he hit upon the idea of the story. This, when it was written, greatly satisfied him. It brought all his inner feelings about what the mouse meant into focus. The story also continued to be a help to him in remembering and living what the attitude, the mouse and his relationship to it symbolised. Here is the story.

THE SHINING MOUSE

There was once a time, and there always will be, when a man lived alone in a little house. He was really quite happy, because the house had most things he needed in it. It had a number of rooms, a cellar, five windows, and all that went with them. He never really went out of his house, but he often watched people out of his windows. This didn't seem to bother him too much, because he managed to get all that was necessary; but he did feel lonely sometimes.

It was during one of these times of loneliness that he first heard the noise. It was not a noise he could really describe and say, 'Ah yes, that's running water,' or, 'Of course, it is the fire crackling.' No, it was just a faint noise that set him wondering what it was, and where it came from. He had just been thinking that he really didn't know what to do about his loneliness when it occurred. He got up and looked all through the house and out of the windows, but could find no trace, for there didn't seem to be anything about that would cause such a noise.

After that he began to hear the noise quite often, and he used to make himself quite ill trying to think what it was. Or at least, he would think so hard he would get a headache and not eat his tea.

Well, this went on for a long time, and he was getting headaches all over the place, till one day he thought, 'This is silly, I don't know what the noise is. I have looked everywhere and can't find out where it comes from. And if I don't know what it is, or where it is coming from, how will thinking about it help? All I get is headaches.' So he gave up trying to figure it out and began to eat his tea again. The strange thing was though, that the same evening, while he was sitting by the fire darning his socks, and eating his tea of brown bread and honey, he saw the noise.

I know that sounds silly, and one doesn't *see* noises, but what I really mean is that he saw what had been making the noise all along. As I said, he was sitting by the fire, really not thinking about the noise, when out of the side of his eye he saw something shining in the corner of the room.

It was a little shining mouse as bright as sunlight, yet not casting any shadows. It was brilliant, yet you could look straight at it without being dazzled. Now, as soon as he saw the shining mouse he didn't feel lonely any more. He didn't mind darning his socks; which had always seemed a tiresome job; and he didn't even mind eating brown bread and honey instead of cream cakes. In fact he didn't seem to mind anything any more. He even thought of asking somebody in for tea one day. Maybe not straight away, but it was an idea.

You see, this all came over him in a flash. You know, like when you trip over, wonder what's going to happen, then manage to stop yourself falling, and lots seemed to have happened very quickly. Well, it was like that. Seeing all this very quickly he thought, 'I must have the shining mouse!' and he ran to it to catch it. But something very strange happened, for as he ran to it the mouse got bigger and bigger. At first it was the size of a rat, then of a cat. Then it was as big as a house, and then as big as the world. The man was so startled by this that he stopped and looked around, only to see that it wasn't the mouse that had got bigger, but he who had got smaller. Then he looked back, but the mouse had disappeared, and he was his normal size again in his room.

It had gone—almost as if it had never been there. Not even the noise that its shining made was there. For a little while at least he carried on darning his socks without minding. He ate his brown bread and honey without thinking, 'I wish I could have cream cakes. I have brown bread and honey every day.' And he carried on thinking vaguely about inviting someone in for tea. Then it gradually wore off, and he hated darning socks, he longed for cream cakes, and he didn't think about inviting anybody in for tea, at any time.

So the days passed, and he wondered about the mouse. 'It must be a magic mouse,' he said to himself. 'If only I could catch it I could do all sorts of wonderful things with it. Just think! I would always be happy. I could set my heart on anything and do it without being put off by being lazy, or doubtful or anything. I could show it to other people as well. It would make the troubled happy, the sick well, the unloved lovely; and I would become a very important man, and be thought of as very clever. Just think of that! People all over the world would want to come and see me!'

This time it wasn't headaches he had, but sleepless nights. All the time he was wondering how he could catch the mouse. It became so terrible for him that he even set traps to catch it alive. Nowadays he often heard it, sometimes even saw it, but it always managed to elude his grasp.

In the end he became desperate. He took his chopper and began knocking holes in the walls, chopping up floorboards, poking about in the cellar, and moving everything upstairs; which made an awful mess, because some of it had got so dirty over the years. He ate hardly anything. He didn't sleep very much, or wash, he just tore the house apart. But, oh dear, he couldn't find that shining mouse. He couldn't even find its nest or dwelling place. And then suddenly he began to cry. He really did cry; and the tears made white streaks down his face as they washed the dirt off. Then he fell asleep and had a long rest.

When he woke up he saw how his greediness and desire for fame had made him almost destroy his house. So, slowly he began to repair all the damage he had done, and clean up all the mess. In the same way that he had given up thinking about the noise, he now gave up trying to find the mouse. He was just so pleased to know it was there at all, and to see it occasionally.

And do you know what? Because he no longer chased it, that little

71

mouse became so tame it slowly began to be about the house most of the time. When I last heard, it had started eating brown bread and honey for tea. He is the happiest man in the world.

So, if ever you are invited to tea by a man who doesn't mind darning socks, or eating brown bread and honey for tea every day, just ask him if you might have a peep at his shining mouse!

It is interesting to see how such stories follow a similar type to fairy stories. Also, they usually express themselves again in symbols, or at least, in relationships, that amplify the dream, expressing its meaning. In this case the house is the man's inner self. The rooms are his different feelings or functions. The windows his senses, cellar his unconscious, while the noise is his realisation of something that is missing from his life, realised because of his loneliness, and so on. The difference between this and a dream, however, is that the dreamer is conscious of the meaning of the symbols used in his story; while the symbols of a dream may need a lot of digging into oneself to understand. The story also *extends* the dream, explains it, carries it forward to conclusions. But it is not suggested that one use this method, or attempt to use it, on all dreams. There are only certain dreams which really lead to this easily. These we can call big dreams; those full of meaning, that do not just cover present difficulties, but offer wisdom about life in general. While some people may never find they can work on a dream in this way at all, if it is possible, it brings into focus things that have a very strong influence on the dreamer's conscious life.

As for how one goes about writing such a story from a dream, the attempt to explain the interpretation to oneself in simple terms is all that is basically necessary. We then look for symbols we *consciously* understand, and let the events dictate how these symbols interrelate. Therefore, if I realise that a dream has told me I have been pig-headed for years; and it tells me the cure lies in allowing my sympathy and love to influence my opinions and emotions, a story already emerges. 'There was once a man who had grown up to be terribly ugly. Adults found him awful to look at, but children would run from him screaming with fear, for he had a head like a pig. The older he got, and the more he saw how people disliked him, the stronger became his desire to look like other people. One day he was walking through the woods in despair, lost and not knowing which way to turn, when he met a little peasant girl. She was dressed very simply, and although plain, was somehow lovely to look upon. But then the man approached her and she saw him, and although she gasped with surprise, she did not appear to be frightened or run away. When he told her his plight, she took pity on him, and took him back to her house.' etc., etc. The girl is sympathy, who the pig-headed man meets in his own depression. She is self-sympathy, his own feelings of being sorry for self, taking pity on self because of his plight. But if we continued the story, the man would learn from self pity that others have similar burdens, and his sympathy and pity be extended outwards, and his head become normal in unselfishness.

In writing such stories about what we have learnt from dreams, we clarify our inner situation. Through turning the parts of ourselves into symbols, we can also see how they relate to each other. We can therefore definitely class this as a means of interpretation, and also as an art, an expression of ourselves.

DREAMS AND POEMS

A number of people dream poems or prose. Samuel Taylor Coleridge dreamt his poem *Kubla Khan*. Unfortunately, he was only able to write down a portion direct from dream memory. He was then called out of the house and forgot what followed, and had to write the rest of the poem in the usual manner.

The following poem was also dreamt by a man, and remembered in full.

> *My dear, when I am gone think*
> *of me sometimes with a prayer.*
> *Make that prayer like a homely*
> *room that one can enter, full*
> *of memories like books against*
> *the walls, that one can open*
> *and read; with pictures in of things*
> *we did together. Carpet the floor*
> *with words of love I spoke, like*

falling leaves to make your
pathway easier. For light,
sort out the wisdom from my
follies and use that. There will
be warmth enough; for burning
there upon the grate will be my
feelings for you, like hot coals.
And in that warmth, and in that
flickering light, among those
books, love me a little and
remember, that I gave you the
heart of a man.

As can be seen, this does not lend itself easily to interpretation, as it is a direct expression of feelings. But usually poems in dreams either instruct one in a new idea, or conjure in a few words the essence of the dream. In the form of instruction, one dreamer had the words, 'Each life is a gap in eternity,' which had very deep meaning for her. It was like being told that her conscious life was only a fragment of her total self. The self she knew was but a part of her awareness, lost in time, a short forgetting of her eternal nature to experience the problems of individual life—a gap in eternity. The same woman had another dream that is illustrative of words, poems or prose catching the essence of the dream. She dreamt that a community of people were looking for God. They had decided that someone amongst them should be chosen as a mouthpiece for God. This would mean that the spirit of God would possess the person and talk through them. Therefore they were trying to choose someone who was most worthy and pure for this task. As they were trying to decide, a man amongst them stood up, obviously under the influence of spirit. This was a shock to everyone, as he was not a person they would have chosen, being rather uncouth. Then he began to teach them under the direction of spirit; and the words the dreamer remembered were *'The vessel God chooses is worthy, the cup God fills is pure.'* In the dream the woman felt that it was God's choice, not the people's, while the sentence meant that whoever is chosen is thus purified by the spirit.

But the reason we are dealing with poetry here is not because it is a part of dreams, but because of the manner it can be used to aid interpretation. Just as stories and fairy stories can express more clearly the difficult part of a dream, so also poems and prose can sometimes help to express the incommunicable. In his book *The Living Symbol* Gerhard Adler quotes the poetry of a woman patient. She suffers from claustrophobia, and is seeking help. In the poem she tries to describe the anxiety and experience of her problem.

She writes:

> *The lightning strikes the granite peaks;*
> *They cannot writhe, they cannot scream.*
> *Their wounds bleed stones; their helpless rocks*
> *Roll grinding in the glacier stream.*
>
> *All night a mad, malignant wind*
> *Buffets the ridge with blow on blow,*
> *And from the high tormented crest*
> *Draws out a shrieking plume of snow.*
>
> *The bridge of logs is swept away,*
> *The path stops short on the moraine*
> *At that black gulf where nothing lives*
> *Except the nights' inhuman pain.*
>
> *No voice, no face, no living soul—*
> *Only the two of us are there:*
> *The eye looks at the Wilderness,*
> *The Wilderness returns its stare.*

The poem is still in symbols, but nevertheless bridges the gap between intellectual understanding and pure feelings. As Gerhard Adler points out, it illustrates the patient's problems extremely well. Her intellect, represented by her 'eye' has only a painful, fearful relationship with the Wilderness of her natural forces, emotions, instincts, etc. The snow and the rock, beaten by the wind and water, can also easily be seen as her hardened or frozen feelings and emotions, battered by nature's moving forces of growth and continual change.

Some dreams are difficult to interpret. Several factors lie behind this. It may be a preferring not to know these things because they are painful; we may unconsciously resist the forces of change as the woman does in her poem; or we are having trouble in clarifying an understanding of those areas of experience the dream is dealing with. If we take pen in hand and try to put in words the 'feelings' of the dream, sometimes the words will come readily and easily.

It must be understood, however, that we are not trying to become a famous or acclaimed poet. One is simply trying to put into words what is cloudy, obscure and unformulated within oneself. Therefore, in setting out to express a dream in prose or verse, we need not stick rigidly to the dream. To do so may prevent the emergence of the interpretation the poem represents. Remember that it was said interpretation is the dream plus consciousness. One often adds something to the dream to properly understand it. One does not alter the dream, because that is like cooking the books, or twisting the truth. But one can say, 'That reminds me of this,' which wasn't dealt with in the dream, but complements it. Therefore, when we try to express the feelings of the dream in poetry, we have to stick to those feelings, but we can include *any* related material or images that occur to us as the poem begins to take shape. It may even be that the poem 'comes alive' as we proceed, and emerges in its own direction, and this is all to the good. It means that parts of us that have sought expression and consciousness are pouring out.

Not all dreams are usefully rendered into poetry. Often it is quite unnecessary to do so. But sometimes there will be a quality about the dream, a hidden content that we long to grasp, a meaning that we grope for, when a natural impulse will arise to express the dream contents in verse or prose. At such times it is well to follow the urge or the haunting idea.

DREAMS AND PAINTING

Some years ago, a very interesting book was published on dreams and paintings. It was written by a psychiatrist about a young woman who was his patient. She had a bad skin condition, was

painfully thin, and suffered other neurotic symptoms. During treatment she showed the doctor a painting she had done of a dream.
It was of a bird, a gate, and a winding path to distant mountains.
Neither she nor the doctor understood the meaning or symbolism
of the painting at the time. All she could say was that the bird
wanted to fly to the mountains, but it could not get past the gate.
The doctor encouraged her to paint more dreams, and gradually,
working on the changing relationship of bird, gate, mountains,
colours, and other intervening symbols, understanding dawned.
The bird was the woman, the mountains the freedom from sickness, and the gate represented an event in childhood. An uncle
had assaulted her near a gate, and the resulting fears and inner
situation, prevented her from getting better. As the paintings went
on, the woman dealt with the difficulties, and eventually the bird
got to the mountains. She was cured.

This, quite by itself, shows how effective paintings of dreams can
be in helping to understand a dream. Most of what has been said
about stories and poems also applies to this type of interpretation.
But paintings often have an even deeper impact upon us than
words, even if the words are poetry. By this I do not mean that
paintings are greater than literature. What I mean is that any
word is only a description which, due to the quality of limited
meaning words possess, effects us largely through our understanding of the word. A German sentence might be quite meaningless
to an Englishman, and *vice versa*. But a German painting is beyond
the limitation of words, and is as likely to be understood in England
as in Germany. A painting, due to its forms and colours, their positioning and relationship, can make us experience or realise things
we might find difficulty in expressing with words. If we see a
painting of a man holding his injured child, with tears in his eyes
despite the strength of his outer appearance, it evokes in us feelings
it might take many pages to express fully in words. Also, the picture
would be universal, words would not.

Why this is so is very revealing. It is because the picture is an
extension of the actual dream images. It is because a painting or
drawing uses forms and symbols to express, just as a dream does.
Therefore, when we paint a dream, we bring it to conscious reality.
We bring it out into the open to be examined. We also make it
secure, hold its images caught within the colours, or the strokes

of the pen. Seeing it outside of us in this way enables us to examine it more carefully, and see what the forms make us feel. Just as on looking at the man holding his child, it would stimulate our associated feelings, and we would know them.

Later in the book, under the subject of mandalas and yantras, the idea of painting dreams is taken up again, and extended in its use.

SEVEN

Active imagination

The most necessary personal quality to interpret dreams is imagination. By imagination is meant the ability to find or group associated ideas and images round a given subject. If I write the word HORSE, what ideas or associated images can we link with it? It can be big, small, brown, black, stallion or mare. It can be weak, strong, old, young, tame or wild, friendly or aggressive. A horse links with images of saddles, reins, bridle, cart, whip, jockey, race-course. It can run, jump, pull, trample, bite, kick, plunge, buck. We can ride it, be thrown from it, mount or dismount, sit easy or with difficulty. It can carry us or a load, and so on. This all links with what has already been said about association of ideas. But there is another aspect of imagination which can be used as a sort of 'diver's suit'. By this I mean that its use often enables us to dive deeply into ourselves, and contact parts of us difficult to reach by any other means. It cannot be used for all dreams, but where indicated, its results are sometimes in the light of revelations to the person using it.

This method is called active imagination; and although often mentioned in various technical or popular dream books, a detailed description of how to do it is seldom given. Yet once it is grasped it is one of the simplest types of dream interpretation or methods of self discovery possible. But before we deal directly with the method, it is necessary to take a further look at imagination.

Earlier we looked at some aspects of memory, and which attitudes of mind inhibit or release it. These attitudes of mind also are largely responsible for the fullness or poverty of imagination. Not that what was said covered the issue very well, or that it can be covered adequately in this book, for many other factors act upon memory and imagination. These range from diet to atmospheric conditions, glandular balance to social influences. All affect our memory and imagination. In the consideration of active imagination, however, for a working knowledge of the technique that

79

follows, a few further remarks on memory are necessary. Earlier it was said that by correctly conditioning our state of mind, we can often remember dreams that had never before been conscious. Possibly re-member is the wrong word, because the dream had never been consciously known, to be forgotten. But at least we are recalling an experience had by us at a different level of consciousness. It was also said that some dreams are difficult to recall because they portray parts of our nature we are ashamed of, guilty about, or frightened of. These factors also control our imagination.

It is therefore fairly obvious that our code of morals also has an enormous influence on what we *allow* ourselves to remember or imagine. The reader may have grave doubts about this, believing that they are free agents as to what they think or imagine; but this is wishful thinking and its falsity will be demonstrated as we proceed.

Memory and imagination are almost one and the same thing, for we cannot imagine without memory. But imagination is the forming of images and ideas into new arrangements or previously un-thought-of relationships. Sometimes imagination simply appears as what one generally calls 'fantasy'. That is, we may see ourselves meeting the Queen or President, and giving them vital information about the country, for which they reward us and honour us. Or else we see ourselves facing up to some bully or superior in work or life, and 'wiping the floor' with them, or really telling them a few home truths about themselves. If we are honest we call this wishful thinking. It is, however, a form of imagination. It is also a safe means of letting off steam, releasing emotions or aggressiveness, or hopes and longings, if we afterwards have the honesty to smile at ourselves.

On the other hand, imagination can be creative. We may be faced by the problem, as my small son was, of keeping two tall canes upright to support a badminton net, yet not be able to push them into the hard ground. He remembered, however, that nearby were bricks with holes in them. In his imagination he saw that the canes could be held upright through pushing them into the bricks. This he did, and created a new relationship he had not seen before. Most creative imagination is an extension of this ability to place the 'known' into new and useful relationships.

Active imagination is not quite like either of these two. It is not simply memory; it is not wishful thinking, nor is it only creation of new and useful relationships from known facts. It seems to be a combination of them all with another factor thrown in—the intuitive discovery of the unknown. Its activity is conditioned by our ability to be receptive as already described, and, as far as possible, in temporarily putting aside our morals, preconceived ideas, fears and desires for self. Because of this, and despite its simplicity, many people find they cannot do it until much of themselves has already been realised and in some degree dealt with. If used correctly though, some dreams will release their meaning to almost anybody. Having said that, let us look at the technique itself. Let us slowly delve into the strange inner realm disclosed to us.

If the reader conscientiously tried to do the exercise of expressing thoughts in images instead of words; or if the idea that prior to speech mankind probably thought in images, was well understood; then this was the first step in understanding active imagination. Also, when our conscious self expresses dreams in story form, poems, drama, paintings or modelling, this also can be a type of active imagination. But, and this must be clearly understood, it is *only* active imagination when, during the creative procedure of writing, painting, or modelling, one feels as if the dream images have somehow come alive and are directing the course of events. At such a time there is a feeling of being moved by something other than conscious decisions or will. Not that one is powerless to stop the course of events. It could be interfered with, and that is why active imagination cannot be experienced in any great depth by those who have not learnt to sit back and watch. While a person persists in controlling and interfering with this spontaneous expression of their inner self; while they constantly block its expressions through their moral principles or preconceived ideas, then this work cannot take place. Yet with the right attitude, one is not possessed by this unconscious direction, but works with it as a partner to create new understandings, new forms, new life in oneself.

The contacting of this spontaneous outflow of the innermost being, has always been the highest aim of the world's great religions. It was possibly the driving energy behind all the new forms of art at their inception. In our own social scene we see that the use of LSD and similar drugs have also been undertaken by many because of their ability to release in some this same contact. Sometimes the contact is expressed in body movement, such as the dance; sometimes vocally as in drama, oration and singing; sometimes through the hand, as in art, sculpture, love; sometimes in realisation, such as religious experience of bliss.

When we think of the early Quakers, we see their 'Quaking' as an expression. The first Wesleyans often knew similar effects. While today we have the Latihan experience of Subud; the spontaneous movements of Reichian therapy; and LSD. All of them, to be effective, require the attitude of mind already mentioned. All of them also are a co-partnership between the deep self and conscious self.

As for how we may contact this influence through our dreams, we must begin with simple experiments to obtain correct understanding. Let us start by building up an image of driving a car. To understand what is being explained, one must sit without distraction and with closed eyes and imaginatively enter into driving a car. As you imagine this, see yourself driving down a very steep hill, with a steep drop on the left. As the car goes down and down, the bends in the road swing this way and that—and suddenly a bend comes up and the car is going too fast to make it. There is a terrible slope, and the car goes right over the edge.

Before you read any further, please go through this whole sequence in imagination, noting carefully what happens. Then read on.

One of several things may have occurred. (a) You may not have been able to imagine it. (b) You saw it but it went before the car crashed off the road. (c) You went right along and the car crashed down the hillside.

Without making any comments yet, I now want you to do the whole thing again. But this time, as the car goes off the edge of the road to smash down the hill, you must try to make it simply fly up into the air gracefully and land safely lower down the road. Try this before reading on.

Once more, several things may have happened. Basically, you will probably not have been able to control the car once it went over the edge of the road. It either crashed—or you could only slow it down. If you could control it then it shows a high degree of direction of your images. But why have we done all this?

Really, to show how difficult it is to produce the image, and then to control it once we have got it moving. Also, most people's car will have crashed, even when they try to stop it. Yet these are simple images of which we are supposed to be in control. We see in this the conscious working of the *because* factor. Are we then, captains of our own mind?

With a little thought, the reason we cannot make the car do as we wish is obvious. The image of the car is moved by our desires and wishes. Therefore, because our *fear of crashing* is involved, it takes hold of the image and crashes it! In other words, because we cannot master our fear of crashing, it controls the image we have produced. Having realised this, we can then learn to *face fear* and move the image where we wish, until another *fear or desire is involved*. I do not have to spell out the tremendous meaning and possibilities of that. It is enough to say that through the manipulation or observance of our own images, we can discover, trace, change and live in our own innermost processes. This is not done by simply following the line of least resistance, as in day-dreaming, fantasy or wishful thinking. It is done by attempting to manipulate, trying to face, what is revealed by spontaneous fantasy or dreams. That is the therapeutic side of active imagination. The creative side lies in the sphere of discovery and expression of our own latent possibilities, wisdom and emotions. The fact that we may discover a 'fear of crashing' through indulging in the above experiment is important enough, but, even greater significance lies in the experience of not being able to stop the car from crashing even if we wish to. This shows that our fears or apprehensions, those subtle often unknown parts of our nature, are *constantly influencing our behaviour*. This may seem exaggerated until we realise that such fears control our thoughts. They control our memories and our imaginations. It is our thoughts, memories and imagination that are the basic causes of our actions or inactions in life. When not interfering in our actions, they are certainly modifying in many ways the manner in which we respond to outer circumstance.

It is difficult, by means of the written word, to hit on an image that will definitely show us how we are controlled in the way we think, do and respond. Many people may easily deal with the car situation in their imagination, or else not be able to see the point of it. But if we could experiment, we would probably find certain images which are terrifying or loathsome to attempt to deal with. Some we may not even wish to *think* about. Yet they are only mental images; nothing is being asked in the actual physical realm. All they involve are our own emotions, fears, prejudices and morals. Therefore, if the car fantasy has not provoked any feeling, try imagining sexual intercourse with one of your parents. Being such a taboo thought, it is almost bound to negatively involve much of our inner life. It is sufficient, however, if it is clearly understood that these images have a life of their own because our feelings, morals and fears are involved. To condense things we can call these parts of us our 'psychic' life, or soul. Therefore, if we realise that our soul is involved in the fantasy, we can take the next step in understanding active imagination. It is also hoped that through what has been done with the experiment of imagination, the forces that produce dreams are also more clearly seen. For if we cannot imagine something while conscious and bending our will to do so; the images that arise while this will is sleeping, come as direct results of the interrelationship of our different fears, hopes and psychic life. Just as the car crashing is a direct expression of our fear, and inability to control it, so in a dream, a car crashing would be just the same.

Although this subject is of enormous interest and application in many realms, such as child education, creative art and personal relationships, we have to explain it here, only in its connection with dreams. What is most important to understand, is what type of dream we can use it with effectively, and how to use it with such dreams. Very generally, it is the dream that faces us with problems we cannot get beyond; or figures in the dream we do not understand. While the way to use it is to put ourselves back into the dream situation and consciously move along with it, or manipulate the symbols.

Earlier in the book, while dealing with dream series, a dream was mentioned where the woman saw herself entering a tunnel. She then met and passed a 'rather frightening little animal', then a larger animal, and finally a 'real monster, rather like a 60-ft caterpillar with a lion's head and fore feet'. This last was not passed, but she only got half way along, and woke. Literally, she woke in the middle of it. This was explained as of 'possibly sexual nature' due to the shape of the symbol. The fact that it was too big to get by, or cope with in the dream, makes it an excellent subject for active imagination. The size of the creature represents its emotional impact on the dreamer. Such 'big' emotions often need our conscious co-operation to deal with. The dream, by itself, might not find a way out of the difficulty. The speculation about the meaning of the symbol also invites us to try to realise its implications in active imagination.

The woman in question did use active imagination on this dream. She waited for a time when she would be undisturbed, made herself comfortable, and then tried to get back into the dream using her imagination. Her description is as follows: 'Several things surprised me. To begin with I could not re-create the feeling of fear. I stood where the dream had left off and waited. Occasionally I saw the end of the tunnel and it opened out into light. Occasionally I saw a small white light just above and beyond the caterpillar's back. Then I decided to climb on to its back to see if that produced any results. None. So I decided to crawl towards its tail. As I went along I found that its fur was full of an unpleasant slime; but I couldn't decide exactly what it represented (apart from filth). I tried to decide what it meant and what I should do, but all the while now the far end of the tunnel was becoming lighter, and so I concluded that I had failed to discover anything useful in this experiment. The only bit that had come alive was the slime on the caterpillar's back, and my revulsion at having to put my hands in it.'

At first sight this appears to be almost a failure. However, it shows that the tunnel's end is in sight, and anyone trained in interpreting dreams would see that the discovery of slime on the caterpillar's back is very important. But we do not have to speculate over this, as the very next day the whole thing 'comes to light'. In fact, the caterpillar episode was very near to the 'light of day', or consciousness. The woman says, 'I suddenly saw the meaning of the slime on the caterpillar: it was semen. It brought partial memory of the four-year-old's sexual shock. I was somehow trapped, probably in the rather crude open-air toilets in the recreation ground, by a man who exhibited himself and almost certainly made me touch the phallus with my hands during ejaculation. Being small I had to reach up. My hands were 'soiled', and my face could have been. I am pretty sure I must have been sick. When I remembered the above I shuddered again and again and at last broke into tears. I've surely released a lot.'

Yes, she had released, *and* realised a lot; because her conscious self had sufficient courage and receptiveness to go along with, and investigate what her unconscious self was pushing up for her notice.

A similar experience of active imagination is shown in the following dream, by a young woman. In the dream she walked across the Rye, which is a large park, in a new 'Maxi' coat. The ground was like a bog, but she did not sink in, although she knew she had come to commit suicide. She lay on top of the bog, quite happy and ready. Then she saw a man walking towards her, only his legs visible. She knew she must now die, and thrust herself through the bog.

The first part of the dream was fairly easy to interpret. She had recently had an emotional shock through seeing her husband kissing another woman at a party. This was terrible because although such an action was not uncommon to her, she always felt very insecure emotionally, and her husband's action was a blow to her security. The Rye was a place where her early courting took place, and represents her own sexual feelings, and the bog that underlies them. The 'Maxi' was a thing that she did not own, but hoped for. She was taking her outer hopes and life, on to the thin surface that covered the threat of her sexual feelings of insecurity. She was willing to face these feelings, though her old self might die in doing it. This much was understandable. It was the man's legs that could not be fitted into the interpretation. They could have been interpreted as a threat of sex, but this did not provide a satisfying picture of the dream. Therefore the woman sat quietly, imagined herself back in the dream, and saw the man's legs approaching. She was then asked to look up at the man's face, and see who it was. She did so, and with great surprise said, 'It's my father!' The realisation of which helped to show the part her father had played in shaping her emotional background.

Another example of how active imagination can help us to understand a symbol is again shown in the following dream and the active imagination.

'I had, or was, a deformed baby, having four eyes, and a somewhat "not normal" face. The eyes were operated on, two being removed. But the baby grew up to be a dwarf, very lonely and shy.

'The dwarf and normal I, were one, yet somehow separated. He lived downstairs and would often climb the stairs and stand outside my door, hoping I would see him and befriend him. I, inside, vaguely felt his presence, but whenever I got near the door, his shyness made him retreat downstairs.

'Then I met him on a footpath between steep meadows. I asked him why his other two eyes had been removed, and he said, "Because I could see too many (confusing) things with all my eyes." That is, too many images were presented at once, and could not be interpreted clearly.

'He said, "Now I can see differently." Pointing at the meadow he said, "Really there are no cows there at all."

'I looked and saw a lot of cows, and struggled to understand what he meant. While I was pondering he walked along a bit and said, "No, I was wrong; there is one cow there." I looked and saw a very beautiful cow among the herd.

'The next thing was that a large male dwarf, and two female dwarfs came along the footpath. The two men (whom I now was) recognised they were deeply related to each other, and ran into each other's arms with great love. As they held each other they (I) felt that two incomplete parts had now found each other.'

Trying to interpret this rather long and involved dream without outside help, the dreamer found it difficult. He therefore held a picture of the dwarf in his imagination, and talked to it. Here is the record of his conversation.

Q. Why were you born deformed?

A. I am the part of you *born* deformed. Your sins from the past. The sins of the parents.

Q. Why did you have four eyes?

A. Because I looked for too many things. Through trying to look in too many directions there was confusion.

Q. What does it mean that you stood outside my door?

A. It means that we were so close all the time, but did not meet.

Q. Why was there only one cow?

A. There is only one cow because all the others are reflections, false images of the one. The others have no soul. You see the cows, because you have not lost the eyes as I have done. I can only see things with a soul, real things.

87

Q. When you met the large dwarf, what is that?
A. Now we have met. You are but a larger, not complete dwarf. Together we make one person. The large dwarf is two thirds grown; I am only one third. Together we are complete.

When reading this one may feel that some of the answers are as confusing as the dream. It has to be realised that the conversation takes place within a particular person, between two parts of himself. This is something we do all the time, but not as consciously as in active imagination. If one wished to emigrate, for instance, but had aged parents who needed help, the desire to emigrate, and the desire to stay, could be represented as two people in a dream. These could talk and discuss their different desires, trying to find an agreement. But this conversation uses the education and background of the person. Therefore, a history professor might easily use terms foreign to a bricklayer, when talking to himself. The answers are therefore meaningful to ourselves, or become meaningful with a little thought. The man in question was helped to realise certain things about himself. As a child he had been extremely shy and lonely. At thirteen this had become such a problem that he took up various interests and activities to alter himself. In this way he developed the ability to meet people even more confidently and successfully than most; he spoke in public, and so on. So he felt, before the dream, that he had developed beyond his shyness, but the answers the dwarf gave him made him realise that in fact he had learnt to shut his shyness out of his life, 'downstairs' in the unconscious. For years he had not met this part of him due to the very differences in these two parts of him. But he could now see that his frequent blushing when certain topics were mentioned, that his conscious self had no 'feelings' about, suggested this other part.

This shy part of him had looked in so many directions for 'real' relationships with people, only to find confusion and dissatisfaction. So much so that he had had to 'cut out' his looking, to stop being hurt. While the cow is explained by the dreamer in these words. 'I didn't properly understand the bit about the cows, even after the dwarf had spoken to me. I knew that in India it is regarded as a sacred animal, and I thought of it as a sort of mother figure. Then I realised that it is a source of sustenance and motherhood. Milk is our first food, our first contact with mother. To see so many false cows was to see false sources of security and sustenance that a mother provides. I had made false 'cows' out of my desire for love and affection. But my shy, sensitive part, because only the real thing could satisfy it, could see through these shams.'

The same man had another interesting experience of active imagination that demonstrates several of the other principles involved. As can be gathered from the above, he had been dealing with the relationship between himself and his mother. That is, not his present relationship, but the effects of his relationship as a baby and child. In this instance he did not use a dream as the focal point of the active imagination. It is important to understand this, as when we start working on dreams, some feelings, emotions, or memories, are unlocked by what we are doing, and may attempt to come up outside of our dream life. Unless we know how to deal with these 'risings' the development of our work will be much delayed. Here is the man's account of the experience.

'I was quite alone in the church; just sitting trying to allow my thoughts to become quiet. Usually, this was fairly easy for me, but on this particular day I could not keep my thoughts from turning to a woman I knew. Eventually, realising that some inner unrest must lie behind this constant desire, I gave myself over to it. I suppose it is meaningful that I had previously been contemplating a banner with the Virgin Mary and baby Jesus on it—the mother and child. In any case, as soon as I let my thoughts go where they wished, I saw myself at the woman's breast. For several reasons I immediately drew my thoughts away from this. Firstly, I came to church not to fantasy sexual feelings, but to find something that helped one through the mire of personal relationships. One could go on and on fantasying sex. I had nothing against it, but such imagined scenes gave neither satisfaction, nor did they ever end. No satisfaction = no end. Also, I was married, and sexual fantasies with other women involve the very feelings that are needful to make one's own married life complete. They divert the very emotions that are necessary in making a good home for wife and children.

'Due to my past experiences in this realm, however, I felt I ought not to push these things aside out of hand. It was better for peace of mind to let such fantasies come up and out, rather than be bottled up inside. Therefore I put my reasons and morals on one side, sat back and watched. Immediately I went to the woman's breast, as a baby might to its mother. There was a tremendous feeling of satisfaction and fulfilment, and gradually without trying to push it away, the whole scene lost its potency and faded; the emotions and desires having found release through the fantasy.

'For a moment all was quiet. Then a thought came to me of its own accord. It was—"But that was only a substitute!" I naturally asked myself, "A substitute for what?" Immediately the reply came, "Your mother's breast."

'It is impossible to describe the flood of realisation or revelation this brought with it. The many women I had longed for outside of marriage, now took on the form of substitutes for the love and affection, fulfilment and satisfaction I desired at my mother's breast. Realising this, I thought, "Well, I will imagine myself at my mother's breast. Again, the shock of revelation is difficult to describe; because, the simple fact was, I found I could not do it.'

On this revelation of not being able to imagine himself at his mother's breast, despite all his efforts, this period of active imagination ended. Later sessions, carrying on where the last left off, gradually revealed that it was feelings of uncleanness and rejection that prevented the image forming. This, in turn, led to the man reliving, during active imagination, a babyhood memory. In his own words, 'I could not understand why I should have such strong feelings of uncleanness and rejection about an imagined picture of my mother's breast. In fact I couldn't get the picture. But by simply allowing these feelings to develop fully, as I had done with the original "substitute" experience, it began to move. Suddenly I was at my mother's breast. I was a baby, I was re-living it. There I was in her arms, and I loved her so much, so enthusiastically, that I was sucking and expressing my pleasure by my body movements. I realised that a baby experiences infantile sexual feelings while at the mother's breast. They come as a sort of blissful oneness with the mother.* But then my mother smacked me, or scolded me,

---

* It must be understood that a baby does not separate the different parts of its being. Its emotions are not distinct from its thoughts, or its thoughts from its sexual feelings. When it does something, even as simple as shaking a rattle, it does so with all of itself, emotions, sexual feelings, hungers, etc.

because she felt that such feelings were unclean. I can understand this, as she still cannot accept my father's feelings in this direction. And that, in a nutshell, is where my own sexual conflicts began, which now try to find substitutes outside of marriage for my sexual feelings. For I saw that a man replaces his mother with a wife, with whom he now shares and *gives* his deepest feelings. But his wife is his new mother. If he could not give himself to his mother because she made him feel unclean, then the same feelings of uncleanness pervade his attempts to give himself to his wife. It must be a problem that many men and women face, all begun at the mother's breast, because the mother feels that sex is filth.'

The important thing to note in this description is the need to 'go along' with the images and feelings being released, without passing judgement on them. This allows them to rise, and reveal their source, which may be an event in early life, or a relationship between parts of oneself. The willingness to plunge again and again into unsavoury emotions and images, can also be seen as a necessity. The beautiful is often hidden in the dirt, or grows out of it. It is only when we see that beauty grows out of dirt that we realise dirt is not 'filth', but earth. It is the basic stuff of life, the material all growth emerges from; the stuff that our life forces transform in the process of growing. But if we are out of touch with the earth of our nature, our energy has nothing to transform into the flower of our manhood or womanhood. In the East, the lotus growing out of the mud has always been a symbol of this.

No attempt has been made in this description of active imagination to show its use in art, poetry and dance. This is because the chapters on dreams and poetry, painting and stories, cover this. It is also hoped the reader will, by grasping the general principles, be able to express what arises in his own way.

EIGHT

LSD—hypnosis—meditation—the dream

There has always been a great deal of criticism aimed at dream interpretation. It has been called many things. Those who have not investigated it have denied any truth in it. Others have said that most dream interpretation was in the head of the analyst, and dreams were meaningless. This has been due to the various interpretations one can give to a dream, and the difficulty of arriving at any interpretation in the case of some dreams. Like an ink blot one can see all sorts of faces in it. But the ink blot is really just a blot, and depicts no face at all, or if it does it is pure coincidence.

When one begins to attempt an interpretation of one's dreams, especially if doing it alone, these criticisms become important. To start with, dreams present a shifting phantasmogoric world in which one is a stranger, and cannot find the way. It is a world of changing shapes and shadows; a land of hinted meanings, where nothing holds still long enough to determine its real character, and a snake can slip into the form of a frog as easily as a man can become a stone, or learn to fly. It would be unusual then, in this land for which there can never be a fixed map, due to its changing contours, if one did not suffer serious doubts about finding one's way, or arriving at meaning. This is because different values apply in this world than those of the outer world. To get somewhere in the dream world, we cannot simply follow a road as in the outer world, for the road may quickly become a trackless bog or change into a seashore covered with ferocious lettuce leaves which threaten to eat all the hair off one's body. It is the world of Alice in Wonderland, of Hercules and the Heroes, it is Fairyland, where one gets somewhere 'because', and not by walking at all. Therefore, if we judge this land with our old ideas based on outer, conscious life, we shall certainly be dismayed. If we persist in the face of such difficulties, however, then gradually we shall develop new senses, new values, and the ability to move around in this strange world. We will then be able to converse with the natives of this land.

and understand what they are saying. For the natives are symbols and allegory, and their language is not usually in words.

It is fortunate, therefore, that to help our doubting mind in its persistence to understand, evidence does point to the feasibility of dream interpretation. What has already been said about symbols and imagery being an early type of thinking is a part of this evidence. We can test it for ourselves. In the same way, our experiments in active imagination also demonstrate to us personally, that dream images do arise from our psychic values. They can, therefore, through analysis, be traced to these underlying emotions, and thus be understood. When we arrive at an interpretation of our own dreams that thoroughly explains us to ourselves, this too constitutes personal evidence. There are other sources of evidence, however, and because these throw light on another method of interpretation, they will be mentioned.

During the early part of this century, investigators set out to test some of Freud's conclusions regarding dream symbols. Three men, Gaston Roffenstein, Karl Schroetter, and M. Nachmansohn, used hypnosis for this aim. They hoped in this way to throw light on three dream factors; the dream censor, the symbol-making process, and whether dreams help us to stay asleep.

For one experiment, Schroetter used a 24-year-old female pharmacist he calls 'Miss E'. Having put the subject into a 'deep hypnotic sleep', he then told her she would dream of having homosexual intercourse with her female friend L. Schroetter comments that Miss E is Aryan, while L is Jewish. The dream that followed during the night was of Miss E sitting in a small dingy café holding a huge French newspaper. Talking with a strong Yiddish accent, a woman twice asks her, 'Don't you need anything?' Miss E doesn't answer, but the woman comes a third time, and is recognised as her friend L. She is holding a worn suitcase with a label that reads, 'For ladies only!' Miss E goes out of the café with her, and walks along an unfamiliar street, while L hangs on to her. She doesn't like this, but does not like to be rude by telling her to stop. They arrive at L's house, where she pulls out a huge bunch of keys from a rag. She chooses a key and gives it to Miss E, saying, 'I trust only you with it, it is the key to this case. You might like to use it. Just watch that my husband doesn't get hold of it.' L then leaves her with the key.

As, according to Freud's symbology, a case is a woman, a key the male organ, and walking up a strange street, new sexual conquest, this dream is very interesting. It can be seen how a forbidden idea is hidden within the symbols, and how the symbols express the hidden idea. As Miss E had no knowledge of Freudian concepts these symbols are spontaneous products of her own dream state.

Roffenstein, because he wished to be quite certain of the subject's ignorance of formulated dream symbols, chose a 28-year-old nursemaid. She is described as of sub-average intelligence, totally uneducated, and quite innocent of his proposed experiment. She was likewise hypnotised and told to dream, amongst other things, of having sexual intercourse with her father. The dream was of her father. He gave her a large bag, and with it a big key. It was a very big key, like the key to a house. She felt sad, but opened the bag. Then a snake jumped out of it against her mouth, when she screamed and awoke.

Once more, the bag and the key, and one other classic sex symbol, the snake as male penis. If there were not other evidence but this, we still have to admit that they do not suggest dreams being meaningless. Unfortunately, because Freud's ideas were being tested, which reduce most symbols to male or female, we cannot see how the dream expresses religious feelings, concepts of life, or ambitious drives, but we can see this for ourselves in our own dreams.

Although the two dreams mentioned are full of information and evidence they were nevertheless induced. Another source of evidence helps us to see dreams from a different direction. In the hypnotically induced dreams, the dreamer does not interpret them. But there are cases where dreams are interpreted spontaneously, without conscious attempts; or intervention by an analyst to inject their opinions. The most evidential of the ways in which this spontaneous interpretation or understanding takes place, is during the dream itself. While one may not have a lot of dreams where the understanding takes place during the dream, it is by no means uncommon. Most people have such a dream at one time or another, and some people have a whole batch of dreams that are understood while they are taking place. Below is a description of a dream, and the spontaneous interpretation that arose with it.

'A young girl kept coming up to me and placing my hand on

her breasts. She was just developing her breasts, and they felt so very beautiful. Then, while still dreaming, I asked myself what it meant, and an answer came without any effort. The girl represented my desire for sexual satisfaction. That is, not just physical, but also the mating of emotions, mind and soul. I caress her breasts due to the fact that my sexuality is still developing. This means that the other levels of union, such as mental and spiritual, develop out of the physical. So I have to allow this stage to go on being experienced so that the other levels can unfold from it. The girl also represents the Divine Mother, or the female, unconscious counterpart of my outer, male nature. She herself develops as my feelings mature, and this suddenly threw a new light on all my sexual dreams in the past.'

Not only can we see how the interpretation beautifully fits each aspect of the dream, but it is also interesting to see how much longer the interpretation is than the dream. This shows just how much information a small dream can contain. The example gives us the ideal of interpretation as well. It should arise out of the dreamer as understanding, and fit each part of the dream.

Another way in which dreams can be interpreted spontaneously is during hypnosis. The hypnotic state is similar to sleep in some respects, the most obvious being that critical sense, full reasoning powers and conscious judgement are to some extent less active. This is possibly why one can solve the riddle of dreams more easily, and also why they are so fully understood. As we have seen with memory, or active imagination, preconceived ideas, or moral judgements, prevent ideas or inner contents from surfacing. We can see exactly the same process at work in our conversations with others. Certain events in our life we may easily be able to talk about to one friend, but find it impossible even to mention to another. This is very often because one friend is sympathetic, interested, broad minded, does not ridicule, judge or criticise; while the one we cannot tell misunderstands such things, thinks less of us for them, ridicules or criticises. We do exactly the same to ourselves. Because of our attitude to parts of ourself, they can never 'talk' to us or tell us about themselves. In sleep or hypnosis, many of these attitudes are put aside, and a more direct contact made with these parts of us. Also, because, with an ultra conscious attempt to understand dreams we may hold the wrong idea in mind, the right one cannot come through. Or else our doubt may press back what we need to know. In fact, what was said earlier about memory is worth reviewing in the light of spontaneous interpretation. In hypnosis, the association of ideas to symbols and dream structure, are also easier and more certain. This is because there is less interference from our reasoning faculties. Even a light hypnotic state, or deeply relaxed condition aids this process.

In the book *Three Faces of Eve* by Thigpen and Cleckley an example is given of this. The patient, Eve White, has told of a dream which she cannot relate to any of the events or details of her life. The dream is of being in a huge room, in the middle of which is a pool of stagnant green water. Eve is in the pool with her baby, Bonnie. Her husband and uncle stand on the edge of the pool. She tries to get the baby out, because they both seem to be drowning, but tries to avoid putting the baby girl near her husband. Despite this she eventually puts her in her husband's hands. Then her uncle, whom she loves, pushes Eve's head under the water. The psychiatrist treating her suggested trying hypnosis as a means of interpreting the dream. During the hypnotic condition it was suggested she would be able to explain the dream on being wakened and this in fact she did. The room was her existence, the pool was the religious associations of her husband, who was Roman Catholic. She was trying to escape from being drowned in this Church, and to prevent her baby from being educated as a RC. As in life, her husband refused to help her in this struggle. Her uncle had in life suggested she fulfil her promise and have the child brought up as a Catholic, and this is seen as a pushing under.

Further proof of this type of interpretation is shown in recent use of LSD for therapeutic purposes. C. Newland, in her book *Myself and I* which describes in detail the course of her analysis under LSD, experienced spontaneous interpretation under the drug several times. The analysis was not concerning itself with her dreams. It simply occurred that she knew her dream meanings several times while using LSD. This happened despite the fact that during normal consciousness she had not the vaguest idea what the dreams meant. One of the dreams she mentions is as follows (I here quote from memory). She dreamt that there was a war on. She and a number of other people hid in an underground shelter. They felt that they could last out here until the war had finished, but shock troops attacked and gained entry to the shelter. Some of the people ran off, but the troops were rounding them all up to finish them off. The interpretation, or should we call it 'understanding' that arose, was this. The war represented her own inner conflicts. These had gone into the unconscious because she was unknowingly resisting her own cure. The shock troops were the LSD treatment that broke into her unconscious feelings and revealed them. Even then some parts tried to escape, but were being 'rounded' up and dealt with by the treatment.

The more we consider these dreams, and how understanding of them was arrived at, the more it is seen how necessary it is to have the right state of mind. This method of interpretation (the open state of mind) may not be possible for many people, but some people on trying it, will find it comes naturally to them. It will be as if they have a 'gift' for it. Others will be able to develop it with some practice. For what can be induced by sleep, hypnosis or drug, can also be arrived at through discipline. Which brings us to the other method capable of giving spontaneous understanding. This is the intuitive method, or meditation. With this method, one consciously tries to take up exactly the same state of mind described in the chapter on remembering dreams. If one analyses carefully the state of mind necessary for one to fall asleep, then this is it. There is no effort to go to sleep. One waits without worrying when sleep will overtake you, without trying to control the thoughts. It is an open, relaxed state of being. If we introduce the dream into this; ask ourselves what it means, and simply wait without trying to dig out the answer, ideas may begin to naturally collect around the question. It can be likened to fishing. The conscious mind is rod and line. The dream is the bait, the question the hook. These are lowered into the waters of the unconscious by becoming quiet and passive, letting the question and dream sink into lower levels of consciousness by stilling the upper levels. Then, like the fisherman, one has to be patient. One waits for the line to pull. It is no use thinking.

The following dream and interpretation is an example of this. 'I dreamt I was courting an Indian girl. We were on a beach, and I was making love to her. All her family knew this. Then we wanted to get married, but now tremendous formalities began, and a banquet was prepared, and my question of worthiness brought up.

In trying to find an answer to this dream I sat and just wondered about it. I didn't *try* to find answers for it. Then suddenly it all fell into place. The day before, I had gone for a walk, and had thought about an experience I had the year before. I had seen deeply into myself at that time, and found it very beautiful, often wishing I could reach the same level again. Now I saw that the dream showed me on the beach, representing the borderline of consciousness between unconscious and conscious. It was because I had found a way to this borderline state that the previous experience had happened. As the dream shows, I merged, or made love to, this dark part of myself at the time, but now I wished to reach that level of experience frequently. I wanted to own it, marry it, but this requires the formalities of enquiring into my worthiness. Can I "maintain" the girl by my life. Can I deliberately produce the state of mind that made our former liaison possible?'

While this type of interpretation may be difficult for us, it is at least worth trying when other methods fail. And one may even find one has an aptitude for it.

NINE

Tests of analysis

From all that has been said, a whole collection of methods present themselves suggesting how we can understand a dream. I suppose one could use all these methods on a single dream, and arrive at a whole spectrum of information. But the question now arises as to whether the interpretation is correct. After all the effort, is it right? It is not just a question of whether the answer satisfies us; it must also enlighten us. It must do even more than that. What we arrive at must fit the events and symbols of the dream, and unveil the characters of our inner life that have clothed themselves in the forms and events of the dream. The interpretation should make sense to other people also, so that if explained, they too can easily see the connection between dream and interpretation. The interpretation should be able to stand the test of time as well.

One of the biggest temptations in analysing our dreams, the thing that most often leads to a false interpretation, is to attempt a purely arbitrary translation of the symbols. By this is meant that because one dreams of a bag, a large key and a snake, one should not therefore immediately denominate these as 'sexual symbols'. They may be; and we have to keep this possibility in mind. But the dreamer may be a locksmith who is having difficulty opening an important bag. In which case the symbols represent a problem and not sexual intercourse. And he may have a friend who keeps snakes, by one of which he was nearly bitten. So the snake might mean fear of death. This is why one has to be careful to find one's own associations with the symbols. Only when we cannot find a personal association; or the dream setting does not point to the possible meaning, should we try a general interpretation. Jung has said that if the dreamer finds difficulty in arriving at an association, he would ask him to describe the symbol in his own words, as if Jung knew nothing about it. Therefore, if one dreamt of a table, one would say, 'It is a thing usually made of wood and having four supports. Upon these a flat surface is fixed, so that one can place objects, food, books, etc., on it at a level nearer one's hands or mouth.' Or at least, one would describe it as one saw it.

As for how we can test the interpretation, dissatisfaction is the biggest clue to our inadequate understanding of the dream. If there are factors in the dream which we have not explained, or if the interpretation does not bring to light the inner feelings' that shaped the dream, then one will always have a feeling of dissatisfaction. It is as if two parts of a puzzle have not been properly fitted together, or, although the pieces fit, the colours do not quite match. Thus arises the feeling of not having found the right solution.

On the other hand, when the right understanding is arrived at, a very profound thing happens. There is usually a feeling of thrill, a sudden pleasure of exaltation, a feeling of being on the track. This is usually accompanied by a sense of seeing deeply into yourself, sometimes into parts of your being never bared to view before. In all, there is a feeling of pleasure and achievement, of certainty. One is usually somewhat amazed at the wisdom of dreams, despite having felt the same many times before.

Another test of the interpretation's accuracy, and a guard against arbitrariness, is to see whether it fits everyday experience. A dream nearly always deals with things one has experienced in one way or another. Therefore, if an interpretation does not fit or explain our actual experience, then it should be placed to one side. We must beware of using words we do not understand. For instance, we may read that Jung has said a dark-haired woman can represent a man's anima, or female nature, while a dominant man in a woman's dreams represents her animus. Or that Freud suggests that some cutting or scissors dreams might symbolise a fear of castration. But do we really, *in our own experience*, know what these mean? Can we see them in our own life? It is certainly not sufficient to label our dream symbols this, that or the other. If these ideas are true, then we shall see them in our own experience. We may not give them the same name even; but one that describes them *to us*! This is not to say that a knowledge of these ideas is not extremely helpful. It may even help us to see these things *in our own experience*. But we must beware of using such ideas without seeing them in ourselves. Therefore we have to look at ourselves and ask, 'What part of *me* does this dream symbol represent? What experience is it dealing with?' And when the word experience is used this does not simply mean events in the outer world. It means emotions, attitudes, ideas, response to people and events, relationships with others, with self, and with Life.

Sometimes, however, the dream deals with things that have not yet happened, but are about to happen. I am not here dealing with prophetic dreams. When a woman has a tummy ache and says, 'Ah, my period is beginning', she is not prophesying. She is speaking from past experience. In a similar way, the dream often sees that things are about to begin that are not outwardly obvious to us. For instance, a man dreamt that a bull broke loose and rushed into a field of cows. Shortly afterwards he was almost carried away by a release of sexual desires he had kept 'chained up'. His inward feelings had warned of this in the dream. Yet outwardly he could see no sign of it. So with some dreams we have to see if 'time' reveals their meaning. Or to put it another way, we may interpret the dream satisfactorily but find no signs of it in our experience. Then it is for time to bring it into the realm of the real.

An example of arbitrary interpretation can be seen in this dream. 'An unconventional looking postman delivered a registered package. But I didn't open it.' This was taken to mean that due to an unconventional experience, the dreamer had realised something. Something had 'registered' on his consciousness, but he had not explored the possibilities of it. Although this seemed to fit the symbols, and no other ideas were forthcoming yet the dreamer could not, despite a lot of searching within, discover an experience of something registering that he had not explored. The registered package is a double symbol, because it also suggests something valuable contained in it. Therefore, despite a seemingly good interpretation, when it came down to testing it, no satisfaction was forthcoming. Which makes us realise that proper interpretation lies not only in reading the symbols, but in seeing the understanding applied to our life.

We can sum up the tests for interpretation then, as: Does it satisfy us? Does it explain us? Does it enlighten us? Can we see it as a part of our experience in the past, present or future? Above all, does it help us carry on with the business of living?

TEN

After understanding—what?

We may have discovered in a dream greater self understanding, a knowledge of mankind's origins, new attitudes to outer competitive living, or even suggestions as to what lies ahead. Like the schoolchild, a great many facts and understandings may have been given to us, but the same question must concern us that concerns the child. What am I going to do with them in life?

Remembering the analogy of the instrument panel, we realise that it depends upon us what we do with the information displayed. Dreams, of and by themselves, do not, will not, solve all our problems. Who has ever removed all problems anyway? Those who have found peace and fulfilment in life did not do so through an escape from difficulties. They did it by relating to their problems in a new way. Likewise, we too can use what is revealed in dreams to relate to the old world in a new way, but this can only be done if we bring certain things to the study of our dreams. For there are many who have most profound and amazing revelations, but whose lives remain unchanged. While there are others who glimpse only a passing fragrance of wisdom, but who take it and transform their lives. So one can truly say that it is not the extent of the wisdom revealed which changes a man, but the extent to which a man or woman can use that wisdom in their daily dealings with life, that produces the change.

Through a dream one may see the folly of acting upon desires arising from possessiveness and jealousy, yet one may go on acting from these same parts of oneself. While the same realisation by another person leads them to think twice before expressing them, which changes their life. That is, not repressing these feelings, but simply recognising where they lead to if acted upon. For if we act upon jealousy, it often leads us to imprison another person in our desires, not allowing them their rightful freedom. Thus a child might be prevented from making deep contacts with new friends, or a wife or husband chained to the limitations of one person's affection and friendship; or we imprison other parts of our own nature.

Obviously, difficulties beset our path, but life has found a way around difficulties since its inception on Earth millions of years ago. If life had not consistently found ways to deal with problems, we should not be here now. Therefore, a problem-solving apparatus is built into us, and expresses itself in dreams. But again, if we do not act upon our innate wisdom, how can it be of value? Nor must we believe that there is only one set way to deal with a situation. One person might easily be able to act upon what is revealed, while another may not have the energy or ability to do so. This does not mean that the latter should therefore give in. They are in a different situation, and have to deal with their problems differently. For everybody starts from a different point, and encounters a different stretch of terrain. Instead of feeling inferior because he does not have the same powers as the man who can immediately act upon his knowledge, he should ask himself, his dreams, 'Well, how do I cope with this? I have seen it is not for my own good to act out of jealousy, but I don't seem to have the strength to do otherwise. Is there an alternative? Or can I find strength somehow?' It is such questions, unconscious though they may have been, that have enabled species to survive ice ages, floods, earthquakes, climatic and environmental changes, and famines. The outwardly strongest, the quickest to act, have not always been the survivors; but those who could adapt even their weaknesses to face the new situation, the new challenge, have continued in the face of problems. Men did not say, 'Ah, the ice age is too cold, we have not fur enough to face it'—they put on clothes. So we, too, can find an alternative, even for our weaknesses.

One of the first things to be remembered in dealing with dreams is the persistence in searching for a way to use what we have discovered. It lies in applying our new 'tool' to deal with life. But it is no good either, being lazy when, with a little effort, we could use what has already been seen, without alternatives. There is always the temptation to forget, and to let oneself slide back into old attitudes, old habits. Certainly nobody can be condemned for doing so. Life is often difficult enough, without the additional strenuous burden of changing our ways; but one has to admit frankly to oneself, that although change is thus avoided, one still has to suffer the limitations of the old way of life, and we must accept the latter if we choose the former. In the end, it is usually a pressing and painful problem, the desire for something 'more' or better, that gives us the necessary energy to meet ourselves and face change.

Even if we have accepted this, we still need help, and this is where the 'art' forms of interpretation are invaluable. Unless we have given concrete form in an easily understood manner to the understanding we have gained, it may slip away back into unconsciousness despite our interest in it. Therefore, wherever possible, a record should be kept of interpretations. It is adequate even if only in writing, but if one can catch the essence of it and put it into story form, a new symbol, song, poetry or painting, it becomes a much more powerful aid in conscious life. Especially so if it is then easily seen. In this way, a Christian who carries or wears a cross has a constant reminder of religious resolves through the symbol of the cross.

It is not necessary to do this to all dreams. One usually has a series of 'small' dreams, culminating in one or several 'big' dreams. Here, the size does not refer to length of dream, but to the amount of understanding and help we discover in it. Therefore, it is only necessary to express the big dreams, as they usually collect all the information in the previous ones, and bring it to highlighted meaning.

To illustrate this, let me use a dream which a friend recently sent to me. He teaches art, and says of the dream, 'My art class gets a little out of hand, the students rebel. I try to discipline them but am confused, though not unduly worried, except that I feel I may have failed in the task of teaching them as they should be taught.' We will interpret this purely arbitrarily for the purpose of explanation. We can say that it shows that the controlling factor(s) in his conscious life have become 'confused'. Any crisis makes all our being act together as a unit. When we are struggling to stop from drowning, the questions of whether we like the scenery, should we marry the person we are engaged to, or is premarital intercourse right, do not bother us. They are all 'sub-merged' (unconsciously united) in the problem of survival. Once the problem has been overcome, however, these other issues may 'rebel' and become unsettling influences. Similarly, when we are very sure of our direction, doubts, problems are all 'submerged'. But if we become uncertain, or wonder whether we should not have chosen another direction, all the voices of our other opinions and doubts can rise up. We then find it difficult to discipline them, lacking certainty ourselves.

All of which suggests that the dream points to loss of certainty in a previously ruling attitude or direction in life. Let us *imagine* now that he dreams the class is out on the beach. One of the class looks in a dustbin and finds a beautiful and glowing shell. All the class gather round and wish to paint the shell. If this is now interpreted, we see that the shell is something from deep within that one has discarded. In the light of the first dream, the class has left the restrictions of the old attitude represented by the classroom. The discarded feeling or idea is re-discovered and it draws the whole class to a common end again, uniting them in purpose. If the dreamer associates the shell with intuitive feelings he has had for some time, but discarded due to doubt as to their value, the dream falls into place. The intuitive ideas, the dream suggests, are power-ful enough, carrying inner light or energy, to unite once more the conflicting aspects of self. If the dreamer now paints this inter-pretation, he has a constant reminder of the understanding arrived at. This could be depicted as a group of people sitting around a shell painting it. If he frequently sees or thinks about the painting, he is thereby often reminded of what he has learnt about himself. This helps him to allow his intuitive feelings to centre or guide his actions, instead of allowing only his conscious fixed attitudes. These last remarks, and the second dream, of course, are purely specula-tion to illustrate the use of a painting or symbol.

THE MANDALA OR YANTRA

In many books on dreams, where symbols are being mentioned in regard to expressing the essence of a dream, or series of dreams, one finds comment on Mandalas. The word usually refers to a simple or complex diagram or pattern within a circle or square. The pat-tern of a maze can be considered as a mandala or yantra. Or the interlaced triangles of the Star of David, if within a circle or square, can also be thought of as yantra or mandala. We do not have a word, or words, in the English language that mean quite the same thing. Therefore, to define their meaning, one could say that they are a symmetrical or meaningful diagram, usually held within a circle or square. If looked at, thought over, or contemplated for any length of time, especially under guidance, the mandala or yantra is seen to symbolise or synthesise knowledge we were previously unaware or unconscious of. In other words, the Star of David could symbolise the interlacing of the visible and invisible forces in the universe. If we carried on thinking about it, we could gradually collect, or realise, more and more about the relationship of seen and unseen. The symbol continuously unites in our mind all this information. It also represents all that remains consciously unknown to us.

Therefore mandalas or yantras are powerful symbols in uniting, making conscious, yet reminding us of the still unknown contents of our own conscious and unconscious being. As symbols they remind us of what we have discovered of ourselves, and of what remains to be discovered. They help us to apply what we have learnt, while remaining receptive to further growth. They can also summarise a whole series of inner events which have already happened, while pointing to the unknown but possible direction these events are leading us to.

Having defined the mandala and yantra, perhaps it can already be seen how the idea can be used to synthesise the understanding of dreams. In the dream already discussed, where a painting showing a circle of people painting a shell was suggested, we could make this into a mandala. The purpose being that in a very simple design, the elements are easier to remember, and can often *suggest* more powerfully than a more complex symbol. Thus, when looking at an ink blot, we can imagine more faces than if a proper face were drawn. This is because it allows the creative function of our imagination more scope. It also gives our unconscious contents a more plastic form to project upon. Therefore, the simpler the symbol, the more of our inner unconscious contents we can continue to bring up and incorporate into it. The cross, for instance, can symbolise Christianity as a whole. When Jesus is added, its meaning becomes more restricted, and so on. Thus, to make a mandala out of the dream example used, we have to look for the most basic elements. In this particular dream, we have the shell, representing the known, the becoming known, and the still unknown of the depth; and the circle of people representing outer creative expression of what has emerged. We can say the basic elements are the shell and a circle. A mandala could therefore be drawn of a shell in the middle of a circle. Or if we wish to cut it down even more, simply a dot in a circle. Despite its simplicity, this would still remind us of all our interpretation, and be capable of integrating further information.

A STEP FURTHER—MEDITATION

Yantras and mandalas are not absolutely necessary. Nothing is *absolutely* necessary, but each thing is helpful when used in its appropriate place. Nevertheless, some things revealed through inter-pretation of dreams, call for frequent application. Using the arbi-trary interpretation of my artistic friend's dream once more, we see that the need to drop a more conscious attitude in order to be guided by intuition, which sometimes speaks with the essence of our total self in its present situation, rather than parts of our self such as ambition, and desire for creature comforts, then it becomes wise to listen. After all, intuition is probably one of the few means of expression which our complete memory and experience have. We cannot recall much of what we have read, studied, felt, done, seen or heard; we know next to nothing consciously of the biological processes that formed us, and intuition, waking or in dreams, is an expression of them. When the part of us we call our conscious self gets a helpful message from this other self, it is important that we consider it. We have to remember, however, that not all things that emerge from within are good, helpful or true. The dream, as instrument panel, merely tells us what is going on. It is for us to decide whether that knowledge is applicable, and in what way. In the above dream and interpretation, however, where it seems an association with the intuitive factors will be unifying, action is called for. The only problem is, intuition can be so easily drowned out by daily events. What can be done? In answering this question, we have to realise it is about a specific dream. This is done to make the method clear. But it is hoped the general effectiveness can nevertheless be seen in what is said.

It must be reasonably obvious that any idea or emotion we dwell on or experience for long periods of time, begins to channel a great deal of our energy. It also influences our behaviour. When we think of Henry Ford, whose central thought and desire for many years was to produce an inexpensive motor car, we can see how this aim and desire influenced his behaviour, and even his fate. Almost any great name in history, when studied, reveals a similar story. They have held to particular ideas and desires, sometimes of a negative character, and this has channelled their energies and shaped their destinies. When working with dreams, our aims are not so much to become an historical figure, as to become a happier and whole person. Nevertheless, we can still learn from the example of the famous or infamous. For our own ends we can apply the method of keeping our attention fixed upon ideas and emotions that are important. Naturally, the demands of each day bring forgetfulness, but if we set aside a few minutes before starting work, or at mid-day, or before sleeping, then we can make a habit of remembering.

Returning once more to our hypothetical dream, we have reached the point of capturing the dream's essence as a mandala, or if not this, then we have at least reduced it to the idea of the outer conscious self, directing its attention in a receptive manner to the centre, or intuition. As far as the dream is concerned, this is important, and will lead to uniting conflicting emotions and tendencies. If the dreamer, having got this far, now simply forgets the whole thing, little or nothing will have changed for him. His outer life may continue to be 'confusing' and rebellious; but if he spends some time each day practising what has been revealed, then his life cannot help but change in some degree. Even if nothing stupendous occurs the very fact that he practises in itself shows he has *changed his attitude towards himself*. In and by itself, this makes him a more unified person, for he is attempting to listen to his whole spectrum of desires and ideas, directions and needs, rather than just a portion of self. If he practises this new attitude of mind regularly for a long period, then his energies will gradually be diverted from their old course, and begin to express in this more fulfilling direction.

It is repeated that here we are dealing with a particular dream, and one's own dreams may suggest an entirely different course; but the rules remain the same, the direction of one's energies can be slowly changed by practising the new attitude of mind as a meditation. As to how this can be done, and what its results will be, I will now try to explain. All that is necessary is to take the mandala or synthesised interpretation, and consider it for a period of fifteen minutes to an hour, depending on temperament. This should be done once or twice each day. By 'consider' is meant to think about its meaning; to wonder whether we have applied it; to try to see its implications and results. But more important than thinking about it, *one should practise the attitudes of mind and emotion suggested by it.* In this case it means that the dreamer should become outwardly still, quieten his thoughts and conscious desires, and then direct his attention to those feelings or ideas suggested by the shell. For the period of the meditation this should be maintained. Each time the attention wanders or attitude changes, it should be gently but firmly brought back. Very little of interest may occur at all during these periods. In fact they must not be thought of as reaching for the spectacular or phenomenal; but as practice sessions, just as one might exercise the body so that it remains strong and supple. This will require a great deal of discipline, but will be seen, after some months, to be worth while.

It is necessary then, to understand the dream, grasp its essence, and practise this; but such dreams only come very seldom, and so we shall not be constantly practising new attitudes. What usually happens is that eventually, after having dealt with one's dreams for some time, a dream of great importance occurs, summarising all that has gone before. If the message of this dream is applied and practised as suggested then another dream appears much later adding to our understanding and slightly modifying the practice. In this way one slowly progresses through a very personal and intimate course of instructions in self development.

The man who dreamt of the white mouse, and wrote *The Shining Mouse*, used the story as a starting point for meditation. The white mouse he associated with contact and experience of his deepest life-giving self. If this was to be gained, certain attitudes had to be changed. As the story shows, the mouse cannot be caught by searching for it, grasping it, longing for it or thinking about it. The dreamer realised that he had to give up trying to 'grab this inner experience to make me more important or wonderful. I saw that I didn't even know the dwelling place, or source of this part of me. So I had to give up looking. Because, after all, I did not know where to look. I simply had to be quiet and let the Shining Mouse come to me in its own time and way. When I first tried to assume these feelings, everything in me rebelled, and I often gave up the practice, or thought some other type would be better. But I came back to it and kept on, until gradually it began to be easier and natural, and slowly it began to change certain parts of my life.'

GROUP WORK

Wherever possible, it is of enormous help to work on dreams as a group. This is difficult because many people cannot find others as interested in dreams as themselves. But even two people working together can be of great help to each other; but it is safer, where the two are of opposite sexes, to be part of a larger group, unless man and wife. This is said not out of prudishness, but because a great deal of sexual energy is often released in the process, and can cause difficulties unless understood.

One of the main things about working with others is that their questions make us talk, or allow us to talk. Time and time again, a difficult dream has been suddenly understood through talking to somebody else who is interested in dreams. This is not necessarily because they help us to understand through their greater insight. It is as if the meaning pops up as we speak. As if speaking draws it out. This has to be experienced to be believed, but one can be quite hopelessly clueless one moment, and the next moment the answer is there. Possibly this has something to do with the act of speaking, and thus expressing ideas. The fact that one talks about the non-understanding, and unsatisfactory ideas about the dream, seems to clear them out, and make way for the real answer by making one receptive.

Another group benefit is that several different viewpoints and types of questioning about the symbolism of the dream, are often more helpful than simply one narrower viewpoint. Seeing how other people's dreams are dealt with, and the difficulties they face, also aids us in gaining insight into our own. At first, any such group are almost certainly shy of each other. This is because dreams deal with such intimate and personal aspects of our lives, that to reveal them to others in dream interpretation is not easy. But gradually, as each person realises that everybody else has similar inner contents, these barriers fall, and a great depth of contact, encouragement and love can spring up. The contact comes because we see each other without our social masks and reserves; naked so to speak. The encouragement lies in the fact that because others have similar problems, and are dealing or have dealt with them, this gives us the courage to face them also. While the love arises through sympathy, and knowing the deep spirit that lies beyond the outer tangle or 'show' of each person.

Because another person can stand aside from our own situation, they can often see our dreams better than we can ourselves. We may unconsciously not wish to know or understand, and a group helps us to be honest with ourselves. Sometimes, a small advertisement in the local newspaper is all that is necessary to put us in touch with others thus interested.

PROBLEMS AND DANGERS

It is difficult in this book to give anything more than a hint of the difficulties one faces on the 'dream journey'. It requires a book itself to map out the various experiences one is likely to meet. But fortunately others have already written adequately on the subject, as in P. W. Martin's *Experiment in Depth*. Perhaps we can sum up what he has said as follows:

One of the big perils is releasing more emotion or inner contents than we can easily cope with. We see this in the dream of the bull rushing among the cows, and the dreamer being nearly carried away by sexual desires. It is the old problem of biting off more than we can chew. Usually, however, dreams will have given us a method of dealing with this before it happens. This may take the form it did with the dreamer of the shining mouse, where he practises the attitude of quietness and not being moved by doubts, fears or desire. Thus, although not repressing the inner contents, one is learning a technique of calm amidst the storm—of finding a rock to cling to amidst the sea's turmoil. But unless such methods are practised, they cannot be effective. Martin calls this danger being 'Swallowed up by the unconscious'. Those who retreat completely from everyday life, to live in their inner world can be classified under the same heading.

The balance being a unity between inner and outer life.

Another problem occurs if we start the journey of seriously delving into self, and after a long period, suddenly give it up. For things have been glimpsed, possibilities seen that will not let us rest, but cause us a sense of frustration and loss. Or else problems have been released but not dealt with, and haunt us. *Obviously, such events do not occur to those of us who are only mildly interested, and merely try to unravel one or two dreams every so often.*

The danger of what psychologists call inflation, or hubris, is also met along the way. Contact with the inner wisdom makes one feel 'special', 'different' or 'superior', and here is the danger. For if we feel superior or different, we may act in the same way. This not only alienates us from all except those who seek a new messiah or leader to follow, but it gives us the false impression of being above normal care and events. Thus it can easily happen that one crashes violently with 'the bars of experience' the world provides in the outer life. In other words, physical reality—the facts of life. The person may then either be tempted to retreat from the outer life because it questions or attacks their sense of importance—or else the other extreme is to drop into depths of depression, due to feelings of worthlessness, of having failed because life questioned their ideals.

Martin says that experience is usually the lesson that helps us learn how to keep our balance between the extremes, and walk safely. When we have veered to inflation and depression a few times, we can look back and see that this is not the way. It is not what we seek. To feel 'on top of the world' and superior may seem like an advancement for a while. Only its results tell us its real value. Nor does morbid criticism of ourselves and the world satisfy us.

A further danger lies in taking dreams or intuition as oracular, godly, or supernatural truths, instead of pointers on our instrument panel. This makes them as much a threat to our wholeness as acting only out of ambition, or sexual desires. These too must be only a 'part' of our life, not the controlling factor. After all, not only truths or wisdom are shown in dreams, but also represented are our murderous impulses, homosexual desires, feelings of power and grandeur, etc. All dreams are truths of the inner life, because they represent what is actually going on inside. But we do not therefore have to act upon them all, or believe that the future is ordained by them. This is all a form of irresponsibility.

A danger to women lies in their ability to enter more fully into their inner world of dreams and intuitions, but not being able to construct meaning and purpose so easily as men. They thus may find a man who sympathises with their inner feelings and dreams; who sees great meaning in them, and helps the woman see how they may be applied. This leads to the danger of making the man into a god-like figure who is the soul mate, or spiritual counterpart. This weakens the woman's own powers of determination, or construction. But, to quote Martin, 'This is in no way to condemn the true master-student relationship, where those less gifted or experienced learn from those having special knowledge or insight.'

While the danger for men is to make of the inner journey only an intellectual experience. The man may read and understand, but refuse to free his emotions from the rein of his intellect so that he can experience it. Thereby the man may never *know*, he will only *think* he knows.

These are a sort of basic 'highway code' for those who wish to make the journey into self discovery. If we learn them by heart, and attempt to understand them, they may remain rather dry at present, but on the journey they could easily be living realities.

ELEVEN

Using your dreams

From all the dreams and information that have already been dealt with, an enormous number of conclusions can be drawn. It is hoped that many of these do not need to be enlarged upon; but because it may not be clear from what has been said, the subject of purposeful use of dreams will be explained in greater detail. For instance, it was mentioned at the very beginning that dreams have helped such varied fields of research and expression as science, literature, philosophy, psychology, and so on. It has to be admitted that most dreams that have given such service have been spontaneous, and often unsought, but in a few cases people have purposely set out to gain information from dreams that they could not easily get in waking consciousness. Businessmen, scientists, laymen, and doctors, have each looked to the dream for help in their various enquiries. In some cases they did not understand the process of dreaming, and so were handicapped. Others had gained an understanding by analysing previous experience, and were better able to use dreams as tools in their research. How this is possible must be reasonably clear from the other chapters. The dream emerges as an expression of what is happening in *all* the departments of our being. The unconscious biological processes that have made us a living being—the physical and energetic processes of our body, with its digestion, circulation, metabolism, etc.—the relationships between different parts of our being, such as body and mind, sexual and ambitious drives, self and others, all are dealt with in dreams. Likewise, all that we have ever experienced, read, thought, studied, heard or seen, is all stored in the complete memory of our unconscious. Nothing is lost. This vast storehouse of learning and experience, coupled with the wisdom latent in our very cells, built in from millions of years of life experience, are all available to the dream. A later chapter will show that we are not limited even to our own vast memory, but can pick up thoughts from others through telepathy or expanded consciousness. Therefore, to have a question answered by a dream, is to receive a reply from the most advanced and best educated computer in the world. Even a new-born babe can rely upon the biological knowledge of its cells, which open to it, as instinct and intuitive response, the wisdom of the ages.

The examples of Robert Louis Stevenson gaining ideas for his writings, Kekule discovering the Benzene ring, the dreaming of Kubla Khan, and the dream foretelling the nationalisation of Iranian oil, illustrate a little of this. Another example is quoted in *Dreams, The Language of the Unconscious* by Hugh Lynn Cayce. The dream occurred to a member of the New York Stock Exchange, on March 5th, 1929. He says, 'Dreamed we should sell all our stocks including box stock (one considered very good). I saw a bull following my wife, who was dressed in red.' This dream was interpreted to mean that a crisis was approaching on the stock market, and all should be sold. Unfortunately the man did not heed this advice, and suffered the collapse of the stock market six months later.

Boccaccio, in his *Life Of Dante*, gives details of a dream had by Jacopo, a son of Dante. After Dante's death, it was discovered that the last thirteen cantos of the 'Commedia' were missing. This caused much debate as to whether they had been written, and all involved searched everywhere. Jacopo and his brother Piero were induced by others to try their hand at writing the missing cantos themselves, but before doing so Jacopo dreamt that 'his father Dante had appeared to him, clothed in the purest white, and his face resplendent—with an extraordinary light; Jacopo asked him if he lived, and Dante replied, "Yes, but in the true life, not your life." Then Jacopo asked him if he had completed his work before passing into the true life; and if he had done so, what had become of that part which was missing, as none could find it. To this Dante seemed to answer: "Yes, I finished it", and then took Jacopo by the hand and led him into that chamber Dante had been accustomed to sleep in when he was alive. Touching one of the walls, he said, "What you have sought so much is here." Then Jacopo awoke and although still night, called upon a friend, who went with him to Dante's old house. Waking the present owner, they were allowed in, and on coming to the bedroom and looking at the wall indicated in the dream 'found a mat fixed to the wall. They lifted it gently up, when they found a little window in the wall, never before seen by any of them. In it they discovered several writings, all mouldy from the dampness of the walls,' and found them to be the missing cantos.

It can be argued, of course, that Jacopo must have noticed the mat before, even if he had never seen beneath it. Therefore it could possibly have concealed a hiding place; but what is important is not the question of whether or not he had seen this, but the fact that he had not *consciously* thought of it as *the* hiding place. Even if he had considered it as *a* hiding place and forgotten it with the passage of time, the dream still presented him with a new combination of ideas—the mat and the cantos. If this is the limit of dream perception, and I am not agreeing that it is, then it still puts the dream in the position of a competent computer. It still shows it as having entrance to our complete memory, and seeking deductive answers from it.

Having admitted this much, we are still faced by a problem, namely, how can we get the dream life to respond to a particular question? Suppose we are a scientist researching on cancer cure, or an archaeologist searching for an elusive clue in his studies, or a philosopher seeking to understand life; or just you or me trying to understand how best to use our abilities; how can we go about finding an answer to our problem? The two dreams quoted already help us towards an answer, even though they are not induced dreams in the sense that we are seeking. They help us because they are induced dreams in a different sense. They are induced by the dreamer's interests. For the one dream is by a stock broker who recorded and attempted to analyse his dreams. The dream is induced because his *interests* in life are deeply bound up with the stock exchange. While Jacopo's dream was induced by the search and by others urging him to finish the cantos.

From just these two dreams we can see that a dream response can be induced by being emotionally and intellectually involved in the question or problem answered. Therefore, if we are going to ask a specific question, it will have a greater likelihood of producing a helpful dream if we become as involved as possible in it. A person I once met had a mother much given to the study and practice of positive thinking. The man wished to take his wife for a holiday abroad, but did not have and could see no possibility of getting sufficient funds to finance this. His mother persuaded him to live positively, however, and told him to plan his holiday anyway. This he did, arranging all details. As time drew near he still did not have sufficient money, and began to get somewhat apprehensive as to how he was going to pay fares and hotel costs. This situation lasted right up to a week before the holiday began. Then he had a dream of a particular horse winning a race. Searching through the papers the following morning he found such a horse by the same name, and bet on it, which was something he never usually did. The horse won, and he had his holiday.

I mention this because here we see the man not only intellectually and emotionally involved to a large degree, but also financially as well. These really are the ideal conditions to provoke a dream to answer our question or problem. I have used this method myself with some success, one dream being a direct answer to a direct question. At the time of the dream I had been researching on the psychological effects of Yoga exercises or postures. I practised the postures and tried as far as was possible to discover consciously what they did to the emotions, instincts and mind. I then asked myself, just before going to sleep, if there were inner effects I was unconscious of. If so, what were they? In this way I hoped to induce a helpful dream. In fact, I had several, but one in particular helped a great deal. In it I was on an underground train. Two black men were standing in the aisle. The train was nearing my station and I passed them to get to the door. One would not stand aside, even after I said 'Excuse me', so I had to push past him. This annoyed him so much that he rushed at me with hands extended to strangle me, but I caught his hands in mine, and gradually forced them down from my throat. As I did so, I thought: 'This is what Yoga has done' (i.e. given me the strength to stand against the black man).

The meaning of this dream is not readily understood until it is realised that these black men had appeared in other dreams. In one, he got my throat and began to strangle me, and I could do nothing, but awoke in terror. Here we see the unconscious or black parts of my nature which I associated with my instinctive drives and fears, throttling my conscious life. The second dream is therefore saying that Yoga was developing the strength to face and deal with one's unconscious fears and repressed urges. There is still a conflict, but at least my conscious self can meet its fears on equal terms, which is a very great part of the battle.

Becoming involved in a question is not all there is to inducing informative dreams. Earlier on I suggested that a baby, even though new born, can draw upon its biological past, the result of which is instinct, but the baby cannot ask the same sort of question as we do. Its questions are all associated with survival, feeding, sleeping, relating to its mother, and so on. Even if it could ask a more intellectual question, such as, 'How can one make a better mousetrap?' any dream that *did* give an answer would be quite incomprehensible to the baby. In short, while our dream producing mechanism may have entrance to infinite wisdom and resources, it nevertheless has the problem of explaining it to a very limited intelligence—namely us! In other words, we cannot ask a question that is beyond our present comprehension. If we did get an answer it would be meaningless. The question and answer are all bound up in each other. Dr Washington Carver, in seeking inner intuitive answers to scientific questions, had the same problem. He had before him the task of synthesising various products such as milk, glue, printer's ink and oils, from peanuts and sweet potatoes. He had to modify his questions, however, to get understandable replies.

This faces us with fresh information as to how we must approach the effort to induce dreams. First of all we have to exhaust the limits of our conscious research into the question. We should read about it, study it, experiment with it, becoming involved as deeply as possible. If an answer to our problem is not forthcoming from these conscious efforts, then we have to realise that what we seek does not lie in the *known* areas of our knowledge. With the present information at our disposal, we are not able to arrive at a solution. Most breakthroughs in knowledge or understanding, however, are not explainable with the old facts. So we have to let go of our present conclusions, opinions, concepts and feelings, and admit that these present aspects of ourselves do not appear to hold the solution. Or if they do, we cannot see it. Then we have to sleep on it and watch our dreams.

The result of this might be that:

(a) We have no noticeable response at all.

(b) We have only a partial reply to our question.

(c) We have an amazing dream that reveals the answer.

If there seems to be no response, we have to keep trying, and record any dreams that occur. It might be that the dreams are not properly understood, or else we are more deeply involved in some other issue. If the reply is partial, then further dreams may enlarge upon it. It may be that a total reply would be beyond our present comprehension. This is very noticeable when watching a dream series. As it proceeds, and one has gained understanding of the broad outlines of something being revealed, the dreams begin to portray greater detail, which is understandable in the light of what has been learnt; or else our attitudes and concepts are so fixed in one direction of approach, that we have to be gradually led and introduced to new areas. Then the subject proper can be introduced. In this way, a researcher into the problem of migraine headaches might be directing his experiments along the line of a particular type of chemical, but the dream might hold information dealing with it under a physiological approach. Therefore a change of attitude would have to exist at the very start of gaining what the dream holds in store. We have to be willing to let ourselves be educated by the dream. This can take a long time; but then so does any research, for we need to grow in understanding and ability to the point where we can comprehend and make use of what we are seeking. Leonardo de Vinci designed the helicopter, the submarine and the bicycle chain, but it took technology three hundred years to be able to apply this man's 'dreams'.

Some of those whose insight into the hidden process of human life amount to genius, have claimed that intuition is based upon vast experience or education. This education or experience can have been forgotten, or be the result of years long past, or even, as some claim, from past lives. The point is, however, that this knowledge is tapped, not by remembering it, but in receiving a sort of summary of its entire comments in regard to a particular question. As an example, let us say that a doctor examines a young girl, and has an irrational feeling that she has a rare blood condition. He cannot for the life of him think why, but nevertheless sends her for a blood test to check his feelings. Much to his surprise the condition is confirmed. This makes him really sit down to ponder how he knew; and after a great deal of searching he discovers the reason. In college he had read a novel mentioning a strange mark on a man's body, which turned out to be a sympton of a blood disease. Later, in medical school, he noticed in passing the colour of a person's eyes with a blood condition. Both incidents were lost to consciousness, but his intuition signals the essence of his knowledge by making him 'feel' uneasy about the girl's condition, and irrationally (i.e.

without knowing for what reason) suspect a blood disease.

That is an imaginary example, but there are plenty of real life ones. Seventy years ago, Morgan Robertson wrote a book called *Futility*. Robertson had been a seaman, and also had an inventive ability, having invented an improved type of periscope. The book he wrote was about a ship named 'The Titan'. This had a displacement of 70,000 tons, 800 ft long, had triple screw propulsion, speed of 24 to 25 knots, was designed to carry 3,000 people, and had only a few lifeboats. In the book the Titan hit an iceberg in the North Atlantic and went down.

To understand what I mean about intuition, I have only to explain that the 'Titanic' had a displacement of 66,000 tons, and was 852.5 ft long. Like the 'Titan', it also had triple screw, speed of 24 to 25 knots, carried 3,000 people and had few lifeboats. It too sunk in the North Atlantic after hitting an iceberg.

Heinrich Schliemann not only believed his irrational feelings, he did something about them. The son of a poor German clergyman, he educated himself, worked his way into a monied business; then, at a time when all the world scoffed, he set out to discover the mythical city of Troy. Later, he unearthed one of the richest treasures in the world at the Mycenaean Palace in Greece. All this from believing his inner feelings about the 'fairy stories' of Troy and King Midas. Schliemann himself says it was due to a past life in ancient times, and his irrational feelings were memories from that time he could not explain with present facts. Whether we believe this or not, his intuition, from whatever source, proved correct.

The prophesies of H. G. Wells also stand in a similar light. Working from his knowledge of his day, he spoke of such things as an atomic war, aerial fighting craft, armoured tanks, air-conditioning—intercontinental air travel and television. In a similar vein, as a great devourer of scientific information, Jules Verne prophesied many of the important scientific discoveries and applications that were to follow. One of the most interesting of these amazing intuitive insights into facts is displayed by Jonathan Swift in *Gulliver's Travels*. Written in 1726, the fictional Laputian scientists discover that the Planet Mars has two moons, and one of these travels around the planet twice as fast as the other. It was only in 1877, that Asaph Hall, an American scientist, was able to confirm the truth of this remarkable statement. How Swift came by this information is unknown.

Another interesting case is that of Herr Scherman. As an infant in the nursery he started collecting envelopes because of the various handwritings displayed on them. From then on his consuming passion was a study and analysis of handwriting. As his knowledge of this subject grew, his ability to determine who wrote a particular sentence became more than just a reasoned conclusion; it became intuitive. Cornelius Tabor, a newspaper man who wrote of Scherman's work with the police in crime investigation, said, 'I was introduced to him (Scherman) by Dr E.K. I showed him an envelope addressed by a lady he certainly did not know. He glanced at it briefly and then set to work. He decribed in minute detail the lady's appearance, her figure, the colour of her hair, her features and—suddenly it seemed that she came to life in front of me—he imitated her manner of speech. He seemed to know everything of her character. He told me her life story as if he had suddenly become a part of her very existence.'*

What has all this got to do with dreams? They are simply used as instances of the unusual knowledge, foresight, inventiveness, and powers of insight the human mind can exhibit, especially in its intuitive side. They are but a dewdrop in the sea of examples that could be given, but as long as they bring home one point, they are enough. The point being, that any thoroughgoing dream researcher will never discard ideas presented, just because they do not fit his or her present opinions. We are always enlarging our facts to fit increased human knowledge and experience. Let us not then cast away an idea because it will not fit the smallness of our conceptions, or because it seems ridiculous or irrational. Neither let us believe it without testing it. Once more, the balanced way.

If we approach the dream with an open mind, an involvement in our question, and the willingness to be educated, we are certainly on the right tracks. If we add to this the constant interest and enthusiasm in our subject that men like Scherman have shown, then we bring to the dream an ever widening sphere of experience and knowledge through which it can express itself.

It has to be pointed out, however, that the past 'knowledge and experience' explanation of intuition in dreams and waking does

* *My Occult Diary*—Rider.

not fully acount for it. Scherman's abilities, for one, do not entirely fit into this. If we read the lives of *Andrew Jackson Davis*, or *Edgar Cayce—Man of Miracles*—Neville Spearman, we shall soon see this. A study of their lives does show one interesting fact that furthers our knowledge of dream research. To state it briefly, the question asked, and how it is asked, has enormous influence on the answer received.

This has already been hinted at when mention was made of Dr George Washington Carver and his discoveries. When studying Edgar Cayce's life, we find that several of the important aspects of his intuitive knowledge were not displayed until someone asked him the right questions. For instance, Cayce eventually began to give personal information on people's latent capabilities, talents and problems, but this did not begin until a man named Lammers asked him questions on subjects he had not considered before, and so had never bothered to ask himself about.

I once made the experiment of asking a young man of very unphilosophical nature, a series of questions, rather like the Socratic method. Within fifteen minutes, as the questions awoke a realisation of his own experiences, he was talking pure philosophy, but he could not repeat this alone, without the questions.

The issues that arise from this are probably not of importance to the average person interested in dreams, but for the serious investigator they pose a very real problem; for one may have certain information that cannot be illicited because we do not know what questions to ask, or how to ask it. While this may seem of little importance at present, with very little stretch of imagination, a time can be foreseen when the present scientific method will attempt to incorporate the intuitive type of research into its sphere. Then, those found capable of dreaming or intuiting answers, will be as much a part of a research establishment as laboratory workers are today. Therefore, the framing of the question will be a serious undertaking. Basically, it has to elicit a response that remains understandable, but is not bound by preconceptions and already known facts. It must be more in the line of 'What do I need to know?'—or 'What is best to consider?' rather than a too pointed question arising from already held opinions. In this way we may discover that another intelligence other than our conscious self is working within us, and we can make contact. Of this, Shane

Miller tells the amusing story of the little boy who took a pole to measure the depth of the pool at the bottom of the garden. Each day he measured it, and each day it seemed to show a different depth. He pondered on this, and one day found the thrilling answer. There is Someone, or Something, at the bottom of the pool, moving the stick up and down. The boy realises *he is not alone*!

Working along similar lines, Professor James Bonner of the California Institute of Technology tried to analyse scientific creativeness. He questioned a number of researchers and scientists about intuitive knowledge gained in their work. He then set down his findings as follows:

(1) Define the question. This may itself be a creative act, since to recognise a question that has not been asked before may take great creativity.

(2) Stuff with facts. Once the question has been defined the potential scientific creator must have all the information he can get. He may have to do some experiments; he reads the literature, he gets together all the information that he can imagine bears upon the subject.

(3) Wait. The scientist may mull the facts over; he may worry; but in principle what he has to do now is wait.

(4) A solution pops out. Perhaps many solutions pop out. Often solutions emerge when one is half asleep, or perhaps during a day dream.

(5) Assess the solution. The scientist must now ask himself whether his new creative idea is a useful one or not. Is it good or bad? Does it unify everything that is present to be unified?

Getting down to methods, these should now be reasonably clear to understand. Having worked and worried over the problem, having looked to see what other people have said about it, or what other people have done along similar lines, we now approach the bed, but before actually climbing in, it is best to sit awhile, and consciously go over what you have thought, what you plan, what you hope, concerning the question. Cover the doubts, ideas, difficulties. Try to pierce the veil that hides the answer. If it is a personal problem ask 'What shall I do? What is the best course of action? Or, how should it be approached?' If the question relates to work we plan to do, such as starting a business, investing in a venture, or beginning some undertaking; run through the plans, and ask, 'Have I missed anything? Are there factors I have not considered? Is this for my best interests? Any suggestions?'

Then drop thought of the subject, get into bed, and go to sleep. When you wake, whatever the time if you remember a dream *whether it seems like an answer or not,* set it down lest it be forgotten. If you wake and cannot remember any dreams, lie quietly for a while, trying to remember as explained earlier, and— 'Good Luck!'

SOURCES OF DREAMS

If one is sincerely attempting to use dreams as a way of research, one has to realise that dreams may arise from a variety of sources. This has already been mentioned, but what has been said is perhaps not detailed enough if we want to probe deeply. At the very outset of trying to give further information, however, it has to be admitted that the following statements are not made dogmatically. Very little is known about the sources of dreams. The inner consciousness has not been explored and charted sufficiently to make it common territory. For this reason I have collected several explanations of the main aspects of man's being. Whether these descriptions are true or adequate has to be left to each person's experience. At least it is hoped they are helpful.

In giving the various theories concerning the dream, we have seen that one of the commonest is that they rise from subtle physical sensations. In some cases, disease has been indicated by dreams some time prior to its appearance outwardly. While A. J. Davis goes into some detail as to descriptions of dreams and their possible sources in the bodily functions, he also says. 'There are numerous spiritual phenomena connected with the state of sleep.' That is, he defines levels of consciousness. He says that man's being is the harmonious relationship of seven principles. If we think of dreams once more as the instruments panel, then just as the oil gauge of a car connects with the oil pump, and the thermometer with the water, so dreams can be indicators of these seven modes of being. Davis lists these as the ANATOMICAL, which relates to the body as matter, and its form; the PHYSIOLOGICAL, which relates to the function of the form; the MECHANICAL, which is the energy or force behind the function or form in matter, and can be termed movement; the CHEMICAL, which is decomposition of form and substance, as in catabolism; the ELECTRICAL, which expresses as combination, or anabolism, or the combination of simple chemical or organic substances into more complex ones; the MAGNETICAL, which is the law of harmony allowing the other principles to relate together harmoniously; the SPIRITUAL, or that which relates to attenuation, or growth and development of more extended aspects, or that relates to all other manifestation. Therefore, a dream could arise from any of these departments of ourselves.

Davis, like many other philosophers, gives the over all forces within man as LOVE, WISDOM and WILL. Others express it as Love, Wisdom and Power. As general classifications these include many seemingly separate functions and capabilities of the human being. They may be better understood if we say that Love covers such diverse activities as physical attraction of the opposite sexes; emotional attraction and harmony between any sex or age group; the grouping together of cells and chemical substances in the body seemingly opposite or antagonistic. In fact the law of love seems to be the bringing together and stabilising of opposites or conflicting factions, whether physically, emotionally, energetically or mentally. Similar general rules apply to the other two classifications. Love may unite, but Wisdom gathers experience, looks for causes, understands direction. Power on the other hand relates to all expressions of energy, of will, of force. In human affairs we may see a loving person who lacks wisdom or power to understand and direct their love; or a forceful person may lack love and wisdom and so be destructive and hurtful. Or a wise person may lack forcefulness and love, and so be a dry, fruitless intellectual; and so on with the other combinations.

Dreams can be concerned with LOVE in its various aspects. Here, perhaps the Freudian type of interpretation concerns itself most with relationships of passion and love. Alder is an excellent example of one who concentrated on dealing with the Power aspect of dreams. His life was spent helping people to direct their 'will to power' their ambitions and energies. Without stretching our imagination too much, we can say Jung represents the study of dreams of WISDOM. Such dreams would deal with the desire to understand, to clarify awareness of self, and relationship to life, with its attendant unravelling of the beauty and wisdom of our own and other cultures.

As many other investigators of man's being have listed seven main principles, perhaps I can summarise these to make them more understandable. For the information locked in Davis' remarks may lose its helpfulness without a little further commentary; and philosophical systems as varied as Hindu, Buddhist, Hebrew, Alchemical, Christian, Agnostic and Anthroposophical, have all listed these seven levels. As these could naturally take volumes to explain in detail, an analogy will be used to summarise them. In doing this, the failings of using such a symbol and imaginative method must be forgiven. To start with we have to imagine the sperm and ovum as a seed, planted in the fertile soil of the womb. This seed holds in it a great deal of potential, but it is at present all unexpressed.

MATTER OR PHYSICAL BODY

When we plant this human seed let us think of it as a little piece of earth, of matter, only. If we literally planted a piece of earth in a human womb, nothing would happen as far as growth was concerned. In this sense matter represents just a set of 'materials'. Just as we may use bricks or clay, planks of wood, nails of iron, windows of glass to build a house, so the seed is likewise a collection of materials, which in themselves are inert. This is Davis' 'Anatomical'.

FORMATIVE

When we plant our seed under the right circumstances, however, it already has form, and continues to express itself in forming a developing body. Therefore, one of the things latent in the seed was a sort of *formative power* or process. This same organic formative power, that takes hold of inert matter and shapes it, is one of the first processes of evolution. We see it at work in forming the minerals of our Earth, and the crystals. This is the first of its potentials the seed can express. At its lowest level this formative power is something like the growth of a crystal, of filings shaping themselves round a magnet. At its highest phase it becomes movement such as plants describe in growth. This is Davis' 'Physiological'.

SENTIENCY

In the growth of our seed, further levels of potential can express themselves as the lower stage prepares the ground. The plant cannot use sunlight until the leaves are unfolded. So, sentiency cannot express until a sensitive vehicle is formed. In plants, this sentiency can be seen in the growing toward light, or closing of flowers at night. Without this sentiency or sensitivity, one would never be aware of physical or sensual impressions. Naturally, with the development of sentiency, it changes the direction of effort of the previous processes. In this way a plant directs the formative processes to grow to the light, through its sensitiveness to light. At its lowest level this is a chemical and organic response to impacts from within and outside itself. At its highest level it becomes emotion or feelings. This is Davis' 'Mechanical'.

PERCEPTION

Just as sentiency could not manifest without form, neither could perception without feeling. Perception means an awareness of sensations. It means the ability to add two and two together. When a dog sits too near the fire and burns himself, he learns to avoid such close contact again. The dog has associated the sensation of burning with the image of the fire. In man, such perceptions become more and more complex. A man can take the ideas of pain and fire as abstractions, and add the idea of prevention, thus producing a fire guard. This is thought. At its lowest level, perception is memory to avoid pain, or direct activities. At its highest level it becomes constructive thought, which has emerged out of feeling. This is Davis' 'Chemical'.

KNOWLEDGE

Out of thinking develops knowledge. When we experience a feeling such as pleasure, it is ours alone. It cannot be handed from person to person. It can be stimulated in others, but not given. But Knowledge goes beyond the individual. At this stage a man can look at life and discover that if corn is planted, a harvest may later be reaped. This realisation can be passed on. At its lowest level it is learned response. At its highest level a collection of conscious realisations about life. This is Davis' 'Electrical'.

INSIGHT

This level is often listed as intuition, but with careful thought we see that many creatures possess intuition, but it takes a man of a high calibre to possess insight. Insight is the result of a high level of consciousness, a wide knowledge, plus the faculty of intuition. Intuition is the power that takes hold of experience and facts, and puts them into new orders, fresh insight. Intuition reveals deeper meaning in already known subjects of knowledge, producing insight. Or should we say, insight is the result of conscious knowledge plus intuition. Intuition minus high conscious awareness produces strange knowledge, unexplainable reaction, but it does not produce insight. So here we have consciousness and its contents, opening itself to the unconscious, resulting in insight, the link between the two worlds of seen and unseen, manifest and potential. This is Davis' 'Magnetical'.

SPIRIT

This is the antipode to matter. Matter is the receptive and resourceful womb that spirit enters, and begins to manifest its potentials by using the materials matter presents. A later description will clarify this.

This may all seem very confusing, and, in fact, it is. Such lists of attributes are only a structure which human beings use to hang their understanding upon; but no such structure will stand up to vigorous investigation, and so secondary or alternative structures are built such as the Love, Wisdom and Power explanation. Some thinkers break man's complicated being into a simpler symbol and instead of seven levels, they list three. This is not to say that they thereby miss out parts given by the others; they put them all together instead. The results, however, seem a lot more understandable. In this category we have the thoughts and investigations of such men as Rudolph Steiner, Edgar Cayce and Spencer Lewis. Steiner calls those three levels Body, Soul and Spirit, and Cayce the Conscious, Unconscious and Superconscious, or sometimes Body, Soul and Spirit as Steiner. Spencer Lewis expressed them as Physical, Psychic and Cosmic. Although these three men had their own individual way of describing these levels according to their own genius, I will attempt to summarise what they said.

PHYSICAL OR BODY

We are all familiar with this. We have to recognise that in this category it is mentioned as the body *minus* consciousness, as consciousness belongs to another level. Under this classification of Body we have inanimate, unfeeling matter. It represents those parts of our nature that by themselves are inert, without energy, without sensation or feeling, like a dead body. Forces are certainly at work in such a body, such as disintegration, breakdown. This level represents the power of *Inertia*, of *Limitation*, of *Unconsciousness*. These are stressed because they have a power in their own right, and if we do not understand them, we may miss seeing their expression in dreams. If we take the analogy of a stream, using the water as movement or energy, and the stream bed as matter or inertia, we see that matter directs the expression of energy, but in its turn, energy shapes and gives form to matter. Another example is an electric motor, which is itself inert matter, but which directs the expression of energy. So the elements, form and physiology of the body direct the expression of the energy. In turn the energy gives form and function to the body, for at death, when the energy is no longer active, the form disintegrates, and the function ceases.

PSYCHIC OR SOUL

Our psychic life, or soul life, is the world of our sensations, emotions, thoughts. It is the world of our *individual consciousness* and intelligence. The body cannot feel or sense or know without this soul life. Just as the heat from an electric fire is the combination, or result, of electricity and the inert instruments, so this soul life is the result of a combination between spirit and body, energy and matter. At one extreme of soul life we have alert, concentrated consciousness, with a sense of individuality and self awareness. At the other extreme we have the subconscious, which is a wider consciousness going beyond our sense of being cut off, individual, and touches the next level of being, the Spirit. Cayce calls the soul, the sense of individual activity and decision, the memory of one's personal activities. The energy that gave life to man is universal, but if consciousness remained at that level, no individual realisation could take place. Thus the soul is the record and the experience of the individual outside a consciousness of the universal.

This level includes all the levels of a man's individual mind, ranging from sensual impressions, thought and emotion, memory, and subconscious activities. It is called the psychic because it is the realm that is neither formless as is the spirit, nor bound to form as is the body. Soul experience is a middle way between the extremes, and a dream is a weaving together of formless energies with images to make them understandable. It links the limitation and unconsciousness of the body on the one hand, with all its separateness with the infinite extensions and possibilities of spirit on the other. So man, in his dream life, can dwell in the aloneness of his body, or contact all beings through the agency of his life force.

SPIRIT OR COSMIC

This is that energy which is the very opposite of matter. In itself it represents the infinite consciousness, movement, knowledge, creativity and energy. This is the male aspect of self, while the body is its mate or wife, which it enters and brings forth the child of self consciousness. As consciousness in the body is a mixture of spirit and matter, it likewise blends the two, that is, it has limited awareness. But it can either associate itself with the body, when it takes on more and more of the physical characteristics, such as inertia, unfeelingness and limited knowledge. Or it can associate itself with its energy, which leads to expanded awareness, greater energy and creativeness. The spirit is man's sense of union or identity with his source. This level of man's being is the synthesis of *all experience*. It holds within it the memory of all men, all creatures, all activity, while man's soul is the record of his doings only. But as the soul is an extension of the spirit, it can partake of the greater wisdom, the greater experience by a harkening to that part of itself instead of only bodily experience, and yet still maintain its individuality, just as a man may learn from others yet apply it differently.

To summarise this description of man's being in connection with dreams, they may arise from body, soul or spirit. If they arise from body they will deal with the health, or workings, or intricate wisdom that its form portrays due to it being a reflection of spirit in matter. If they arise from the soul, they will deal with the range of human feelings, relationships, fears, individual growth, past memories, desires, and aspects of the *individual's* life. If they arise from the spirit, they will express elements beyond the limited desires, aims and knowledge of the individual. Such dreams may carry information about other people, about the meaning of life, or be of universal appeal. People living or dead may be dealt with in a meaningful and usually super logical way. For the dead are only dead in body. The memory, the spirit, of their whole experience is caught in the memory of the Cosmic. Therefore, not only our own past may come to us in a dream, but also the past and experience of the long dead may arise in us, if it is connected with our present life in some way.

One other definition of man's experience of himself may find a useful place here. This is Jung's description of man's four functions. These he called SENSATION—FEELING—THINKING—INTUITION. These are the aspects of man's soul life as depicted above. In saying this I am not trying to confuse Jung's ideas with those of other people. I am merely trying to give a reasonably understandable presentation of man's being that includes the materialistic and the mystical, the practical and the psychological. Therefore, to define the four functions, we can say that in the function of SENSATION, man's soul life is directed towards the body. Jung explained that each person had dependence on one main function. Thus a person whose consciousness mainly existed in their physical sensations could be listed under this first function. These are people who are keenly aware of the outside world, and are at home in their physical sensations.

As for the FEELING function, this refers to people who are 'at home' in their emotions and inner feelings. They can cope with relationships on the emotional level easily and constructively, although they, like the others, may be quite lost outside their own sphere.

The THINKING function refers to the man or woman 'at home' in their ideas, plans, opinions and the world of thought.

The INTUITIVE function person has the ability to see beyond the rational, beyond the things portrayed by thought, feeling or senses. He arrives at truths that seem beyond the ken of those using the other functions.

If four such typical people walked down a street together, we might say that the one with Sensation as his leading function would notice the houses, their colours and changes made since his last visit. The Feeling person would be aware of the emotions stimulated by the surroundings and relationship with the people. The Thinking person would perhaps be little aware of the street at all, but be following a line of thought. While the Intuitive might know from his perceptions, much of what the others are thinking or feeling.

So dreams may be expressions of some aspect of these functions in our life. Naturally, each of us has the other functions. although we live mostly in one. As these have to some extent been explained under other headings, I have done no more than mention them.

Inadequate as it is, it is hoped that these sketchy outlines of the various schools of thought will at least direct attention towards a constructively analytical direction. For sometimes, even hints help us to unravel a difficult dream.

The next chapter will give examples of dreams from these various sources.

TWELVE

A dream sampler and sleep experiences

Although a number of different types of dream have already been dealt with, we have by no means seen examples of all the major types. One of the things that makes dream interpretation easier is to be able to recognise what type of dream we are dealing with. In the last chapter, various descriptions or definitions of man's being were given. It was said that dreams may arise from any of these parts of ourselves. It has been left to this chapter to show just how different these dreams can be. Also, certain typical character-istics can usually be found in dreams arising from the different parts of our being. Despite having a limited number of dreams to choose from, I have tried to select those that do express these typical characteristics. Therefore, this chapter can be used as a source of reference in helping us to determine the character of our own dreams. But quite apart from that, it is, due to the very nature of the dreams dealt with, full of information about life in general.

In this 'Dream Sampler' I am sticking to the general theme of 'Body, Soul and Spirit' as defined in the previous chapter. It will also be seen that the title of this chapter includes the words 'and Sleep Experiences'. This is because some of the examples given are not recognised as dreams by some writers. As they occur during sleep, however, I feel it necessary to include them in order to make this chapter more complete.

THE BODY

Science, religion and philosophy have often been at disagreement with each other, or themselves, as to exactly what part the body plays in the making of a human being. Religion has generally argued that the body is temporal and of less importance than the Soul and Spirit. On the other hand, science has often remarked that consciousness and mind are developments of matter, while philosophy has attempted to understand and reconcile these two extremes.

Dreams about the body do not usually deal with it in quite the same way as science or religion. Like philosophy they tend to reconcile the extremes. With Blake they agree that 'Man has no body distinct from his Soul; for that called Body is a portion of Soul discern'd by the five Senses, the chief inlets of Soul in this age. Energy is the only life, and is from the Body, and Reason is the bound or outward circumference of Energy.'

Getting down to the dreams themselves, we have the obvious 'Body' dreams like these of a mother-to-be. Her two dreams are short but to the point.

'Dreamt I should take more calcium and certain minerals.'

'Dreamt that I should be doing exercises to help with my pregnancy.'

It is interesting that prior to these dreams the woman had felt very low in health. She followed up the advice of the dreams and gradually regained her energy and well being. She discovered then that she had been very anaemic, but had now overcome this blood condition.

In the book *Dreams and Dream Stories*, by Anna Kingsford, a footnote to one of the dreams says she 'beheld a hand holding out towards her a glass of foaming ale, the action being accompanied by the words, spoken with strong emphasis, "You must not drink this." It was not her usual beverage, but she occasionally yielded to pressure (from her husband) when at home.'

Generally, such dreams concerning what we should or should not partake of are reasonably clear. But where the dream attempts to depict the results of wrong eating, it may become more symbolical.

Dealing with the body in a different sense, we have the following dream of a man. He had been trying to understand how his conscious self related to the unconscious workings of his body. He dreamt:

'I had been asked to run a sort of mission hall. It was a bare tin hall, wood on the inside. It seemed to be mostly coloured people I had to speak to. At first I simply stood at one end of the hall and spoke to them about God and life. I felt it was hardly worth the effort, believing that they would not understand or be interested. I believe I suggested they work as a team and produce a book. This was to be about their own life and work, and to help them understand and express themselves, and aid me to know them better. Again I felt it was not worth the effort.

'When I spoke again the following week great changes had already been made in the hall. An orderly notice board was on the right of the hall. It was generally brighter and more purposefully united, and a rostrum and microphone were there for my use. Apparently Bob Miller had made these.

'As I was looking at all this, a coloured woman came to me at the rostrum table. She was Afro-Indian and middle aged. She had with her two books produced by the team. I opened the books and looked at them, astounded. They consisted mostly of pictures, with explanatory captions. They were absolutely beautiful pictures showing their place in industry and society. There were coloured men stripped to the waist working in the steel works at furnaces; women busy at production lines, and so on. So wonderful were they, and I could see in every page the effort and loving care, the team work and deep appreciation, love and respect for myself and what I was trying to do with them, that I was overcome by humility and love for them. So much so that I took the woman in my arms and held her close while I wept. It was an ecstatic moment of communion and understanding between us. Then she felt slightly embarrassed and turned away.'

This is a beautiful and unusual dream. So much so that when the dreamer understood its meaning he cried again. It is therefore worth explaining in a little detail, and I will let the dreamer explain it in his own words.

'The meaning of this dream came to me partly through understanding the symbols, and partly through intuition. The Mission Hall is my own body. It represents also my search for understanding and self knowledge. But it shows that what I discover consciously about life or God, is sought eagerly by the coloured people of the congregation. This congregation is in fact the unconscious forces and activities of my own body. I had felt at one time that my body was something to be conquered. This dream shows how foolish and proud this was. The congregation not only need me, but I also depend upon them. I am their ability to think, to analyse, to try to understand life. While they are all the congregation of my inner forces and energies, that keep my body, and thus my physical consciousness, functioning. They work at the "industries" of construction, digestion, circulation, etc. The notice board represents dreams, which tell me what is going on in the congregation. The rostrum and loudspeaker represent my greater ability to communicate with myself. The rest now explains itself. The Afro-Indian woman shows that both instinctive and spiritual drives are expressed in the unconscious, and my humility is a necessary adjustment to my previous attitude. Then, how can I help but love these parts of myself seeing we are co-partners in the business of living?'

This dream covers so many aspects of our relationship with our body, that further examples are unnecessary. Also, those dealing with representations of sickness have already been mentioned in the dreams of the dog biting the dreamer's body. But one more dream must be mentioned, as a further example of the dream as a guide to caring for the body. It is quoted from *Dreams, The Language of the Unconscious* by Hugh Lynn Cayce. 'I dreamed my brother and I with our wives were out on a party with B.B. I fell asleep at the table. We got home very late. My brother left the car and walked home. He and I stopped to look at a bottle of milk that was marked "undistilled milk!"' An intuitive analysis of this dream by Edgar Cayce suggested that it represented the man as having too many late nights. This is portrayed by his falling asleep at the table. It also is said to suggest a need for more physical exercise in the part where his brother walks instead of using the car. And lastly, Cayce says, 'Change from the present supply (of milk) for this shows adulteration in same.'

THE SOUL

Turning from dreams dealing directly with the body and its func-tioning, we now approach those dealing with our emotions, thoughts, drives, relationships, opinions, and the host of things covered by the word Soul. Because so many dreams fall within this category, they will have to be subdivided into further sections. Let us start then with typical worrying dreams and nightmares.

WORRIES AND NIGHTMARES

Dreams that depict worries and terrors are fairly easy to recognise.

Their very emotional and fearful content, quite apart from the symbols, is enough to tell of their serious subject. Here are three 'worry dreams', all from the same woman dreamer.

'Not a very nice dream. I was in a boat, there seemed to be a lot of people in it to start with, and we were fishing. Then it wasn't very light and I was by myself, and between me and the shore was a continuous row of lobster nets, and I couldn't find a way through to get to the shore. It was dark and I was so panicky and I couldn't try to get through the nets for fear of fouling the motor.'

Here we find the dreamer 'at sea'. The darkness and nets represent her feelings and fears of being tangled up in life's problems. The motor is her drive or energy, which is not capable of expressing itself due to fear of failure, fear of entanglement.

'We were preparing for a party and I was trying to make up a plate of strawberries. At one moment they seemed to be strawberries and the next they were flowers, but half of them were bad and I was sorting through what seemed to be a mountain of wilted flowers to find one or two to make a dish. As fast as I found some nice ones, the next time I looked at them they had wilted and the pile got higher and higher until I was almost covered in a dark brown pile.' In this dream all the nice things in life appear to wilt and go bad, giving the feeling of being buried under brown-ness or decay.

'I was going to go across the street and along a lane to collect seven bottles of milk which were in a box behind a house. The mud got thicker and deeper and as I waded I was being sucked down. Then I got to the milk and turned around to go back but the mud was moving like the waves and I was trying to hold the box of milk higher to get it above the waves and it was so heavy. Then, fortunately I woke up and I'd got a splitting headache.' Again, we do not have to find a specific interpretation to see in this dream the feelings of being held back, pulled down, and carried away. Most worry dreams follow similar patterns, distinguishable by the emotions or fears portrayed. But many people fail to understand these dreams simply because they are unable to look at the symbolism of the dream, and see it as an expression of their own feelings. Yet even without the symbols, these dreams are clear because of the emotions involved.

This also applies to nightmares. To understand in detail we have to look closely at the symbols and their arrangement. But a general understanding can be found just from the feelings themselves. Here is a typical nightmare.

'I dreamt that I woke up in bed. A noise downstairs had disturbed me. It sounded like somebody moving about, and I thought about burglars. I could distinctly hear the noise now, and was annoyed because I would have to do something about it. But just as I decided to get out of bed, it sounded as if the person or thing making the noise began to come up the stairs to the bedroom. I realised now that I was terrified. I tried to move but was rigid with fear. I tried to call out to my wife in bed beside me, but could not move my mouth because I was so terrified. But it became even more horrifying because the footsteps seemed to keep coming forever, and thus deepen and deepen my paralysis. It was like an eternity of fear. Then at last the bedroom door began to creep open, and my fear burst the bounds of my paralysis, and I screamed to my wife to switch the light on. Then we both really awoke, and I switched the light on because the room seemed filled with my own fear, disturbing even my wife.'

The difference between worrying dreams and nightmares is really only one of degree. As the pitch of emotion deepens, one usually wakes in fear or terror. If it is just a mild worrying dream, one may remain asleep, but struggling with the situation. In the above dream, the symbols at their face value suggest some upsetting factor downstairs in the unconscious that is beginning to stir about and disturb the conscious life of the dreamer. The dream is saying that he has just awoken to this situation, and is paralysed by it in his outer life. In fact, the dreamer had just begun to discover fears and desires he had previously not known existed in himself.

CHILDREN'S DREAMS

Children's dreams are very similar to those of an adult. It is only that a child is facing slightly different problems that changes the themes. Or at least they are probably the same problems but at a different level and from a different degree of experience. For the following dreams I am indebted to Liz Hayes, a schoolteacher, who collected them for me from a class of schoolchildren. All the dreams are from girls about the age of twelve.

'I am going to tell you about my dream I had last night. It started when I went for a walk in a park near my home. Well, I was happy that day, then all of a sudden a man came out of a bush and got me by my hand. I hit him that hard he let me go and I ran as fast as I could. He came running after me. I ran to the Park keeper but he wasn't there and I got scared. I could have cried. Then I saw an old lady and I ran up to her but she was death. Then I ran to a telephone box and phoned the police. They came and got the man and took him to prison and I got a reward.'

This is either a fear of assault, or what is more likely a representation of her own sexual desires. As yet they are too big to deal with or handle on a relationship level. Several methods are tried, and in the end, moral conscience locks the man up safely.

'One night I dreamt that I was drowning on a boat and there were strong winds blowing against the ship. I was the only one on the boat and the ship was nearly touching the sea and the waves were over the boat and suddenly the boat went over and I fell out of the boat and the waves came right over my head, then I was screaming and shouting for help and then I found myself awake.'

Obviously things are a bit rough going for this young girl. A boat usually represents the frail craft of our personality structure, with which we set sail on the sea of life.

'One night I had a strange dream that I was walking down a dark road on my way home from my friend's when a car drew near me. I began to run up an entry and when I reached the bottom of the entry I saw two men with stockings over their faces. I ran back but the man in the car was behind me and I bumped into him. I dreamed that he stabbed me with his knife and dragged me in his car. Then I woke up very scared.'

Shades of Freud? No comment!

'I had a dream and this is what it was about. There were some men who threw me down an attic window. The attic was only about one and a half yards wide, but it was very high. I landed on the floor and there was my aunty with her little baby in her arms sitting on a chair. There was no other furniture and the attic was painted all white. There was a very big fierce lion there. I screamed and yelped as the lion came at me. The lion sprang on me and I died. As it was a funny dream I came alive again. The lion sprang at me again. I started shouting and screaming. There was blood bleeding all over. Then I woke up. In the morning my Mom said, "I heard you screaming and shouting for help." I told her about the nightmare.'

This dream by a young Indian girl possibly represents jealousy over the affection given to a baby. The other dreams in the 31 sent to me deal almost entirely with violence, drowning, assault or chasing.

SELF

The large majority of dreams deal with general aspects of ourselves. Most of those already quoted in the book are examples of this, and one could go on forever with them. So, just a few dealing with common themes will be given.

A house is one of the commonest symbols in a dream. It was seen in the very first dream in the book, and in several others. Here is another house dream.

'This house belonged to me, and I let some of the rooms to other girls. The furniture, apart from University stuff in some of the rooms, was mine too. I came in one evening and was sticking posters on the walls in my room when I realised that the chest of drawers—only in the dream it was a bookcase—was only about half its normal size. I couldn't think why and then someone said one of the girls who lived here had stolen half of it. I was absolutely furious, and went on about letting my house and furniture, and how I couldn't put a lock on my door because it looked bad when friends came. It was the middle of the night but I rushed downstairs trying to find the girl. A girl sleeping on the landing said she was out with her boyfriend. I went to her room and burst in— her room-mate woke up and said she and the bookcase were out at Mearweed. I kept trying to remember the address but couldn't —eventually wrote it down. The housekeeper or caretaker or someone came down to the kitchen with us and made coffee—she handed me one before I had a chance to refuse (I don't like coffee). There was a big tin of gingerbread which I thought would take the taste away but someone covered it with biscuits. I kept saying

"Dammit, it's all my furniture," and, "But it's my house!" The housekeeper said, "All right, we know, but it all froze up last winter." I said, "I know, but if people are willing to put up with that sort of thing I am willing to put up with them living here—it's a reciprocal arrangement." Someone had left the gas on. I turned it off and said, "Try to remember not to leave it on." One of the girls apologised in a mocking sort of way, calling me "Ma'am".'

This was dreamt by a young University student, which explains why some of the furniture was the University's. In other words, some of her inner ideas and opinions are not hers yet, but have come from her studies. Without attempting a detailed analysis, which is not the aim of this chapter, the dream is a good example of a house dream. The different girls and rooms represent different attitudes of her own, and the dream revolves around the conflict between her outgoing self represented by the girl with boyfriend, who relates well with the opposite sex, and doesn't mind sharing things, shown by the girl in her room; and the dreamer's other attitude of not liking her personal belongings, i.e. her feelings, ideas, etc., shared with others. The caretaker is probably what we might call her common sense, and the freeze up an emotional withdrawal or coldness.

DESTRUCTION

Many dreams deal with the subject of destruction, or even cataclysm. These usually occur when the dreamer is going through great doubts, cynicisms and soul searching. Events may question religious or moral beliefs; break down self confidence, destroy the concepts one has of the world and life. Here is the dream of a girl educated as a Roman Catholic, but finding many of her beliefs threatened by the materialism of society, and the experiences of her life.

'There was a group of people (none of whom I knew) in a room with metal walls, reached by a trapdoor in the floor, with a ladder down to the ground. There had been a nuclear explosion or some sort of world shattering disaster, and these were the only people left, and they read aloud to keep themselves amused.

'They went outside—the air was heavy and foul with poisonous gases. They walked through fields of dead, brittle plants, through barbed wire fences, past a pylon, and came to a small patch of land which they'd reclaimed and were trying to grow things on— a few small shoots were starting to appear. They walked over the brow of a hill and suddenly came upon the ruins of a cathedral. All that remained was the tower and a rectangle formed by the nave arches and the wall above, which formed a sort of lacy pattern. It was just an empty shell but was very beautiful—they hadn't realised before that it was there. They went back to their room and watched a film of Leeds as it was before the disaster—it was very colourful and nostalgic. The camera followed a road through Leeds—quite a complicated route, and the final shot was of the underside of the trapdoor of their room.'

The whole inner disaster that many of us face is portrayed here so well. Our intellectual schooling, and social influences in their commercial and political leanings, leave us in a difficult state of mind, leading nowhere, surrounded as we are by material and harsh values, unfeeling and unsatisfying. The outer life seems no better, one's spirit is poisoned by the social scene, there is little if any natural growth, only that induced by particular effort on one-self, none induced by our society. Painful restrictions, destruction and seeming hopelessness. Yet although the dreamer's religious beliefs have been shattered and much destroyed, the dream suggests that what does remain are the foundations of her own spiritual life, and these are beautiful. Then the dream looks back on the way things used to be before this inner destruction took place, and portrays the meandering complicated series of experiences leading to the present situation. Nostalgia for the past is felt; but what now? Will a living faith be built, and new growth arise from the debris of the old world? Such is the path dreams often take.

DEAD BODY

Another common theme is to discover a dead body and realise that one is somehow implicated with its death. A dream I do not have a written record of, but which was told me, runs approximately as follows. 'I discovered a blood-stained cloth, and realised I was somehow involved in a murder. I hid the cloth behind a bush.'

Another such dream is, 'I and some other people were burying a corpse, we weren't concerned about the murder that had been committed, only that we might be found out—and I seemed particularly involved because a piece of paper with my address on it had been left by the grave. There was a part in this dream where I definitely became involved in it. I was watching the digging but taking no part in it. It was proceeding very slowly, so I got down and began to scrape at the earth with my hands. The moment I touched it I thought, "I'm involved in this. I can now be done as an accessory after the fact."'

In these dreams the dead body often represents some part of our feelings or capacities that we have killed off, but do not wish to admit. For instance, through our marriage vows, we may kill off through guilt our feelings of warmth towards other people. But this may also 'kill' our warmth towards our children and partner, and so be represented as a dead body in dreams.

Of course it can be other parts of self we have killed, and we must look to the symbols for details. A point to make particular note of in death or murder dreams is whether it is oneself who is to die or is dead, or whether it is some other person. If it is oneself, this means that one directly associates oneself with the feelings or ideas involved in the death. We see this in the dream of the 'holiday bed'. But if we do not choose to feel connected with such parts of our being (i.e. evil feelings within people were at one time projected upon the Devil! This made them easier to deal with in that the person did not feel directly connected with them. But it is only a temporary help, because the feelings represented by the Devil remain within to haunt us), then we see them in a dream as some other figure than ourselves.

WASHING

Bathing or washing is another symbol often experienced. Here are two dreams from the same person. They occurred in the order given, within a week.

'I was amongst a lot of people, some known to me but I forget who they were, and everything in the building was getting into a greater and greater muddle. Things wanted tidying up and generally cleaning, but instead, everything got quite chaotic. I decided to have a bath, but found it impossible.'

'I decided I wanted a bath. I went to a woman who was somewhere in the building in her own flat and she said that she had just had something done to improve the plumbing and that since then the water was always dark brown, muddy or rusty. We ran two bathsfull but it was no good, we could not get through to the clean water.'

The meaning of washing is here made quite plain. The muddle of the house needs cleaning. Bathing is a rite of purification and cleansing. Therefore the bath is a cleansing of her inner muddle.

MARRIAGE

Marriage in its various aspects is another well-worn symbol. The following dream, by a married woman, is both beautiful and instructive. In it we can see how one can feel 'on top of the world' in early marriage; then drift apart emotionally and physically, the pain of which can sometimes stimulate the partners to discover a deeper relationship than ever.

'Dreamt that there was a green and beautiful place on top of the world. It had crags and cliffs and vales and hills, and all was covered with bright green grass and moss. In a deep dell, more green and beautiful than the rest of the place, a young girl met a young man, and married him; for what reason I cannot tell, except perhaps that the place was beautiful. Now the young man was an alien from another planet, but he did not tell the young girl in case she would not marry him.

'As time passed the young girl and man drifted apart and slept in separate rooms, still on top of the world, and the young girl grew to hate the young man, although he seemed unaware of it and quite content.

'This then was their state when I arrived. I immediately leapt and skipped over the hills to the place where they had met, but found it no different in appearance to the rest of the hills: no more beautiful, no less. I then went to see the young man and talked to him. I explained to him the feelings of the young girl, and that it was because she did not understand him that she felt the way she did. Whereupon he immediately went to her and confessed to being an alien, and she accepted him as he was. Then they grew together again and slept in beds side by side and peace filled their nights and beautiful children one after the other were born to the young girl. And the young man was surprised and amazed beyond his comprehension.'

GOING UP HILL

Going up hill means that things are difficult, but leading to higher things. Here is a typical 'hill' dream.

'My husband, children and I were going up a terrifically steep hill, almost vertical, in our car. It was so steep I did not know if we would make it and I knew that once we started rolling back it would be difficult to stop. Nevertheless, although we had to put the brake on and stop a few times, I felt very strongly that we would make it all right especially as we were almost at the top.'

The fear in the dream can clearly be seen. At first the doubt about being able to overcome the difficulties one is facing is in control. As the dream develops, however, the doubt is replaced by feelings of certainty. If they had not been replaced, this would have been a 'worry' dream. Or, if the car had begun to roll backwards, then it would have been a nightmare. If this dream, and the underlying emotions, is thought about, the inner workings of a human being become much clearer, for it can be seen how our confidence can banish worries that would otherwise have caused us to slip into despair and hopelessness.

SEX

Dreams that often occur, but are seldom mentioned, are those involving our sexual feelings. Our society has such strong guilt and filth feelings about sex that it is difficult to talk openly about the subject without being misunderstood. But because they are as much a part of our life as our worries, ambitions and strivings, they have to be mentioned here.

Many, if not most, sexual dreams, are just plain methods of relieving the pressure of our feelings. When one has gone without food for some time, and the biological hunger grows, we dream about eating. Similarly, a pressure of sexual energy and hunger for a sense of completeness in the male-female union, also gives rise to dreams. But whereas dreams of eating do not fulfil one's hunger, dreams of sexual union can, if one's feelings of guilt and filth do not interfere at this level of consciousness, release the sometimes agonising tension and loneliness. Here is a reasonably straightforward dream of this type.

'My aunty, whom I have often thought physically attractive, came to me in the garden. It was dusk, and we were quite alone in the quiet of the warm summer evening. She looked at me searchingly and came close taking my hand. "Do you not like me?" she asked; and as she spoke she passed my hand beneath her blouse on to the softness of her breast. As I felt her nipple between my fingers it was as if a charge of energy flowed into me and my breathing quickened. She spoke again, saying "Maybe you do not love me, but have you felt no passion for me?" I explained that I had, and that my coldness had not been disinterest, but that "I did not wish to rush things." Then we were undressed upon the ground, and beautifully and leisurely I expressed in her waiting body all my withheld desire for her.'

Kinsey found that such dreams occur in most age groups, and in both sexes. The next dream is that of a married woman, struggling with her own sexual feelings in the face of her husband's disinterest.

'Dreamt that I ought to let myself go and practise active imagination to get rid of the weight of depression that I felt. As I did this my hands moved of their own volition to my husband's bed, and I knew that the answer to my problem was to get in with him. I shook him and told him I was cold and asked if I could get in with him. He was irritable and surly and told me to leave him alone, which was just the reaction I had expected as I knew him to be tired and worn himself. I did not, under the circumstances, like to persist and yet I knew it was the only answer. I got back into my own bed still knowing it was the only way to lose my burden.'

Sometimes our sexual dreams may hide problems we do not consciously realise. One man, reading about Freud's views on a boy's desire for his mother, felt that he could not honestly see any such desires in his own life. That night he dreamt 'I was in a very dark and strange street. The police were after me, and the street was a cul-de-sac. Fortunately it was so black they could not see me. I groped to a door at the end of the cul-de-sac, and knocked on it. It was opened by an elderly woman. Without saying a word I grabbed her and had intercourse with her. Her flesh was cold and smooth, and she moaned and cried with fear and pleasure. This awoke her passions, and she took me upstairs, as she had not had sex for twenty years. Her husband knocked at the door but somehow she got rid of him for good.'

What could be clearer? The 'old woman' is frequently used in dreams as a symbol for the mother—or 'old man' or King for the father. As with Oedipus, the father is 'got rid' of so that the mother can be possessed by her son. The reason we have such dreams is because the feelings and desires of early childhood (when such desires are natural) have not fully developed into the different relationships of adulthood. The dreams mentioned earlier under the section of hypnosis, will serve to illustrate those symbolising homosexuality.

Having said that the early desires change as we mature, let us look at an amazing dream that expresses the whole struggle an individual faces in developing towards sexual maturity. The earliest phases of sexual development are represented by the baby loving its mother during breast feeding or cuddling. This gradually develops into a sort of self love (Narcissus) in adolescence which may be expressed as masturbation. It is at this point that the following dream takes up the struggle, but does not quite solve it.

'A couple of nights ago I had a strange experience that summed up my sexual situation perfectly. It was all in a sort of dream, yet not in pictures but in thoughts and realisations. First I was masturbating in my sleep without knowing it. In some peculiar way the act has always been hidden or camouflaged by a host of confusing images and pictures. For instance, I might dream that I was pumping a bicycle pump, but in fact was masturbating. So there was always a sort of excuse or cover up for the real action because I felt guilty about it. But I had recently tried to drop this guilt, and now I gradually began to see through this screen of confusing images to what I was doing. When I awoke to the fact that I was masturbating, a question flashed into my mind: or at least, it was like a terrific type of realisation that posed a question. The realisation was that a man's upright penis was more than just a "sex organ". It was a sort of symbol for his whole manliness, his whole masculinity. Whatever way he chose to express this wonderful power of manhood, that was the direction the whole current of his life would flow, and I saw that masturbation was a type of selfishness. Hidden in it was a wonderful feeling, and this feeling should be shared—nay—given to others. So the question was, "Is this the way you really choose to express your manhood—all on self?"

'I realised that deep down this was not what I wanted. Then an amazing thing happened. It was as if my decision had thrown a switch, and there was a complete change of scene and mood. The pressure of desire for fulfilment was still very strong; but instead of masturbation, images of various women arose before me as an alternative. First of all I realised that they were phantoms, but the idea was presented that I could save the pressure of my desire for the real women behind the images.

'This seemed a likely solution, but I was married, besides which, an intuitive realisation of the results of such relationships came to me. I saw that to find or discover the deepest secrets of my manhood, I had to give my manhood to others. Not necessarily sexually, but through affection, protection, encouragement and so on, but one had to give this manhood in a particular way. The deeps of it could only develop through constancy and courage, the very two things not expressed in relationships with a variety of women. And the courage here is not that of a soldier in battle but of the human soul facing the tedium and emptiness of daily contact with the same person for years on end, and discovering wonder in it. It is the courage of putting aside promises and rumours of *greater* things, so that you can concentrate on discovering the secret beauty of the *little* thing you have.

'All this I saw, and to the question as to whether I wished to spend my manhood on these other women I answered "No". Again a sudden scene shift, and all the images disappeared. This time just the awareness of the awful tension that sought relief devoid of any images. Wondering where to turn for help I prayed. "Dear God, what can I do with this part of myself?" Immediately another scene change this time directing me to my wife. But, dear God, I couldn't find the love, I couldn't find the ability to overlook her human failings, that would allow me to fly to her with tenderness and give my manhood to her.'

If you are puzzled that a man finds it difficult to sleep with his own wife, perhaps you are either lucky, or do not understand the problems of marriage. The reason lies in the dreamer's own statements. Marriage where it provides a deepening experience of each other and oneself, also confronts one with deepening demands and sacrifices. If we cannot meet these demands and sacrifices, then we may attempt to break free of the union or revert to earlier forms of sexuality or affection. The dreamer here finds himself as yet unable to give as much of himself as his particular level of marriage demands. Also inherent in the above dream lies the idea that one discovers deeper possibilities of self as one matures sexually in marriage.

The next dream in this series helps to show how greater self awareness, higher consciousness, or the 'third eye' as some people call it, is also bound up in the development of what the last dreamer called his 'manhood'. As he explained, this means the whole current of life, not only sexual urges. Just as we saw in earlier chapters how the snake can represent male sexuality, in the next dream the creature represents this also, but is probably better described as the underlying energy that can express as sex, and also as love, affection, understanding, ambition, aggression, etc. We can therefore call it Libido, Kundalini, or Spirit.

'I was with a group of people going to a meeting place, or house. We were passing through rolling hills. On our left, a rounded hill had a hole in its centre, surrounded by brushwood. I understood that a great fish or creature lived in the hole, and it was dangerous. On getting to the house we gathered together and we were there to call up the great fish. It appeared slowly and gracefully through a trap door in the floor. It was very beautiful and symmetrical in every line, silver in colour; but as it appeared I saw that it was not so much a fish as a great creature, a mixture between a black panther and seal, with a smooth legless body. It reared its head, and I saw it had an emerald at its brow, just above its eyes. Our reason for calling it up was to get the jewel. Then somebody—the man who had called it up—said that the next thing was the most difficult. The beast then came out of the hole and changed into an enormous eight foot tall woman who was tremendously obese and cruel. She had huge water-filled breasts hanging to her waist. Everybody scattered in fear.'

The centre of this dream is to get the jewel, which represents consciousness of the eternal, and wider vision, but this cannot be done without dealing with the creature from the unconscious, the earth, the physical energy, the rapacious huge mother who could swallow you up in a gobble.

In some dreams, we find the ancient gods appearing, even though consciously we may know little about them, their powers, functions or symbolism. The following dream was dreamt by a young man torn between love for his wife, and the imaginary (not actualised) pleasures he could find with other women. He is also struggling to understand what are merely his ideas and beliefs, and what is reality in life. He says of his dream: 'I was at a party in a very large house set in its own grounds. I found the party frivolous, surface talk only, and unsatisfying to my inner feelings. It was dusk outside, but I stepped out of the french window on to the sloping lawns around the house. A large wood rose at the edge of the lawn and I entered it, eventually coming to a lodge house. The gatekeeper, the man who lived at the lodge house, told me I ought to be careful in the wood, as many strange creatures lived in it. I told him I thought I would be all right, and walked on. There were wolves in the wood, I saw them, and a strange serpent jabberwock type of creature that was forever moving through the trees, but they did not harm me. I walked on and suddenly came to a clearing deep in the wood. It was still quite light and in the clearing stood the most beautiful girl I have ever seen. She was naked, yet some-how this was natural, as she was brown, and like a creature of the woods. We stood and looked at each other, people from two different worlds, and I knew that if I left my ordinary life, and went into the woods with her, I would find a love such as I had never believed possible. But I also knew that I would be lost to the world; that I too would become a creature of the woods. I was in doubt what to do. Then, to my amazement, out of the shadows at the edge of the wood, where he had been standing all the time watching me, the god Pan walked to the girl and looked at me. Around him walked tiny creatures of the forest, rabbits, mice, deer and others. Without words, he offered the girl to me and tried to persuade me to come with them to unearthly delights. Then a voice spoke to me, telling me to save myself, to resist or I would be lost. I felt a tremendous power of attraction from the girl, as if I longed for her beyond all else, as if she were the answer to all my longings and dreams; but the voice kept on at me, telling me to think of a woman I loved in the outer life, any woman, and thus save myself. I did, for I knew I would be lost otherwise, but there were tears in my eyes as I did so; and the scene faded, and I was back in the wood again, a wood without magic, or fairy love, or unearthly delights or the strange presence and power of the gods. It was just a wood, and I turned away.'

The wood here represents all inner ideas and opinions and also the inner self beneath consciousness, the strange unearthly world of the unconscious that can make the drab world magical and full of meaning, turn women into goddesses through projecting strange powers and emotions on to them. Yet it is dire to lose oneself thus, for one may lose one's sense of identity, be possessed by the gods, or powers of nature active in oneself, and lose contact with the outer life, and family and friends. This is why the dreamer had to think of someone in the outer conscious life he loved, to re-establish ties with them, to re-stimulate his awareness at that level.

The next dream is not directly sexual, but is included simply to show how some dreams explain the source of this energy in us, and how it can be blocked by fears or ideas.

'I was in the basement of what I assumed to be work. Les came in, and we said we would start the machine. I somehow knew that this was a contraption that had a windmill on the roof, and a driving belt that came through the floors above straight down into the basement. Here it ran a machine that drove all the equipment in the building. We slipped the belt on to a flange and it began to move, but then jammed with some noise. Les shouted something like, "It's stuck!" and he looked up through the hole in the ceiling where the driving band went. Looking up myself I could see that some rags and paper had torn away from the ceiling of the room above and jammed the belt. Somehow this was causing an electrical shorting in the machinery in the basement, so I threw the switches to off.'

As a quick interpretation of this dream, perhaps we can say that the Spirit, Prana, or Libido, is the main cosmic energy that drives the unconscious or basement processes of our body, which generates energy for the functions throughout our being.

INITIATION

In looking at the sexually orientated dreams, it becomes easy to think of sexual experience as an experience of energy. Or if we think of the energy that lies behind sexual pressures, possibly we can define it as vast potential lying hidden within a human being. We see that 'manhood' can be discovered, or the 'jewel' won from the creature of the depths, while in the basement dream it depicts a release of the energy or force from the blockages. In each case it shows the possibility of finding something MORE in our life or in ourselves. It symbolises growth, discovery of new faculties, emotions, energy or riches, and when a human being discovers a way of realising a further part of this 'potential', and releases it into their life, it is called Initiation. Initiation is the conferring of some new and expanded wisdom, or power, or capacity for love. In such organisations or Orders as the Freemasons or Rosicrucians, initiations are conferred upon the candidate by means of ritual and its impact. But it is acknowledged that initiation in its most vital aspect comes from within the person. In fact we can gain an understanding of this in thinking upon Paul's experience on the road to Damascus, or Jesus' baptism, both of which illustrate initiation. Needless to say, dream experiences are the commonest type of initiation open to each individual. Some examples were mentioned earlier in dealing with dreams in early societies, where individuals sought initiation during fasting and solitude; but even in our own hectic society, the process continues, for initiation is a vital aspect of life and growth. A few examples of dream initiation are given here.

'Dreamt that J.A.'s Guru was coming to see me. I was waiting in some kind of reception hall. Suddenly he came with his followers. He gave the impression of being Eastern. He wore a long white gown and his arms were full of harvest produce, fruit and vegetables. He explained that he ate once a day and ate everything at the one meal. He then put down the food and took both my hands, palms upwards. He examined them for a minute and then pointing to a place on each hand told me I was capable of being very efficient; also something else I can't remember. He then looked at me and told me there was something I should have done but didn't, but again I cannot remember. He then told me to look at his forehead and see what was written there. I looked and saw the lines on his forehead were placed so that they spelt out a word explaining what he was. It was something like MEEK. He then told me to look again and I would see my own self written there. Again I looked, and this time saw the word BITTER. The other people there could not see the writing, and he told me everyone had what they were written on their forehead. He then pointed into the audience and said, "But you will do the thing you came to do. You will do it!" He pointed beyond me, but I felt the words were for me.'

This particular dream is really more of a prelude to initiation, but it does explain many things. First of all, what we have called the 'potential' is often symbolised in dreams as a holy man, guru, yogi, master, saint; or as Jesus, Mohammed, Krishna, or some great person. His arms are full of harvest because this part of our being holds all the fruits of our experience, as well as the future possibilities of self. It is therefore very important what this being tells us in our dreams. In this case, the woman found that after the dream repressed bitterness poured out of her for some months. In the next dream by another person, initiation is taken a step further.

'I was walking along a street in London, and my wife came hurrying up to me. She looked very excited and said, "I have found a Master" (a saint or holy man). I was very sceptical and told her so. Nevertheless she insisted, and asked me to come and see for myself. We walked to a printing firm nearby, where a few people were already waiting for the master. I reviewed my scepticism, thinking that this was probably a man who was very clever and spoke much occult nonsense, and so everybody thought he was godlike; or at least, all those who desperately wanted to find a god-like man. Just then a man walked down some stairs from the building and said quietly to those waiting outside, "He's coming." Outside the building was a loading bay a few feet high. On to this walked a slim man of middle height, in his thirties. He seemed very ordinary and was bald except for the sides of his head, where his hair was a sandy ginger colour. He appeared a very passive man, and began to talk quietly, with little emphasis, his gaze above our heads, as if looking beyond us. As he talked I thought to myself that I had heard all this before. I had read it in the Bible and a number of other books, but it hadn't done me any good. Neither could I see myself even beginning to live up to it. In fact I dismissed the man as a dreamer. He didn't talk for long, however, but soon finished and came down from the bay. We all walked slowly along the street, some of the people asking him questions. When we neared the end of the street he stopped. We also stopped, and were facing him in a small irregular semi-circle, there being about six of us. He didn't speak, but looked at the person on the extreme left for a few moments. Nobody said anything, and he then looked at the next person. I watched him but had no idea what he was doing until his gaze turned to me. Suddenly it was as if a bolt had struck me and pierced me to my inmost being. I knew this man understood every fragment of my life—more than that—he loved me as I have never been loved before. A floodgate opened in me and a torrent of emotion and love swept over me. I stumbled forward impelled by the current of my feelings, and embraced this stranger with a fervent love. As he held me the turbidity smoothed and became a calm love, and I stepped back. His gaze turned to my wife and I saw her expression change under the impact of his eyes. Now I had no doubt—he was a master.'

In the East, one of the ways a master confers his grace, or initiation, on his pupil is by 'look'. Here we see this dramatically experienced in the dream. The dreamer is suddenly 'opened'. His attitude to inner power is changed, and the spiritual power of the Bible is seen as a living reality in the master. Also, his love, once held at bay by reason and scepticism, is released and received.

Sometimes the initiation is not given through the symbol of a holy man, but some other thing as seen here.

'I was walking across open moorland, followed by a crowd of people. I was their leader, and was supposed to be leading them to "Salvation". The only thing was, I had no idea in which direction salvation lay. We came to a barbed-wire fence and stopped. I was considering the best place to cross, when I noticed a rabbit beyond the fence. My dog was with me, and leapt on the rabbit to kill it as in my previous dreams, but this time the rabbit fought back and bit his foot, and he stood back respectfully, as he would if a cat clawed him. I now saw that the rabbit had turned into a huge and powerful hare, with four pink furry babies. Then the hare spoke to me, saying, "Where are you going?"

'I told him we were looking for salvation. He listened, then quietly said "Turn back. Go back to whence you came." At this I became irritable and said, who was he to tell us what to do. There were so many so-called authorities telling people how to discover truth, and yet most of them either disagreed or hadn't found it themselves.

'The hare looked at me and suddenly disappeared. Then, in a few moments it reappeared. This impressed me tremendously. I felt it was a sign of complete self mastery, and knew the hare was the master. He then said again, "Go back, and carry on with your accustomed tasks. Do not seek wildly the Kingdom of Heaven, for you already have what you seek within you. Your seeking only hides it." Then we all turned around and went back to our village, and carried on our usual tasks, knowing that in time, we would realise our heaven.'

This is an initiation of instruction and wisdom, it is a re-direction of the activities or energies of the dreamer. The dreamer interpreted the hare to mean his faculty of intuition which speaks of the inner wisdom. He was amazed to later find that the hare has been used as just such a symbol in many countries and cultures of the world. The next dream is also initiatory, but once more uses a different symbol.

'I was in a large room—very sparsely furnished—rather like a warehouse. The walls were of brick with a light coat of whitewash over, but you could see the brickwork underneath and that it had been meticulously done. I was told that this building had to come down and whilst feeling a little sorry that such good craftsmanship was to be demolished, I quite accepted it. It seems I had prepared some kind of a stew—chicken, I think—and it was in a large (oval) cauldron ready for cooking. There was a square table in the room with a sort of flat plate (made of metal) in the centre. I put the cauldron on this thinking that it would then be ready for cooking when required. . . . Then I must have gone away because when I returned, to my surprise, the stew was boiling furiously and steam was puffing out of the lid. I couldn't think where the heat to cook it was coming from, and then saw that the flat plate was connected by a thick dark cable to a huge battery-like contraption under the table.'

The main initiatory factor in this dream is the realisation of the hidden power. We sometimes speak of being in 'a stew'. But a stew is also broken down pieces, and can therefore relate to various aspects of self. The square table is at once the material 'surface' of our life upon which we work—a working surface—and also an altar upon which we can sacrifice self to the unknown power *underlying* matter, or the square table. For we *can* thus sacrifice self in our material affairs. Then the unseen power behind life can be seen, for it transmutes the elements of our life into an integrated whole. But only when we sacrifice or surrender self in this way does the hidden power have a chance to manifest in our lives.

PROPHETIC DREAMS

In the dream where the guru looks at the dreamer's hands, he tells her that she will do what she has come to do. This is a prophetic statement, but in this dream it is ambiguous since it is not clearly defined exactly what the woman had 'come to do'. Many dreams are much clearer, and so their statements can be tested against the reality of later events. We have to realise, however, that dream prophecy is often nothing more than a knowledgeable deduction. Not that I am belittling knowledgeable deductions, it would be helpful to make them more consciously. But really, a person's actions can be almost pinpointed due to their latent and expressed tendencies. For instance, if a detailed and careful analysis were made of ten men, and they were then taken to a holiday town and set loose, one could prophesy with a fair amount of accuracy what they would do. Their very make-up acts as a sort of filter keeping them away from some places, attracting them to others. In the same way it decides the sort of people with whom they will associate, and so on. Obviously many factors have to be taken into account, and one cannot be dogmatic, but one man is almost certainly likely to go to the pub frequently : another may seek out the quiet places : yet another associate with as many women as are willing to accommodate him. If we think about ourselves, we can easily make such prophetic statements about our own future movements. Many dream prophecies fall into this category, but a large number are quite different and portray events it would be difficult to have deducted from past experience. The dream of the winning race-horse is in this category. Sometimes this can be explained by telepathic contact with others—sometimes only by conjecturing a higher consciousness that synthesises the experience of all things everywhere, and prognosticates from this. People have said that God is the great mathematician or geometrician; but we might also coin a phrase and say that God is the great Prognosticator.

The next dream given here is one of my wife's. It falls possibly within the classification of self-knowledge prophecy.

'I dreamt that I was in prison and I wanted to escape. There were no locks on the doors and the evenings when the officers went off duty presented the best opportunity. The first time I tried I was caught almost immediately, before getting clear of the grounds. The second time I got right away and went home to the flat where Tony was living. We sat talking and I was planning how we could leave the country and start a new life together. I knew that if I did not finish my sentence I could never return here. As I sat talking, a hand fell on my shoulder. I knew it was a policeman come to take me back to prison. I also knew in that moment that there was no escape, as I would probably have to serve a little longer now. My sentence was for three years, and I had about eighteen months left to do, and Tony and I would have to wait until that time was completed before starting a new life. But I knew that he would not start without me, that I was somehow necessary to him in the new life.'

This dream occurred at a time when my wife felt imprisoned and shut in by the circumstances of our life. It has a great deal of philosophy in it such as open prison doors, but the central fact is that although at the time we had no conscious plans, eighteen months later we suddenly moved house, changed occupations, and literally started a new life. The decision to move took place sixteen months after the dream; the house purchase began at eighteen months, and the move occurred at twenty-two months. So the 'about eighteen months' was very clear. One could easily explain this dream as a coincidence, but with some people such dreams occur far too often to be explained away so simply. As I have mentioned the sale of our house, I can illustrate this with dreams that occurred at that time to my wife.

Dream One: 'Dreamt the surveyor would come that evening.'

Dream Two: 'Dreamt the young couple had got their mortgage, and would call that night.'

Dream Three: 'Dreamt that we had won £100.'

With the first dream, the surveyor had sent a card saying he would call sometime that week, and would let us know beforehand. As it happened, no prior notice arrived, but after the dream my wife had all the house looking shipshape. The surveyor *did* turn up, and looked very surprised when my wife said she had been expecting him. The young couple who wished to buy our house were dubious about getting a mortgage, and had no idea when they would know. Because of the dream we sat up late waiting for them. However there was no sign of them and we decided to go to bed. At that moment they rang our bell, and once inside announced that their mortgage was through.

The third dream is not as well defined as the first two. We waited and waited for our premium bonds to present a win of a £100 and nothing happened. But shortly afterwards I was offered a contract to write a book, the down payment of which was a round £100.

There are a great many people who have this faculty for dreaming prophetically. Velta Wilson, who through her own hard work has made herself an expert on dreams, and is, as far as I know, the only person in the UK teaching dream analysis in a Further Education evening class, has sent me some of her own experiences. She says, 'I am walking along and as I look up I see the splendid sight of three golden rainbows stretching across the sky. I am thrilled, amazed and delighted. Various people to whom I told the dream, gave interpretations of good luck. Some time later while turning over the pages of an illustrated book on astronomy—lo and behold—my three golden rainbows! It is a speculative drawing of the view one would have if one were standing on the planet Saturn.'

This is reminiscent of some of the experiences mentioned by Dunne in his book *An Experiment With Time*, where he was investigating prophetic dreams. But Velta goes on to describe two further dreams of an even more interesting nature. 'A friend and I were sharing an hotel room. I had a long and involved dream which ended with my intention of buying books by Edgar Wallace in order to solve a problem. I woke up and lay in bed thinking about the dream. Suddenly my friend spoke; "Don't buy the books by Edgar Wallace. I will take you to the library where you can get them." Amazed, I asked her whether she had had the same dream. She did not answer, she was asleep. In the morning she had no idea what she had dreamt.'

'I dreamt that the fiancé of a girl I hardly knew was trapped in a submarine at the bottom of the sea. All hope was lost but finally the submarine managed to surface. When I met the girl I told her the dream. She went very pale. "That is exactly what happened to him—we never speak about it—who told you?" '

These are prophetic in the sense that the dream informs us of something we have no means of knowing through outer information. Thus they prophesy what can be later known via the senses. A further example of prophetic dreaming was sent to me by Bernadette Fallon. She says, 'A strange thing happened recently. Before Christmas I had a dream in which a man (no one I knew) showed me his room, which was a very distinctive shape, and decorated in dingy brown wallpaper. At the beginning of this term (after Christmas), a close friend of mine moved into a new flat. On going into his room I was amazed to find it was the room I'd seen in my dream—only the walls were white. I described the paper in the dream-room to him and he said that's exactly how it was before it was decorated.'

PROPHECY OR WHAT?

Some dreams, or sleep experiences are difficult to categorise. Sometimes they are not directly symbolic, or dealing with memories of one's past, nor do they seem to be about a logically possible future in one's own lifetime. The following is a dream experience during unconsciousness produced by fainting. The faint lasted ten or fifteen seconds, yet the dream is but one of the many experienced during those few seconds.

'I was in a room filled with people, but not crowded. It was a circular room with windows all the way round, and there were about thirty or forty people in the room sitting casually at tables. People came and went, and there was the impression that everyone knew each other. Neither did anybody appear old. Mature, yes, but there was no age as we see it. There was something different about the colours too. The room itself glowed bright with colour, not artificially applied, but as if its very materials were colourful and brilliantly lit. The people's clothes were also of attractive hues, none of them appeared formally dressed. Neither did any of their garments seem to be quite the same style as any other person's in the room. It was obviously a place where one could eat and drink, but many came just to meet others. Yet in no way could it compare with a meeting place such as we usually know; for the informality went far deeper than the clothes. Possibly, in our terms one could call it naturalness. These people were natural in a way that was true. There was no effort to be a particular type. Nor, as has happened so often in society where groups of people decide not to conform to type, had the effort itself produced another type. These people were themselves, in a way beyond any effort. Each face was frank and open, yet completely individual. Their meetings and partings happened spontaneously, and as relaxed as themselves.

'I realised also that there was no marriage here, although children were conceived and born as usual. But it is not easy to adequately describe their equivalent of marriage. For here there was no insecurity, no sense of possession, no personal self-seeking for satisfaction or grasping for methods to prove oneself. These people were free. Their marriage reflected their freedom and their ability to love freely, which is *not* the same as so-called free love. Here a couple came together because of deep links of common purpose, understanding, and sympathetic relationship. They might or might not live together, it did not matter to them. For how could it matter when there was no attempt to own each other? In our society we cover up our real feelings by social codes and fears of inferiority; or else destroy ourselves through doubt, worry and insecurity. Neither was physical sex the aim of the relationship. It was an event that occurred if and when all their feelings were right and matched. Their sensitivity to the demands of circumstance, relationship of mind, emotions and body ruled out promiscuity. Although again, there were no rules of marriage, written or unwritten, spoken or unspoken, to keep two people together or sexually faithful. For these people were indeed *not* faithful to one another as our vows would have us be, nor yet were they adulterous as we are. For they were not moved by the same fears or passions, graspings or self centredness.

'In our world there are opposing schools of thought suggesting that either children should be reared by one single mother, or else collectively by the state. These people would smile upon all such rules, for they had no rules at all. To take their place, they had a deep awareness of relationship, of the demands of each given situation, an awareness of how each action would influence the society as a whole, and thus, how it would influence their own lives. Therefore a child could stay with its mother or it could live with others. The father might part from the mother, but never in anger or not to see her again.

'It must be added that there was, of course, no fear of being unprovided for, because money did not exist. Neither was there a government, a police force or armies. People worked, or did not work, as they pleased, and each in this way did what best expressed their energy and interest at any time. On Earth this would be called chaos, but for these people it worked because of their inherent understanding and lack of personal avarice. Nor was there any forced education. A child inherited culture through widening experience of life. There were those who enjoyed teaching, and all their energy was devoted to its study and practice. So there was plenty of opportunity to learn, not only in youth, but at any time in life. It was not a rigid system, however. Their culture was a blend of the technical, the artistic and philosophical or religious. It was a blend that had not been imposed by outer rules, or commercial powers, but developed naturally as a flowering of their own inner traits.'

THE SEARCH FOR GOD

In using the term 'Search for God', I do so without referring directly to organised religion. It is used to cover a wide variety of experiences. The search for self understanding, for new insight into life; the attempt to discover deeper relationships with others, or in what mysterious ways we are connected with others, can all be put under this heading. If we take the word 'God' to mean the hidden and revealed of our own life, the general and particular in the universe, the personal and the transcendental, then dreams are definite contacts with God. But generally, dreams relate us to God *personally*. That is, while they do not usually detract from any value or meaning we find in belonging to a religious body or church, they show that our direct connection with God is through ourselves.

We might also call this section of dreams the Upper Reaches of the Soul. This is because a distinctive feature is often noticeable in these dreams. It is that they are much less symbolical, far more a direct experience. They either express a reasonably clear understanding of something, or else are as logically presented as any waking thought or experience might be. This is not always true, but is certainly a feature much in evidence. This can be seen in another of Bernadette Fallon's dreams. Here, obviously, the ideas are no longer presented in symbols, but directly in words. She says, 'On the subject of interpretation of dreams I dreamt the following sentence some time ago: "The purpose of symbols in dreams is to fix permanently the subsequent significance of subconscious elements, which are not always clearly understood, in the conscious mind." '

Bernadette goes on to say, 'I don't really understand it, so I don't know whether it is just a truism or contains anything of any significance.' But possibly we can rephrase it and get at its significance as follows: 'Symbols in dreams act as a record and focus of ideas, gropings, half-felt meanings, that we have not yet consciously understood or defined. In this way the elements that are collected but not quite unified into a new conscious realisation, are nevertheless fixed or held in the symbol; which is still vague or undefined, but can later be worked on further.'

Bernadette's difficulty in understanding is experienced by all of us who meet an experience in these Upper Reaches of the Soul. This is because they are often super-logical. They contain information not yet found in our memory or reasoning. In other words, if we take numbers to represent ideas or facts, we cannot add three and two making five, while we still only have three. We have to discover two before we can add it to make five. In the same way, we cannot reach certain conclusions logically or with reason, if bits of information are missing. But the dream does not always work logically, and so can present higher ideas without their supporting reason. It is often only much later, having rushed around and discovered supporting evidence, that we can understand the statement logically.

Anna Kingsford is certainly one of the most amazing dreamers of the last hundred years. She is also one of the few who explored the possibilities of 'dreaming' information. Her experiences in URS (Upper Reaches of Soul) are superbly clear and astonishing in detail and revelation. Her *Dreams and Dream Stories* has already been mentioned, but her greatest works are undoubtedly *Clothed With The Sun* and *The Perfect Way*. From *Clothed With The Sun* I quote a dream experience to show how clear it can be. In her sleep it is as if someone is telling her the meaning of the prophecy of the vision of Nebuchadnezzar. Here is what is said:

'The King Nebuchadnezzar is mystically identical with King Ahasuerus, in that each alike denotes the spirit of the latter age, that, namely, of mere intellectualism, as distinguished and opposed to Intuition. And both narratives, as well as that of the Deluge and of the *Book of Esther*, are prophecies which are now beginning to have their accomplishment on a scale greater than ever before. For the image shown to the king in his dream represents the various systems of thought and belief which find favour with the world. Of these, the intellectual philosophy which rests upon the basis of a science merely physical is the head, and is symbolised by the gold. And this rightly, so far as concerns the intellect, for it is indeed king of kings, and all the children of men, the beasts of the field, and the birds of the air, are given into its hands. That is to say, all the activities of society, its learning, industry and art, are made subordinate to the intellect. The breasts and arms of the image are silver. This is the domain of morality and sentiment, which under the reign of the mere intellect hold a subordinate place. Belonging to the region of the heart, it is feminine; implying the intuition, which is of the woman (i.e. the feminine receptive principle in male or female), and her assigned inferiority, it is silver. The thighs and the belly are of brass, and this kingdom is said to rule over the whole world. By this is meant a universality under a régime wholly animal and non-moral, where falsehood, cruelty, impurity, blasphemy, and all those deprivations of true humanity, characterise an age of materialism. The iron, of which the legs are made, represents force, and denotes the negation of love, the consequent prevalence of might over right, and the universal rule of selfishness. By the mingling of iron and clay in the feet is implied the weakness and instability of the whole structure, the clay representing matter, which is made the foundation of the system instead of spirit, which alone is stable and enduring.

'The Stone cut out with hands, which destroys this image, and becomes a great mountain filling the whole earth, is that "Stone of the Philosophers", a perfected spirit, and the true gospel of the inner knowledge which appertains thereto. This it is which smites the age upon its feet, or fundamental basis, its materialistic hypothesis. And with the demonstration of the falseness of its doctrine, now being made to the world, shall fall the whole fabric of society with its empire of force, its exaltation of the masculine mode of mind, its subjection of women, its torture of animals, and its oppression of the poor. With its clay, its iron, its brass, its silver, and its gold, all swept away as chaff before the wind, the true knowledge and spirit of understanding, which are of the intuition, shall usher in the kingdom of God, and the "stone" become a mountain, shall fill the whole earth.'

This tremendous outpouring, which as an interpretation of Nebuchadnezzar's dream is clarity itself, is an expression of the intuitive function in dreams. Here we see it as intuition instructing the intellect, information being given to the intellect that has not understood these things. I have also said that the URS dream can be more directly one of experience. Below I give the experience of a friend who *died* for a short time, but then revived. I have to quote this from memory, so I hope she will forgive any slight errors. 'I was critically ill and in terrible pain. My husband had been called and was sitting near me. Gradually the pain began to lessen, and slowly disappeared altogether. I was then floating above my body and looked down on the whole scene. As I did so I began to hear beautiful music in the distance. I felt that something beautiful and wonderful was waiting to be explored, and felt an urge to go to find it. But I could see my husband and somehow knew all his thoughts and feelings. He was in terrible despair because he could see I had died, and felt he could not go on alone, and care for our child. Despite the promise of beauty away in the distance, I knew I had to go back and stay with him. As soon as I had made this decision, I began to sink into the body again. The pain and heaviness returned, and for ages I could not even move. Later the nurses told me they thought I had gone for good, and were amazed that I had recovered.'

We might be tempted to take this as a symbolical dream instead of a direct experience, if it were not for several important factors. One is that her experience coincided with physical events in her body. Secondly, her husband later admitted that her description of his thoughts and emotions truly described his own. Thirdly, her description exactly tallies with that of other people who through electrocution, heart failure, illness, drowning, have died and been revived. All who can remember, describe the separation from the body, the beautiful call, sometimes waiting friends, and then the return.

I turn now to an experience of my own which further illustrates the possibilities of dreaming. It occurred while I was doing my national service in the RAF in Germany. After duty I had remained in the billet reading. Then, feeling rather homesick I decided to have an early night, and lay in bed thinking of home. I wondered whether one's consciousness could reach out across space, and visualised home as clearly as I could. But realising that it was only my imagination I gave up and went to sleep. The next thing I knew was that I felt as if I were being carried upwards in a fast lift. Everything was black and rushing and I felt confused, but like a cork coming out of a bottle. Then suddenly I could see. It was still light, and I was looking down from above the bed, and could clearly see my body asleep below me. I became very frightened, but this passed as I realised my consciousness had projected from my body. The next thing I knew I was flying through the air, knees curled up to my chest, arms clenched round them. I looked down and saw fields and villages below. I noticed something very strange, rising from the ground. It was like ripples or bands rising from particular points on the earth; like rainbows, only with many, many bands going right down to the ground. I couldn't really understand it, but wondered whether it was people praying. I was then over the sea, travelling very fast. I could see ships below. Next I was in our sitting room at home in London, standing behind the settee. I noticed that I was dressed in my civilian clothes instead of uniform or pyjamas. I also saw that my mother was sitting looking at the television knitting. She was alone except for our Alsatian dog Vince, who was asleep in front of the gas fire. I called out to my mother feeling sure she could see me. She paused in her knitting for a moment, as if she were listening, but then carried on. I called again, this time shouting in an effort to make myself heard. She carried on with her knitting, but a strange thing happened. It was as if some deep part of her responded to me and knew I was there, yet her conscious self still carried on unaware; and I suddenly knew why we could not see the dead. But then Vince raised his head as if he had heard me shout. He saw me and came bounding to me behind the settee, which was in the middle of the room. He hadn't seen me for months and barked and yelped with delight and love. The next thing I knew, it was as though I were being put into a a lead suit—I was re-entering the body. Out of it I had felt more conscious, more energetic, lighter, with deep receptiveness. Now I felt the weight of the body, and the dimness of waking consciousness, like a moon compared with the sun. Writing to ask my mother if anything strange had happened that night, she replied that she had experienced a tingling feeling up the spine, and thought of me. Then Vince had leapt up from his sleep in front of the fire, and run behind the settee barking. She had also been alone, knitting watching the television, as my father had gone out.

This experience is typical of those had by many people and is often called astral projection, bilocation, or astral travel. The main feature is that the consciousness is able to apprehend events happening even thousands of miles away. Sometimes the physical environment is not seen, however, and one is opened to tremendous intuitional information about questions asked (as seen in Anna Kingsford's description). Some people claim to meet and converse with the dead, which seems entirely logical if the consciousness can leave the sleeping body. Another feature is that, as seen in my experience, the body one uses is completely plastic. In bed I had pyjamas, while in projection I wore civvy clothes. It seems that whichever way one unconsciously thinks of oneself, this is the form one will take, as the body is formed of one's own desires and thoughts. (The physical body is likewise changed by one's desires, thoughts and attitudes, but not as **quickly**.)

DREAMS OF THE DEAD

Unless our consciousness actually projects, and enters this ultra clear stage in sleep, our contact with others, or the dead, will still be through the symbol-forming function of a 'less conscious' area of our mind. This does not invalidate the reality of the contact. Because a prophetic dream is seen in symbols, this does not mean it is untrue, it simply means it is less direct. Some people who do not understand dreams and have not taken the trouble to examine the workings of the mind are often heard to say, 'Oh, that's *only* a dream.' From the information already presented, I hope it can be seen that contact with another mind *is very likely to be shown in symbols*. But we must not therefore put it aside as valueless. I must state that I am not, in this book, attempting to *prove* anything. For those who are not convinced, then such great works as those of F. W. H. Myers, will be more helpful.

I am more interested in writing for those who wish to know how their dreams may put them in contact with their dead family and friends. To start with, it often happens that we dream of the person in connection with death, before the transition occurs. Or sometimes, just as it occurs. To make this plainer, here is a dream experienced by my father. His own father was Italian by birth, and at the end of the war (1945) he wished to revisit Italy. He had booked his holiday and was going on a Sunday morning. On the Friday night prior to his departure, my father woke from a dream crying. My mother, disturbed by his tears, asked him what was the matter. He replied that he had dreamt his father had died. He also saw two passport photographs of his brothers, with the impression of a plane journey, while in the background was his father, smiling at him. When the family went to see him off, my father felt he would never see him alive again. A postcard came to say he had arrived safely. On the Tuesday week, a telegram arrived saying he had died in his sleep. Then the two brothers flew out to Italy to have his body brought back.

Another example of this prior dreaming is given by Shane Miller, in his excellent article, 'Working with Dreams as Recommended by the Cayce Readings'. What he says also illustrates the 'follow-up' dream.

'Three days before my father's death, in 1953, I dreamed that a woman appeared to me on the staircase of his home in Philadelphia. She said, "I have come to offer condolences on 'the' death," and continued on her way upstairs. End of dream. My father had been ill for some time; the end had seemed imminent time and again, but when I went away for the weekend of that week I took enough clothes with me to see me through a possible trip to Philadelphia, in case the warning was realised. No time of fulfilment was given, but the Cayce readings state that in many cases the deceased will appear *in a dream* to the loved ones to reassure them, *after* three days.

'In a general way I reckoned the time of Dad's death to fall on Saturday; in this case, three days after the warning. The news came at 5.30 on Saturday and the following day we left for Philadelphia directly from there, exactly on schedule.

'I found that my father had died in a coma, that he had passed on without knowing what was happening. The third night after his passing came and went without a dream of any sort. On the fifth night I had a dream which showed him sitting at a table, with his back towards me, as he fitted the *pieces of a jigsaw puzzle* together. The anagram suggested two things immediately; first that he was unaware of my presence, and second, that he was trying to figure out what had happened to him.'

It can be seen that the 'follow-up' dream not only assures the dreamer of the 'dead' person's continued existence, but tells them of their condition. Three further follow-up dreams can be quoted to show their characteristics.

Michael Gornall, my brother-in-law, had this dream shortly after his best friend, Bill Downs had died. (I quote from memory), 'I saw Bill standing by a train. It was one of the long-distance type of trains. He had a bag with him, was dressed in new clothes, and was smoking a pipe, which he never did in real life. He was going on a long journey. The dream left a very deep impression on me.'

Another dream of Velta Wilson's emphasises the characteristics of these 'death' dreams. 'The Ts have moved to another flat, high up, a big flat with many corridors and rooms. Prof. T . . . is sitting peacefully in a chair, but his wife wanders about the corridors desperately. I say to her: "What are you worrying about; now all is well." It turned out that Prof. T . . . had died that night.'

Another dream, told me by a friend, although short and simple, yet has a sense of beauty about it. 'A little while after my father's death, I dreamt he came to me. Taking his old tobacco tin, he opened it, and showed me, inside, a beautiful jewel.'

As a last example of this type of dream, I will quote from

F. W. H. Myers' book, *Human Personality and Its Survival of Bodily Death*. The dream and experience happened to Karl Dignowity. It shows how the dream may develop into a waking experience.

'About a year ago there died in a neighbouring village a brewer called Wunscher, with whom I stood in friendly relations. His death ensued after a short illness, and as I seldom had an opportunity of visiting him, I knew nothing of his illness nor of his death. On the day of his death I went to bed at nine o'clock, tired with the labours which my calling as a farmer demand of me. Here I must observe that my diet is of a frugal kind; beer and wine are rare things in my house, and water, as usual, had been my drink that night. Being of a very healthy constitution, I fell asleep as soon as I lay down. In my dream I heard the deceased call out with a loud voice, "Boy, make haste and give me my boots." This awoke me, and, I noticed that, for the sake of our child, my wife had left the light burning. I pondered with pleasure over my dream, thinking in my mind, how Wunscher, who was a good natured, humorous man, would laugh when I told him of this dream. Still thinking on it I hear Wunscher's voice scolding outside, just under my window. I sat up in my bed at once and listened, but could not understand his words. What could the brewer want? I thought, and I know for certain that I was much vexed with him, that he should make a disturbance in the night, as I felt convinced his affairs might surely have waited till the morrow. Suddenly he came into the room from behind the linen press, stepped with long strides past the bed of my wife and the child's bed; wildly gesticulating with his arms all the time as his habit was, he called out, "What do you say to this, Herr Oberammann? This afternoon at five o'clock I have died." Startled by this information, I exclaimed, "Oh, that is not true!" He replied: "Truly, as I tell you; and, what do you think? They want to bury me already on Tuesday afternoon at two o'clock," accenting his assertions all the while by his gesticulations. During this long speech by my visitor I examined myself as to whether I was really awake and not dreaming.

'I asked myself: Is this a hallucination? Is my mind in full possession of its faculties? Yes, there is the light, there the jug, this is the mirror, and this the brewer; and I came to the conclusion: I am awake. Then the thought occurred to me. What will my wife think if she awakes and finds the brewer in our bedroom? In this fear of her waking up I turned round to my wife, and to my great relief I saw from her face, which was turned towards me, that she was still asleep; but she looked very pale. I said to the brewer, "Herr Wunscher, we will speak softly, so that my wife may not wake up, it would be very disagreeable to her to find you here." To which Wunscher answered in a lower and calmer tone: "Don't be afraid, I will do no harm to your wife." Things do happen indeed for which we find no explanation—I thought to myself, and said to Wunscher: "If this be true, that you have died, I am sincerely sorry for it; I will look after your children." Wunscher stepped towards me, stretched out his arms and moved his lips as though he would embrace me; therefore I said in a threatening tone, and looking steadfastly at him with a frowning brow: "Don't come so near, it is disagreeable to me," and lifted my right arm to ward him off, but before my arm had reached him the apparition had vanished.'

Needless to say Wunscher had died that afternoon at five o'clock, and was buried on the following Tuesday at two. The time of the burial was settled by relatives in the death room immediately after death. This was because relations at a distance had to be told by telegram.

I hope it is obvious from the foregoing, that not all and every dream of the dead betokens a definite link with them. We often use images of the dead as symbols in dreams dealing with some personal issue. Therefore the message of the dream, as always, must rest upon the meaning unfolded from its symbolism and content. The above dreams will help to determine whether they are contact with the dead, or just symbolical.

TOWARDS THE SPIRIT

I find it difficult to draw the line between dreams occurring in the upper reaches of the Soul, and those referring to the spirit, thus the above heading. I open this section with an unusual dream told me by my eldest son, Mark, when he was about three. Mark's bedroom at that time looked out over the village, and the church spire dominated the scene. Every Thursday evening was bell-ringing practice, and Mark had often asked why the bells were rung. One of my answers, which may explain the dream, was that they called the people to church. He then asked me why people went to church, and I said it was to speak to God. A couple of weeks later we were walking through the churchyard together, and at this time he had never been in this church. He said, 'I went in there the other night.' I realised he meant the church, but couldn't think when. I asked him if his mother had taken him. He was quite firm that he had been in, and he had been alone. Realising I was missing information through doubting questions, I asked him why he had gone. He said, 'I went to look for God—but He wasn't in there.' I concluded this was a dream.

We have wandered away from the direct reference made earlier under 'The Search for God', but it is only a circuitous wandering, to encompass the various aspects of our soul experience. And we must wander some more before we deal with the fulfilment of what my son went in search of. This occurs only when the marriage between soul and spirit occurs, the wedding of the conscious and unconscious, the Prince and the Sleeping Beauty. Once more during sleep, Anna Kingsford *dreams* clear information about this.

'Now, there are two kinds of memory, the memory of the organism and the memory of the soul. The first is possessed by all creatures. The second, which is obtained by Recovery belongs to the fully regenerate man. For the Divine Spirit of a man is not one with his soul until regeneration, which is the intimate union constituting what, mystically, is called the "marriage of the hierophant".

'This union of the two wills constitutes the spiritual marriage, the accomplishment of which is in the Gospels represented under the parable of the marriage at Cana of Galilee. This divine marriage, or union of the human and Divine wills is indissoluble, whence the idea of the indissolubility of human marriage. And inasmuch as it is a marriage of the spirit of man to that of God, and of the Spirit of God to that of man, it is a double marriage.'

Talking about birth, she says, 'The process of incarnation, and the method by which the soul takes new forms, are in this wise. When two persons ally themselves in the flesh and beget a child, the moment of impregnation is usually—though not invariably—the moment which attaches a soul to the newly conceived body. Hence, much depends upon the influences, astral and magnetic, under which conception takes place. The pregnant woman is the centre of a whirl of magnetic forces, and she attracts within her sphere a soul whose previous conduct and odic (libido) condition correspond either to her own or to the magnetic influences under which she conceives. This soul, if the pregnancy continues and progresses, remains attached to her sphere, but does not enter the embryo until the time of the quickening, when it usually takes possession of the body, and continues to inhabit it until the time of delivery. A pregnant woman is swayed not by her own will alone, but as often by the will of the soul newly attached to her sphere; and the opposition and cross-magnetisms of these two wills often occasion many strange and seemingly unaccountable whims, alterations of character, and longings, on the part of the woman. Sometimes, however, the moment of impregnation or conception passes without attracting any soul, and the woman may even carry a false conception for some time, in which cases abortion (miscarriage) occurs. . . . Some clairvoyant women have been conscious of the soul attached to them, and have seen it, at times as a beautiful infant, at times in other shapes. Children begotten by ardent and mutual love are usually the best and healthiest, spiritually and physically, because the radical moment is seized by love, when the astral and magnetic forces are strongest and most ardent, and they attract the strongest and noblest souls.'

It may be gathered from this that Anna Kingsford (who was a medical doctor, but who eventually gave her life to a study and promulgation of intuitive researches) found in her dreams mention of reincarnation. In fact, several of her dream experiences dealt with her own past lives. She tells us, but does not offer proof, that the information given in dreams on this subject, was substantiated by outer evidence.

Whether this is so or not—whether reincarnation is a fact or not, does not concern us here. All we are concerned with is covering all the aspects of dreams, and some dreams definitely suggest the possibility of reincarnation. Therefore these dreams will be dealt with. These, like the dreams of the dead, are symbolical of death and rebirth. Others seem to be clear-cut memories. The symbolical can be seen in this dream.

'There was a little copper-coloured boy who found a piece of polished wood shaped like a hand. He found it floating on the water, and used it as a token to buy a riotous and selfish living. After many adventures had befallen him, he realised his error and was so ashamed that he did not want to face the world. So he decided to float upon the waters like the stick. So he lay upon the waters and gradually the waters entered his nose and throat and his head began to roar; and the waters invaded his brain, and the waters were rushing all inside him and his head roared. Then quite suddenly the water took him and flung him violently on to dry land, so that he could not even die in the waters. And the waters scolded and rejected him and left him on dry land to live and to compensate. And the boy lay and looked at the hand, and he knew the meaning of the hand.'

This is a very lovely dream, suggesting in its symbolism that a man cannot find peace even in death, if he has misused the power of his hands, his activity. For death will reject him, and he will have to live again to compensate for his actions.

Here is a less symbolic dream. 'I was a writer in one of the Germanic countries, in the time of swords and women's long gowns. But although I was well known for my writings, I was only an educated peasant, and my notoriety was disliked by the "nobility". It was the "done thing" for me to be "seen" at the balls. In the dream I had arrived at such a ball, at a large house. All evening I danced with the ladies, and was glowered at by the young men. They were looking for a chance to pick a quarrel with me. Eventually one of them was so insulting I had either to rise to the challenge of a duel, or back out as a coward. But I knew the danger of acceptance. The other young men had only one idea in mind, to kick and beat me as soundly as they could. Knowing their intentions I had come prepared. As the duel progressed and the others closed in on me to trip and then beat me I shouted the call of the Zimmermen. At this, the youths from my forest village burst into the hall, and there was a terrific fight. I don't think any particular side won, but we eventually got out amidst the confusion, and walked through the forest to our homes. As we walked we sang the song of the Zimmermen, a rousing marching tune, and there was a wonderful feeling of brotherhood between us. When I woke I remembered the tune clearly, but did not know the meaning of the word Zimmermen. I looked it up, and found it meant carpenter or woodman. I felt I had remembered a past life.'

Two excellent examples of dreaming about reincarnation are

given by Dr Leslie Weatherhead in his booklet *The Case for Reincarnation*. He writes:

'I met a married couple in Australia who told me their amazing experience. The lady had many psychic experiences by which she felt certain that none of her girlhood acquaintances would have any special significance for her, but if she waited, her true mate would turn up. When she was in her middle thirties, she met her present husband at a public function, and both had an overwhelming and simultaneous conviction that, in an earlier life, they had been man and wife. They have now been happily married for twenty-five years and both are convinced that this is their second incarnation. A year or two before meeting her husband, the lady had a vivid waking dream of being in bed after the birth of a child which she never saw. In the dream, her husband had to leave her in this distress to go on a forlorn hope on behalf of the King. The poignancy of parting was terrible, and in the waking dream— experienced, let me repeat, a year or so before she met her husband —the lady wept bitterly. When she met her husband, she knew that he was the father of this child and the hero of this dream.

'Side by side with such an experience we can put one like this: Captain and Mrs Battista, Italians, had a little daughter born in Rome, whom they called Blanche. To help look after this child they employed a French-speaking Swiss "Nannie" called Marie. Marie, the nurse, taught her little charge to sing in French a lullaby song. Blanche grew very fond of this song and it was sung to her repeatedly. Unfortunately Blanche died and Marie returned to Switzerland. Captain Battista writes: "The cradle song which would have recalled to us only too painful memories of our deceased child, ceased absolutely to be heard in the house ... all recollection of it completely escaped our minds."

'Three years after the death of Blanche the mother, Signora Battista, became pregnant, and in the fourth month of pregnancy she had a strange waking dream. She insists that she was wide awake when Blanche appeared to her and said, in her old, familiar voice, "Mother, I am coming back." The vision then melted away. Captain Battista was sceptical, but when the new baby was born in February, 1906, he acquiesced in her also being given the name Blanche. The new Blanche resembled the old in every possible way.

'Nine years after the death of the first Blanche, when the second was six years of age, an extraordinary thing happened. I will use Captain Battista's own words: "While I was with my wife in my study which adjoins our bedroom, we heard, both of us, like a distant echo, the famous cradle song, and the voice came from the bedroom where we had put our little daughter Blanche fast asleep. ... We found the child sitting up on the bed and singing with an excellent French accent the cradle song which neither of us had certainly ever taught her. My wife asked her what it was she was singing, and the child, with the utmost promptitude answered that she was singing a French song.

"Who, pray, taught you this pretty song?" I asked her.

"Nobody, I know it out of my own head," answered the child.'

ON THE PATH

In their search for self understanding a question that many thoughtful people ask themselves is, 'Where am I going?' or 'Where will my life lead me?' The following dream is of a married woman. In a fascinating way it looks at the various values and opinions people live by, trying to see where they lead. She says, 'I am walking with another girl (who seems to be a shadowy replica of myself) outside the studio. Some young men who also work at the studio are following behind us, calling out to us and joking. I say to the girl, "If they ask us to have a drink with them when we pass this public house we will accept, but if they don't, we'll just keep walking." The young men, however, do not ask us to join them. The girl turns back, but I keep on walking. I go down a subway station at Chancery Lane (near where I work) with the intention of going to Oxford Street. (Oxford Street symbolises Life to me.) I board a tube train. It is quite crowded with young girls, who look rather like myself. Suddenly, a charming, softly spoken woman of about mid-thirty (my age in fact) appears and tells us that we are all required to take part in a film. In fact, we have no choice, as our carriage is being driven off to a huge building. We are all ushered into a large room. There is a rather unpleasant man who seems to be the director. In the middle of the room is an enormous iron wheel, and on the end of each spoke is an iron chair, into which, one by one the "victims" from the train are being clamped by iron

175

bands around the arms and throat. I get a distinct feeling of fear and distrust in spite of the charming woman's efforts to reassure me. She says, "You will be released when the film is shot." I do not believe her, and look around for some means of escape. Meanwhile, my turn to be clamped into the chair is coming very close. The other girls seem to give no feeling of fear, they are submitting to the ordeal like sheep going to the slaughter. I am still aware that in the background the sadistic man is gloating about the whole thing. I make a frantic dash to the doorway. Outside there are tunnels leading in every direction. I run down one only to find the end is blocked by an iron gate, through which, grinning at me maliciously, is a ticket collector. I turn and run down another tunnel and suddenly find myself running along the top of the train in which I had arrived. It is stationary. I peer down when I see a group of young people walking along a street which is parallel to the train. They are dressed in "trendy" clothes, but their eyes are devoid of any expression and their gestures are mechanical. They are walking straight into a *cul-de-sac*. I decide not to join them; and turn to look the other way. A group of young children and some adults are playing in the street, yet everything is silent and dim. A man is leering at them. The buildings all around are high, dark and poor looking. I manage to bypass them all and find myself looking at a beach scene. Groups of people are sunbathing and playing on the beach. Yet again I am struck by the lifeless and mechanical actions and their expressionless eyes, as if they are living yet dead. I suddenly get a glimpse of the sea beyond them. It is beautiful, *alive*, moving, a translucent emerald green. The sun is sparkling on it. It is the only alive thing I have seen on my travels. I *long* to get to it. I *will* get to it, and drown myself in its purity and beauty. I start to make my way towards it when sand dunes build up before me, making the journey difficult. The sand slips under my feet, but I struggle on. Suddenly, out of the crowd, a matronly woman comes after me, trying to drag me back, saying, "You shall not escape." I feel anything is better than living like the "puppet-like" people on the beach, and I make a frantic effort to escape her clutches and break away and enter the sea, quite happy to know I will die there.'

This amazing dream has so much information in it, one can no more than hint at its meaning. The dreamer is in fact reviewing the many avenues the world offers in the search for fulfilment, satisfaction and truth. The shadowy figure is her own desires she is aware of but does not express. The men are her desires for attention and affection, and the pub is social pleasure and enjoyment. Outwardly she does not push her desires for love and relaxation, but inwardly there is a desire to 'turn back'. Unable to find full satisfaction in this direction, she looks for 'life' in the unconscious, in herself, deep down in the underground. Within she finds youthful urges for fame, limelight and approval. The 'charming' woman is the outer appearance fame gives, but the cruel, materialistic, grasping man is the real driving force behind these urges, behind this life. The dreamer realises that such a life is more likely to crush than to satisfy. She is then faced by the ticket collector, who probably represents the petty authorities who block our way in life. The 'trendy' young people represent attempts to keep up with the Jones's, which again, is not our true self, but a lifeless mimicry leading to a dead end. The playing children can be called 'innocence'. If we try to remain innocent of life experience, then like the children and adults in this scene, we run the risk of being an unknowing plaything of the 'leering' and perverse. The beach scene is, once more, a direction in which many people seek 'life' and fulfilment. It symbolises the healthy outdoor life, the self enjoyment and relaxation of the playboys and playgirls of society. Once more, the dreamer sees this as a puppet like, mechanical existence, and not true 'life'. But she sees 'life' in the sea, which is her inner self, her contact with the forces of life within her. To live in harmony with one's basic self, with life, instead of only conscious desires, opinions, social pressures, promises fulfilment. But the sand of her intellectual doubts, family duties and social conventions hold her back, until she breaks free, and finds herself.

THE SPIRIT

Turning at last to this aspect of self, apart from contact with the spirit through the guru, or master, dreams concerning spiritual experience are difficult to find. They also do not seem to have any defined characteristics, except perhaps a realisation of eternity, sinlessness, and love. Maybe we can call it a realisation of the eternal spirit behind the transitoriness of mortal life.

First of all, my wife describes an experience she had prior to our marriage.

'I lay in my bed unable to sleep, and because of this decided to try an experiment. We had been discussing earlier the possibility of emptying the mind completely and I decided to see if this could be done. After quite a time had passed in trying I felt it was impossible, gave up and fell asleep. The next thing I knew I was suspended above my body which was asleep on the bed. I felt as if I had returned to the womb, but it was not the physical womb but the cosmic womb. There was a wonderful feeling of love and bliss and being cared for, that completely enveloped me. There was also an awareness of my oneness with God and every other creature and being in the universe, and yet also remaining an individual. There were several questions on my mind at that particular time, and I found that without actually being told the answers I knew them intuitively. I knew my forthcoming marriage was right; also the doctrine of reincarnation and karma which I had at that time been wondering about. I knew that I was surrounded by a love and protection that made all my actions right because I could not go against that which was right in the face of this experience. I wished that I might stay always in this wonderful state and knew that this was akin to what death felt like, and knowing this one should not fear death which was an expansion of oneself. Gradually I returned to my normal sleep-state and woke up, but the feeling of the experience stayed with me for quite a while afterwards.'

Paul Brunton also reached these unclouded regions of his inner experience. He describes his condition as one of trance rather than sleep; and his experience illumination rather than dream. Certainly when we reach these spiritual aspects of self, they often come as greater consciousness, as opposed to the dimness of many dreams. Nevertheless, I quote his description of what he learnt during his two-hour period of *physical unconsciousness.*

'Man is grandly related and a greater Being suckled him than his mother. In his wiser moments he may come to know this. . . . Man does not put the true value upon himself because he has lost the divine sense. Therefore he runs after another man's opinion, when he could find complete certitude more surely in the spiritual authoritative centre of his own being. . . . He who looks within himself and perceives only discontent, frailty, darkness and fear, need not curl his lip in mocking doubt. Let him look deeper and longer, deeper and longer, until he presently becomes aware of faint tokens and breath-like indications which appear when the heart is still. Let him heed them well, for they will take life and grow into high thoughts that will cross the threshold of his mind like wandering angels, and these again will become the forerunners of a voice which will come later—the voice of a recondite and mysterious being who inhabits his centre, who is his own ancient self.... The divine nature reveals itself anew in every human life, but if a man walk indifferently by, then the revelation is as seed on stony ground. No one is excluded from this divine consciousness; it is man who excludes himself.... He who has once seen his real self will never again hate another. There is no sin greater than hatred, no sorrow worse than the legacy of lands splashed with blood which it in- evitably bestows, no result more certain than that it will recoil on those who send it forth. Hate will pass from the world only when man learns to see the faces of his fellows, not merely by the ordinary light of day, but by the transfiguring light of their divine possibilities.... All that is truly grand in nature and inspiringly beautiful in the arts speaks to man of himself. Where the priest has failed his people the illumined artist takes up his forgotten message and procures hints of the soul for them. Whoever can recall rare moments when beauty made him a dweller amid the eternities should, whenever the world tires him, turn memory into a spur and seek sanctuary within. Thither he should wander for a little peace, a flush of strength and a glimmer of light, confident that the moment he succeeds in touching his true selfhood he will draw infinite support and find perfect compensation.' (From *A Search in Secret India*.)

To end this 'dream sampler', I will quote what is surely one of the loveliest dreams ever published. It is experienced and described by J. B. Priestly, and is from his book *Rain upon Godshill*.

'Just before I went to America, during the exhausting weeks when I was busy with my Time plays, I had such a dream, and I think it left a greater impression on my mind than any experience I had ever known before, awake or in dreams, and said more to me about this life than any book I have ever read. The setting of the dream was quite simple, and owed something to the fact that not long before my wife had visited the lighthouse here at St Catherine's to do some bird ringing. I dreamt I was standing at the top of a very high tower, alone, looking down upon myriads of birds all flying in one direction; every kind of bird was there, all the birds in the world. It was a noble sight, this vast aerial river of birds. But now in some mysterious fashion the gear was changed, and time speeded up, so that I saw generations of birds, watched them break their shells, flutter into life, mate, weaken, falter and die. Wings grew only to crumble; bodies were sleek, and then, in a flash, bled and shrivelled; and death struck everywhere at every second. What was the use of all this blind struggle towards life, this eager trying of wings, this hurried mating, this flight and surge, all this gigantic meaningless effort? As I stared down, seeming to see every creature's ignoble little history almost at a glance, I felt sick at heart. It would be better if not one of them, if not one of us, had been born, if the struggle ceased for ever. I stood on my tower, still alone, desperately unhappy. But now the gear was changed again, and the time went faster still, and it was rushing by at such a rate, that the birds could not show any movement, but were like an enormous plain sown with feathers. But along this plain, flickering through the bodies themselves, there now passed a sort of white flame, trembling, dancing, then hurrying on; and as soon as I saw it I knew that this white flame was life itself, the very quintessence of being; and then it came to me, in a rocket burst of ecstacy, that nothing mattered, nothing could ever matter, because nothing else was real but this quivering and hurrying lambency of being. Birds, men and creatures not yet shaped and coloured, all were of no account except so far as this flame of life travelled through them. It left nothing to mourn over behind it; what I had thought was tragedy was mere emptiness or a shadow show; for now all real feeling was caught and purified and danced on ecstatically with the white flame of life. I had never before felt such deep happiness as I knew at the end of my dream of the tower and the birds, and if I have now kept that happiness with me, as an inner atmosphere and sanctuary for the heart, that is because I am a weak and foolish man who allows this mad world to come in destroying every green shoot of wisdom. Nevertheless, I have not been quite the same man since. A dream had come through the multitude of business.'

DICTIONARY OF DREAMS

and their Symbology

Your dream symbols

I hope it has already been made clear in this book, that no symbol in any dream can be given *one* meaning. We cannot simply say that a house stands for oneself, a river for the flow of life, a baby for the infant self, etc. Not only do symbols change their meaning according to the way each dream uses them, but also, personal associations must determine the symbol's meaning. Because of this, no person other than yourself can really interpret a dream. The most they can do is to suggest a meaning that can then either be confirmed or denied from one's own personal experiences.

Therefore, the descriptions that accompany the following symbols are but suggestions. They must be pondered over to see whether they really do make your dream, your own self, clear to you. In many cases, what is said may be only half the truth, a fraction of the meaning the dream implies. It may give but a hint. If it does only that, then I shall consider all the work of description worth while. For in my experience, it has often been the tiny hints other people have given in their analysis of symbols, that have helped me at last to unlock the truth in my dreams.

IMPORTANT INSTRUCTIONS ON HOW TO USE THE DICTIONARY

To make the dictionary of reasonable length, key words have been given as often as possible. Thus one may read aggressiveness, self opinionation, dislike of criticism. In such cases, each word stands for a separate possible meaning of the dream symbol.

As many meanings as possible have been given for each symbol. These include everyday speech associations, sexual meanings, meanings suggested by the symbol's shape and function, and it's religious, philosophical and psychological significance. Therefore, in attempting to understand the dream, you must decide for yourself which, if any, of these meanings really fit the symbol *as it appears*; and whether it makes sense to you, describes something you can really understand and is not just a jumble of words.

To keep the descriptions as short as possible, I have made free use of such words as spirit, God, soul, feeling values, material values. Each of these words has been used in a distinct manner, which does not apply to their general, public use. They have been used to avoid the necessity of constant re-iteration, or highly psychological words that are not readily understood. To make this method clear however, great pains have been taken to describe clearly each word, so as to avoid misunderstanding. It is therefore suggested that the words *God, soul, spirit*, be looked up and studied first. These can be found described in the dictionary. As for *feeling* values and *material* values, these mean any course of action or thought that arise from the value or emphasis we place on them.

A

The letter A is directly associated with the Greek Alpha, and Phoenician Aleph. In all such languages, as with Hebrew, A has stood for the beginning of something, some process. Thus, in Alpha and Omega is the symbol of beginning and ending, and this always refers to some physical or soul process, in time, for in eternity there is no beginning or end. It also denotes something singular, as the beginning of something always starts with ONE.

ABANDONED   When abandoned in the sense of being left alone, this expresses a feeling of loneliness, of being unloved, uncared for, and insecurity in relationships. When abandoned in the sense of giving way to feelings, it represents a dropping of the moral code, finding a new freedom, releasing pent up feelings.

ABBEY   Religious feelings—the inner place of quiet. That is, those areas of feelings and thoughts that are quiet, strengthening, and inclined to consideration of the meaning in life.

ABDOMEN   This may be a body dream, where health or diet needs attention. But as a symbol it refers to the process of digesting and absorbing new experiences in life, new facts, also feelings of attraction or repulsion, of passion.

ABNORMAL   To see an abnormal feature on self or others in a dream,

183

shows that there is an unconscious feeling that parts of the being have not developed in the way they should.

ABORIGINAL   This symbol often occurs in dreams, and usually refers to the instinctive, less conscious side of self. Sometimes it represents all the unconscious, black parts of the mind and emotions. Also the less rational or logical side, the part of us moved by feelings, magic, ritual, odd beliefs. In other cases it symbolises the repressed sexual drive, or unregenerate side of self. But it is the side of self that is closest to nature, with keener senses, and it is more intuitive and less rational, and does not regard itself as distinct from the natural forces that produced it, or the other wild creatures of the earth.

ABORTION   To lose, or purposely abort a baby may refer to the loss of some new development in one's nature or relationships with others. It may also refer to actual physical events.

ABOVE   When something is above you, it suggests that it is either beyond reach, understanding, or grasp. Sometimes it refers to the intellectual side of self.

ABROAD   May refer to the exploration of new interests, or new areas of self or of being in a situation or area you are not at home in. Or if you have been to that country, might associate with the events or emotions that occurred.

ABCESS   A collection of poisonous thoughts, emotions or opinions, that cause you irritation, and need to be healed and cleansed.

ABSORB   Two separate qualities that merge into one.

ACCEPT   To be willing to admit or receive what is symbolised.

ACCIDENT   Sometimes this simply suggests the feelings it gives rise to, as shock, fear. Or something has shocked and hurt some part of us.

ACCORDION   Like most musical instruments, it represents an expression of feelings, a coming into harmony or accord with things or self.

ACE   The controlling factor, the vital point. Also, ambiguousness, as the ace can be high or low.

ACHE   An ache is a warning that all is not well, or some part of the body has been hard used. Thus a heart-ache might suggest emotional hurt.

ACID   The power to corrode and eat away. May mean fears, cynicism, or criticism as in an acid tongue, which undermines confidence or determination.
Acid test means the test of real value, as gold will not corrode, but lesser metals will. Therefore corrosion denotes material, easily destroyed things. Where acid refers to LSD, see *Hashish*.

ACNE   To have spots on the face in a dream would symbolise an inner condition that was making it or part of the self shewn to the world, unclean and spotted. In fact, upsetting one's image, and social contacts.

ACORN   Often used as a spiritual symbol representing the tiny seed of spiritual experience or truth, from which a mighty growth can come.

ACCOUSTICS   An inner condition allowing you either to be clearly aware of delicate inner feelings, or disrupting your consciousness of self.

ACROPHOBIA   Fear of heights. May represent an actual conscious fear, or symbolise the fear of falling. That is, you can fall from grace, fall from social favour, fall in other people's opinions.

ACTOR   You are acting a role, not being your true self. Sometimes there is a spiritual significance, you are an actor on the stage of life, and the true self, off-stage, is God or spirit. Or it can represent a desire for public acclaim or notice.

ADAM   Adam can mean your father. He can represent a condition of being; of following, then turning from the divine will, or your innermost feelings. Adam is the symbol of all mankind and is not singular. ADM means A, the beginning of physical manifestation, the first activity in matter, the beginning of human development. D, growth and development. M, multiplicity, the spreading and becoming many, in consciousness and individuality. Thus all individuals were contained in what Adam represents. Adam has not self-will, no self consciousness, until eating the apple and falling into a state of individual instead of group, instinctive or divine consciousness. Adam incarnated as the first human consciousness and fell. He therefore also represents the bodily or sensuous nature in man or woman.

ADDER   See *Snake*.

ADDICTED   This suggests that the motivations for your activities in life are not arising from a sense of will, or responsibility, but from the emotions and fears, symbolised by that to which you are addicted. It shows a power has taken over your life. See *Obsession*.

ADDRESS   An inner situation represented by your outer environment.

ADMIRAL   The power of directing the many facets of self across the sea of life experience. Sometimes used instead of guru or master. The admiral may therefore stand for the higher self, a representative of God or destiny. Also denotes authority, power.

ADOLESCENT   Time of greatest sexual growth, and development of new ranges of emotion, intellect, sensitivity.

ADORATION   See *Surrender, Worship, Pray*.

ADORN   Those things you are adding to self in an attempt to beautify, extend abilities, hide defects, or symbolise position.

ADRIFT   Without any determining direction in life, or anchor, such as family ties, sense of duty, etc.

ADULT   A flowering of those possibilities only latent and unrealised in baby and youth.

ADULTERY   That union and giving of innermost feelings, to persons or objects for whom you do not have a deep affinity. A union caused by physical or emotional hungers rather than any deep spiritual or sympathetic links, or to love, which considers not only your needs, but other people's feelings and situations. In another sense, it means a giving of self to union with the material desires, ambitions and concepts of life, instead of marrying the will to spirit.

ADVERTISEMENT   A means of bringing to consciousness, or special attention, something you were previously unaware of.

AFFECTATION   Mannerism that is not in accord with your deepest feelings or character.

AFRICAN   See *Aboriginal*. Generally appertains to the instinctive side of life, and its mysteries. South Africa may at present represent the whole situation involved in colour bar, within onself. That is, the refusal of the conscious self to share or allow the expression of unconscious desires, opinions and activities, especially in governing one's affairs.

AGE   Usually refers to the prevalent opinions, experiences or attitudes at that period of your life. Although youth represents a time of growth and expansion, of looking ahead; age often symbolises physical decay, looking back, experience.

AGGRESSIVENESS   Aggressive feelings are one of the main expressions of our energy, along with sex, ambition and study, and generally speaking, it is not wise to hold them back even though in an awful and destructive phase, but rather to seek a more satisfying and constructive expression for them.

AGONY   Tormented and in great pain through some opinion, attitude, indecision, emotion, or as the dream suggests.

AGORAPHOBIA   Fear of open spaces. As with fear of falling, this may represent an actual fear. Symbolically it means a fear of being exposed, of being seen, of possible attack, and of having nothing to hide behind or under.

AGREEMENT   A harmony of previously unreconciled opinions, emotions, beliefs, etc.

AIM   Directing energies and desires to some goal, or target.

AIR   In the Bible it states that God breathed into man's nostrils the breath of life, and man became a living soul. Dreams use air in very much the same way, as an intermediary between the invisible life source, God, and consciousness. Air represents the activity of spirit upon our feelings, thoughts, our soul. The wind moves the waters, see *Water*, and thus can direct the inner life.
Also, air connects earth and sky, the cosmic forces and material life. It is the medium in which birds or man can fly, which represents a rising away from material experiences into the abstract realms of speculation, and idealism. Naturally, one can fall from these heights. To breathe in is to be filled with spirit, to become connected with universal life and consciousness. To breathe out is to become more individualised, more aware of self.

AIR RAID   A threat from thoughts. New ideas descend out of the blue. Sometimes, glimpses of your spiritual nature have been gained, and are threatening present aims, prejudices, etc. See *Zeppelin*.

ALCHEMIST   Similar to a master or guru. The power of transforming base qualities into golden ones. The alchemist is an expression of those human attitudes that can release the transforming influence of spirit.

ALCOHOL   Jesus turned water into wine, which is similar to alchemy. It represents the activity of spirit upon us, changing our actions and lives. Also represents stimulation, relaxation, and an outer way to face inner anxieties, even if only temporarily. See *Coffee*.

ALCOHOLISM   See *Addicted.*

ALIEN   Someone you do not understand, and therefore have few links with. Refers usually to some misunderstood part of personal urges or nature, that seem foreign to the rest of the character.

ALLERGIC   The thing symbolised irritates.

ALLEY   See *Road.*

ALLIGATOR   Often used as a symbol for one of the Gods in some countries. By Gods is meant, basic cosmic forces. The alligator or crocodile is similar to the serpent and is the power of the unconscious emotions and fears to swallow us up. That is, of being carried away, or possessed, by fears, urges, ideas, arising from within, or fear of the irrational. The Egyptians worshipped a crocodile as a guide to the dead in the underworld. It represents not only a threat, but also a wealth of wisdom about unconscious things.

ALPHABET   The basic components of words and language, or ideas and expression. The alphabet represents the basic parts of one's being, processes of being, or basic lessons in life.

ALTAR   Symbolises the sense of awe in face of life, nature or God. Also willingness, in face of this, to sacrifice some personal desires, to that of a universal desire. Schweitzer has said that a man who picks a worm out of a puddle is acting for life as whole, not just personal self.

AMERICA   Often found to represent the attitude of trying to grasp as much material experience, worldly success and power as possible. Outer life. Success in a worldly sense.

AMOEBA   Basic expressions of spirit in matter, in yourself.

AMPUTATION   To lose the power of that limb. See *Leg, Arm, Left, Right.*

ANAESTHETIC   Something, some attitude, that is making you un-

189

conscious of what is going on, deadening feelings and sensitiveness.

ANALYST If someone is helping you analyse your dreams and appears in a dream, often is similar to guru. Represents the understanding of self that can be gained, or the things or urges that have led you to seek such understanding. Or the relationship with the analyst.

ANCHOR Some part of the make-up that holds you firm to a task or code, such as determination, love, etc. But it has a deeper meaning, for the anchor reaches the sea bed, or deepest part of our unconscious self, or inner self. Thus it suggests a power of resolve coming from deep within. Or of being tied down.

ANCIENT A part of self relating to biological knowledge of the cells, instincts, that are older than the personal self. Or may suggest aspects of self from previous lives. Knowledge, wisdom of life through long experience.

ANGEL Angels, in visions and dreams, very often give us information, wisdom or directions, of an intuitive spiritual nature. They are the messengers of God, or ideas and active forces of the spiritual part of our own being. Thus they can represent the usually invisible moving forces and intelligences behind phenomena. Or they can be our own spiritual perceptions, our higher senses that look upon the face of the Lord. The two angels are Yes and No, Positive and Negative, Denial and Assurance.
Angels can be associated with death, or the world beyond the grave. Thus one dreamer dreamt that all her family had become angels and flown away, which was a gentle way of getting rid of them.

ANIMAL In dreams these represent levels of consciousness, or instinctive drives, passions, hungers, or similar animal traits.

ANTIQUE See *Ancient.*

ANUS Pertaining to the forces of decay and destruction. The cleansing of waste matter. All the things we leave behind us in life. Infantile pleasure.

APE   The purely physical, instinctive, wild, animal man.

APPLE   Material temptation. Apple of one's eye, something we treasure in outer life. Also can represent wholeness, knowledge of the world or of self, as when it is a golden apple.

ARAB   Masculinity, passionate manhood, possessiveness.

ARCHER   See *Aim.*

ARENA   Area of conflict. Circle of conscious awareness and experience.

ARK   A personality, or area of self, that has been shaped by following the divine will, or innermost urges and intuitions, as opposed to those arising from fear, passion, ambition. Or something can come out of the ark and thus be old fashioned.

ARM   Arms represent our power to express emotions, desires and ideas, to construct or destroy. See *Left* and *Right.*

ARMOUR   The rigid emotional or intellectual barrier we sometimes put around ourselves as protection from being hurt, frightened or influenced by others.

ARMS   Guns, spears, usually symbolise aggressiveness and destructive urges and wishes. Or male sexuality.

ARRESTED   Literally, to be stopped; if by a policeman, then blocking of actions due to moral conscience, or whatever the symbol is.

ART   The exteriorisation of some inner idea, feeling or direction. The expression of inner content, and thus a source of self realisation.

ARTIST   One who is expressing himself. Usually refers to more irrational parts of self. Creative ability.

ASCETIC   Restraint of physical desires, usually in an attempt to realise inner self, but often from inner personal drives. Cleansing of material desires and motivations.

ASH   The purified aspect of whatever symbol has been burnt.

ASS   The lower nature under the direction of the spirit. Humility; lack of intellect. Instincts and natural energies.

ASTHMA   Out of harmony with the air principle. The receptive, life giving, intuitive process is not functioning well. See *Air*. Feelings of being suffocated by work, relations, environment.

ASTROLOGER, ASTROLOGY   Similar to the spiritual teacher. One who explains your inner being, relationship with life as a whole, and destiny or direction. Astrology in a dream would pertain to these things.

ATOM BOMB   Appears in many dreams now. Represents mankind's self destructive philosophy, the destruction man lets loose within himself by following prevalent social ideas, commercial and political influences, instead of trying to live in harmony with his innate nature, which would put him in accord with life in general.

ATTIC   Used in many ways. Memory, when old things are in it. Reasoning and intellectual nature. Often used to represent an extremely intellectual approach to life or a situation, devoid of feeling. It is the high and mighty, or difficult and precarious position we get into through an unpractical or purely idealistic outlook.

AURA   See *Glow*.

AUSTRALIA   Opportunity, hard headedness, practicality, dubiousness about the irrational.

AUTOGRAPH   See *Name*.

AUTUMN   Time of harvest, reaping rewards of labour. But also of beginning of withdrawal from physical activity to inner functions.

AVALANCHE   See *Snow*.

AVATAR   See *Guru.*

AWAKE   To become aware of something.

AXE   See *Arms.* Power, authority of material nature.

B

Corresponds to Beta in the Greek, and Beth in Hebrew. Whereas A is the symbol of a beginning, B stands for what is latent, or within. It refers to man's mouth as an organ of speech. It represents the within as an inviolable retreat, a central dwelling, to which one can retire.

BABY   Your infant self. Or some part of the being that is still in the early stages of development, and needs nurturing, encouraging, caring for, lest it perish. Inner possibilities.

BACCHUS   God of wine, or spirit, of vegetation and growing things, of the soul and its experiences, and sensual pleasures.

BACK   The back of something, or someone, usually refers to the unconscious, unknown things. One seldom looks behind oneself, and so does not know what is going on.

BADGE   Usually expresses a very important idea in dreams. The badge is a sort of synthesis, or potent focal point, of the inner self, a representation of our true inner state, our real being or possibilities.

BAG   Female sexuality. A receptive, containing condition.

BAKER   An aspect of guru. One who transmutes physical and sense experience into understanding or wisdom, into something we can eat and digest.

BALANCE   Law, justice, order. Conscience, that weighs outer acts against the innermost self or spirit.

BALD   See *Hair.*

BALL   Represents the complete being, known and unknown, conscious and unconscious, manifest and potential, visible and invisible.

BALLET   See *Dance.*

BANANA   Male sexuality.

BAND   The various parts of yourself going about their individual functions, but all in harmony and co-operation.

BANDAGE   Injury, healing, death.

BANDIT   Male sexuality in its adolescent, aggressive stage.

BANK   Money often symbolises energy, power, authority at a physical level. It is sometimes used to express male or female sexual potency, or power of sexual feelings. To hoard it therefore expresses a fear of sharing, a fear of losing power and virility. To give too lavishly is to use manhood·or femininity unwisely, and so on. A bank would therefore suggest stores of energy. A banker is the representative of power.

BAPTISM   A symbol of a cleansing of our emotions and mind; a letting go of feelings, opinions and prejudices. It means that you are undergoing a change of heart, and a change of mind. The inner being is becoming more fluid, less set in its ways, ready to be guided by new ideas, new intuitions, by the spirit. This is why Jesus is shown as receiving the Holy Ghost, and at such times many people do receive this influx from their spiritual nature, their potential energy, or whatever you call it. This readies them for the experience in the wilderness. See *Water* and *Desert.*

BAR   Any rod or bar usually represents male sexuality, or the positive, dynamic, constructive and forceful parts of self. It is an expression of the Spirit, or Libido. What we do with the rod in the dream shows how we are using our energies or will power. See *Reed.*

BAR (Room)   A public bar can either represent the sense of pleasure, love of company and entertainment, or sometimes the place where you drink spirits, or higher power. See *Alcohol*.

BARBER   See *Hair*. This is the aspect of self that deals with our hair or how we deal with our emotions.

BARE   To have your motives, feelings, secret hopes and fears, revealed. Sometimes represents a desire to reveal self to others, to have them see us as we are underneath, depending on dream content.

BAROMETER   Showing the state of inner pressure or emotional climate.

BARRICADE   The defence used against others, or events. May be in the form of an excuse I'm too ill to go to work, or I'll never get anywhere, so what's the use of trying. See *Armour*.

BASEMENT   Very often used, and symbolises hidden motives, unconscious, unknown feelings, memories or past experiences, your biological past, and the place where the individual contacts hidden powers, universal wisdom, contact with other minds, deepest feelings. Sometimes it means base deeds, low morals, underlying dislikes. It is from the basement, below, or within, that libido or life force arises. Fears and terrors sometimes come from downstairs. So also the understanding of our deeper nature.

BASTARD   Some desire, action, part of one's nature, born through personal, selfish, uncaring expressions, instead of activities arising from marriage or unity of soul with spirit. That is, actions directed by our deepest self.

BAT   See *Rod*. The flying bat is usually associated with the devil, night or death. It is a creature that can see in the dark, lives in caves, and so is an aspect of unconscious inner workings, that go on in the darkness, or the part below our conscious awareness. Sleep, digestion, memory, spiritual contact.

BATH   See *Baptism* and *Water.*

BATTERY   Energy, life force.

BAYONET   See *Arms.*

BEACH   The borderline between unconscious and conscious self. To find something on the beach is to find something that has come from deep within. See *Sea.*

BEAD   See *Ball.*

BEAR   Sometimes said to represent a possessive mother, and the feelings this has aroused. See *Animals.*

BEARD   Male sexual power and virility. It is also often used to represent great wisdom, authority or even saintliness, as when the person has a white beard. If the beard is very long, it can symbolise great age, eternal life, wisdom of the ages. See *Hair.*

BED   Rest, sleep, unconsciousness, unawareness, sexual pleasure, dreams, escape from the world into sleep.

BEE   Hard working, social life, order. Mass power, individual weakness. Unity of effort.

BEER   See *Alcohol.*

BEETLE   Sometimes used a symbol of eternal life, of fate, or cause and effect.

BEGGAR   The negative side of the self. The parts of your nature that are not usually allowed into everyday affairs because you are ashamed of them. Or it may be a sense of inadequacy, of being an outcast. In a few cases, a wise man lies hidden under the rough exterior who can tell you the secrets of your life and destiny.

BEHIND   See *Back.*

BELL   Warning, signal.

BELLY   Sensual feelings, passions, hungers, the physical side of self. Or in Body dream may refer to an internal organ.

BIBLE   The sense of rightness, spiritual knowledge, expression of innermost self. Symbol of organised, orthodox religion—the letter that kills rather than the spirit that quickens.

BICEPS   Physical strength.

BIG or BIGNESS   If something is very large in a dream, it usually denotes the emotional and mental impact of the thing, as 'It was a big thing in my life. It was bigger than both of us.'

BILLIARDS   Most games, in their winning and losing, their tactics, skill, luck, represent the game of life, with its difficulties, triumphs and despairs. May also represent sexual intercourse.

BILL   To receive a bill often symbolises a bill of reckoning. In other words, something you have done or thought, now is producing consequences that have to be paid for.

BIRD   Freud said the bird represented the male phallus, and flying means the sexual act. Many countries use the word bird to mean a girl or woman. In Italy it means the male organ. But to dream of a bird may also mean a sense of freedom from material ties. In ancient myths, birds denoted the soul, spiritual knowledge, or experience. Thus a dove descends on Jesus at baptism. Sometimes it represents aspirations, thoughts, or ideals. The Egyptians used the bird with a human head to represent the soul leaving the body at death, while the phoenix stood for the new rising from the old. See *Air*. Also *Intuition*.

BIRTH   A new beginning, a fresh start, starting life under influence of a new power. In Christianity the new birth was caused through the power of the spirit. Birth dreams can also be expressions of actual infantile memories of birth, with all its difficulties, terrors and events. In this way the unconscious emotions and fears may be made conscious and dealt with. We have to remember that birth of one part of us cannot help but be death to another. The womb experience dies when the baby is born to outer life, the baby self dies as the youth emerges, and so on.

BIRTHRIGHT   The innate qualities you are born with, but may never receive, or unfold in life.

BLACK   Unknown, unconscious, evil, death, absence of knowledge, or ability to see or understand. Inner activities we are not aware of, but which like earth, are rich in possibilities, and have all the elements of growth.

BLACKBIRD   Sometimes thought of as messengers of the dead.

BLACKSMITH   Expressive of physical and masculine power, in shaping the metals of life, the possibilities of your nature. Forcefulness, material creativeness. See *Iron*.

BLASPHEMY   A denial or cursing or your own innate self or latent possibilities. A turning of the will away from the possibility of direction from within.

BLEAK   Unfeeling, difficult emotionally.

BLESSING   A release of the innermost energies into outer life.

BLINDNESS   An inability or unwillingness to understand or agree to something.

BLOOD   The life energies, conscious life, physical energy. Blood is the physical substance that interpenetrates every part of our body. It carries or produces, sensation, life, consciousness. Its lack causes coldness, lack of sensation, powerlessness, death. Blood, symbolically, is the substance through which the spirit, or formless, expresses itself. In magic, blood is used so that demons can materialise. There is the saying There is bad blood between them, or bad feelings.

Also, It's in his blood, that is, in his very nature.
In Christianity, the wine symbolises Christ's blood, or love and sacrifice. Inwardly this means that the spirit loves and sacrifices its life and self to us despite the way we may abuse the very life and consciousness thus produced in us. Blood also represents kinship, brotherhood, family or racial ties, or similarity.
At another level blood may express fear of pain, dirtiness, or physical uncleanness.

BLOSSOM The unfolding and expression of what was latent within from the beginning.

BLUE Relates to the mind, religious feelings, spirituality, the sky. If a dark murky blue moodiness, depression, witchcraft or evil wishes. See *Colour*.

BOAT Methods used to deal with the world. For instance, during bad times we may say, just press on, all things come to an end. This is the personality structure, the ship used to sail across the seas of life.
Often found used in dreams when we begin to investigate the contents of the unconscious, and stands for our adventure into the unknown, and our means of coping with what is experienced, found is not the right word as we experience our inner contents totally.
In Myths it is used to carry the soul to the underworld or land of the dead, and here denotes contact with spiritual realms. In some cases it is also used to represent sexual adventures.

BODY The temple of the soul, your physical instrument and means of discovering yourself through the difficulties with which physical life faces you. It is the visible expression of your inner content and past experiences. See *Arm, Leg, Head, Belly, Feet*, etc.

BOIL See *Abscess*.

BOMB Some explosive emotions or fears that terrify. Your anger may explode and do you and others damage.

BONE   Your convictions, bone of contention, beliefs or opinions that give you support; or backbone in life. Strength of character.

BOOK   Memories, ideas, record or expression of self, or others.

BOSS   The prevailing major driving force in your life, as ambition, desire, love. Sometimes as guru.

BOWEL   See *Anus.*

BOY   If no one you know, may represent your own growing male, constructive, intellectual qualities. The means with which you deal with outer life. In some cases represents the divine child, or growth of spiritual contact; that which has been born from the union of your conscious will with spirit, God, deepest self.

BRAIN   Thinking, intellectual faculty. Organ of consciousness, reasoning. The directing influence of our physical life.

BREAD   Bread symbolises the physical needs or sustenance of the body. Also general outer needs. Inwardly it represents fellowship, unity of all life, and its common purpose. It is the universal substance, or body of God, which all creatures partake of, for the body depends upon matter, bread, while the soul depends upon spirit, wine, for its existence. Bread may also symbolise what you have learnt from life.

BREAST   An expression of female love and nurture. An expression of female sexuality. To go to a woman's breast in a dream may represent an expression of the baby's desire to be fed, loved and made feel secure. That is, a regression, or reliving of infant desires. A woman expresses male sexuality through her breasts, in that she fulfils the body of the infant. May also represent emotional security.

BREATH   In many myths and beliefs, breath is synonymous with life. Breathing takes in life force, prana, or vril. The breath is in this sense the energy holding in potential all capabilities, knowledge and power. See *Air.*

BRIDE   Any marriage is a unity of opposites but affinities, which in their union form a new state of being. Hydrogen and Oxygen, when combined form something different from either, water. The bride is the receptive, intuitional, negative, material side of the union. Mary is the bride of God. The bride is synonymous with water, sea, earth, nature; with the power of growth, fertility, fruit-fulness, of form. She provides the receptacle, the material condition, the environment, into which the seed, the energy, idea, desire, is sown. Activity in the inner intuitive sphere. The energy or potential uses the materials provided in the being of the bride, earth, and takes on form, which is conditioned by the bride or mother.

Also symbolises the desire for physical marriage, love, children; to leave home, experience marital pleasures and responsibilities.

BRIDEGROOM   The bridegroom has often represented Christ, Spirit or God. At another level the bridegroom is the conscious mind and intellect that marries the unconscious or intuition. He represents energy, dynamic power, activity in the world, consciousness. Again in many dreams it expresses the desire to be married, or to find a loving partner.

BRIDGE   A link between opposing or different emotions, desires, directions. A way to deal with difficulties.

BRIGHT   See *Glowing*.

BRONZE   Warlike passions, force, energy. Emotions, but under the sway of greed, self interest, and plunder.

BROOCH   See *Badge*.

BROOK   See *River*.

BROOM   Cleansing, clearing away unneeded or harmful ideas and feelings. Broom can also represent male organ.

BROTHER   Probably represents your feelings for your brother.

BROW   Intellectual capacities, thoughts and mental attitudes to life. A gem or eye in the brow symbolises insight into life and people of an intuitive and unusual nature, or higher levels of consciousness than most enjoy. In many myths, the inner character is said to be marked upon the brow, as with Cain, marked for murdering Abel.

BRUTE or BRUTAL   Physical consciousness unrelieved by love, affection, wisdom. Physical power and awareness without the faculties of feeling, sympathy, insight.

BUBBLE   Often used in art, literature and dreams to represent the transiency of the world, worldly ambition, our physical lives. Sometimes is used to represent the soul and consciousness which are but short lived, as opposed to the spirit which is eternal. The bubble may burst, but the consciousness, spirit, that experienced it, remains.

BUD   Some part of self that has not developed yet, but is forming prior to expression.

BUDDHA   Represents the eternal part of man's nature. See *Christ*.

BUILDING   See *House*.

BULL   Usually male sexual desires, or male power. In many rituals and dreams, the bull is sacrificed, as in India, Egypt, Mithraism, Israel. This represents the surrender of sexual and physical appetites to the will of God, or spirit. It does not mean the killing or denial of sexuality, but an offering up, so that these may be transmuted into higher, more satisfying forms.

BURGLAR   In women's dreams often represents a fear of sexual intercourse, of being entered unwillingly. In male dreams it may be similar to the symbolism of Beggar or Tramp or Aborigine. Or feeling of guilt about stolen love, or goods.

BURIAL   This is obviously connected with death. So it can represent fear of death of self, or loved ones, unconscious desire to see others dead, or at least out of the way. But it also is often used when we feel buried away from society, or buried under the events of life. Sometimes we bury or repress a memory, emotion, desire or talent. Our past is buried within us. In some religious rituals, the candidate is buried and then resurrected. This symbolises the dying and burial of his old self and life, and rebirth due to spiritual forces awakening in or ruling his being.

The earth also can represent our mother or the past. Burial may therefore symbolise being killed or ruled by an overpossessive mother, or inability to break from her dominating influence. Being weighed down by past actions, sins.

BUTCHER   A butcher may denote a fear of another person's anger; or being a butcher symbolise your own aggressiveness. Or it can represent material philosophy, worldly attitudes, lack of love and feeling.

BUTTER   As used in the phrase butter them up, it depicts flattery, or something like soft soap.

BUTTERFLY   The beautiful that emerges from the unpromising, or ugly. The spiritual that emerges from physical experience. Transmutation.

C

The third letter of the Hebrew alphabet is Gimel, and so does not directly relate to C. Nevertheless, as C is similarly the third letter, its qualities can be associated with Gimel. Gimel symbolises the throat, or half-closed hand when grasping. This represents matter enveloping spiritual forms; the consciousness of man grasping spiritual realities or ideas. The throat gives material form in speech to ideas, an outer expression of what is within, thus is spirit taking on form.

CACTUS   Something upon which we are likely to be hurt.

CADUCEUS   See *Snake*.

CAFE Meeting point of different parts of your nature. See *Food, Bar (room)*.

CAGE Repression, morals, social custom, fear of being held back or restrained, or feeling of being trapped.

CAKE Similar to symbolism of bread, but more luxurious, less practical. See *Bread*.

CALENDAR Time.

CALF Youthful love and sensuality, calf love. Worldly pleasure of the gay frivolous kind. Also, worldly riches, savings, luxuries, as in fatted calf. Calf or leg represents our physical ability to get about in the world. See *Gold*.

CAMEL Ability to journey through the dry places of life. That is, to press on through ordeals or duties for which we do not have the inclination or emotion of pleasure, to energise us. Patience, long suffering, perseverance. Having inner stores of spiritual sustenance. John the Baptist clothed himself in Camel's hair. This means his patient, persevering seeking of God despite living in the wilderness of intellectual doubt, lack of spiritual experience, emotional aridity.

CAMERA Memory, the recording of impressions, the attempt to capture a fleeting idea or experience.

CANAL A means of directing our emotions, usually self created, or consciously worked out.

CANADA Masculinity, adventure, opportunity of self expression, without too much emphasis on worldly goods, as America.

CANCER A part of our nature, or emotions, that do not harmonise with the rest of our being, and so pose a threat to our existence. An individual who steals, destroys, plunders and kills, is not working in harmony with the world, he is thus a social cancer. As a person, if we follow the promptings of the spirit, not church dogma, but our innermost self, that is universal, and not our own selfish desires, then we are a healthy cell within the body of life. In this way, if the cells of our body follow the good of the whole, which includes their individual best interests, the body then functions as a unit, lifting the individual cell to new power and consciousness. Working for self alone, the cells produce disease.

CANDLE   Male sexual organ. Also a symbol of wisdom and understanding. The flame gives light, consciousness, ability to see or understand, and transmutes the matter of the stick into heat, energy and wisdom, or light. It thus symbolises the seeking mind of man trying to understand material existence, and thus gaining wisdom or light. See *Light*.

CANE   Aggressive, sadistic sexuality.

CANNIBAL   The part of us that lives off the lives or efforts of others, instead of producing for ourselves.

CANNON   Male sexual organ. Aggressiveness of destructive desires.

CANOE   See *Boat*.

CANYON   See *Valley*.

CAP   See *Hat*.

CAPITAL   Such as London, New York, Rome, represents the centre of our material interests, our physical life. But obviously, for Roman Catholics, Rome would probably represent religious beliefs.

CAPSIZE   To feel upset. Fear of failure, of being overthrown.

CAPTAIN   See *Admiral*.

CAPTIVE   Fear of being bound or subject to other people, or trapped by circumstances, marriage, work. Guilt about deeds or desires; prisoner of moral beliefs, ideas, opinions or emotions, depending on dream.

CAR   Feelings about the particular car. The ideas, ambitions, drives, ideals, desires that get us somewhere in life. A vehicle or means of getting somewhere. Desires to get on in life; our journey through life. Or general outer experience in the sense of getting somewhere. Status, social standing. Self control or lack of it, in driving.

CARBON   Elementary physical experiences that can transmute into spiritual or eternal values or wisdom, i.e. diamond.

CARD   Fate, luck, unexpected or unplanned events in life. Sometimes associated with the devil or bad luck.

CARPENTER   The ability to shape desires or ideas. The power of reasoning that controls emotion. Logic that is limited by the revealed facts of life, as opposed to intuition which goes into the unknown. Joseph, as carpenter, represents intellectual wisdom, or justice, which while limited, acknowledged after some doubt the intuitive formative function of Mary, and protected her from the world. Joseph extends, guards, the intuition. That is, reasoning seeks to understand and use intuitive information. See *Wood, Tree.*

CARPET   Luxury, richness, splendour. Sometimes symbolises insulation against worldly influence or physical desires, or flights of soul or imagination. In a few cases, the carpet represents the handiwork of God. The differently coloured threads, know not in themselves where they are going. To them, their journeying here, there and everywhere in weaving seems like chaos or accident. But the Master Weaver knows the beautiful design, and out of the seeming chaos arises the splendid pattern. So with the lives of men.

CARROT   Male organ. Or fruits of the earth culled from worldly experience. Promise of reward, as used with Donkey.

CARTRIDGE   See *Bomb.*

CARVE   Similar to carpenter. To work on the self and bring out inner qualities. Leave indelible marks, memories, fears, regrets, on our feelings or thoughts. To work hard at difficult situations and carve a niche for yourself.

CASE   See *Bag*.

CASH   See *Bank*.

CASKET   Secret hidden memories. Wonders hidden in ourselves. Special things.

CASTRATE   Represents a fear of not coping sexually. Losing sexuality. Cutting off deeper feelings, sympathies, ambitions and energies. To cut off the penis or testicles is to repress the feelings, emotions and urges represented by them. This cutting off may be done by a fear of uncleanness, feelings of guilt about sexuality, conviction of inferiority, dread of pain or being repulsed or thought repulsive.

CAT   Luck, good or bad. A cat is essentially feminine, or is associated with femininity, also it can see in the dark. Thus it symbolises intuition and knowledge of the unconscious or psychic functions. A cat can be a warning of some coming event, a message from the unconscious intuitive part of self. It symbolises the mysteries of the unknown, dark world within ourselves, of which the cat is a native. It dwells in the psychic realm of self, the irrational, the land of death. It can represent a fear of bad luck or death, or a warning of same; or be a messenger of good luck, or as a warning for safety. If our own cat is doctored, it may refer to a cutting off of our irrational feelings, emotions, or love.

CATACLYSM   Time of great inner changes, fears, doubts, searchings for security, understanding, spiritual certainty. See *Atom Bomb*.

CATACOMB   An exploration of our inner contents or past lives. A descent into the unconscious, the realm of death and rebirth, deception and wisdom. A search for our inner self, lasting values, underlying abilities.

CATERPILLAR   Sexual intercourse, sexual feelings. Material and worldly experience. Spiritual blindness.

CAUL   Sign of second sight or intuition.

CAVE   Woman's sex organs. Womb, or experience of life in the womb, or prior to birth. Contact with the past, with the inner life. A going back into the past levels of our consciousness, where treasures or fears may be found. Or we may find a spring, the source of our feelings or life. Christ is said to have been born in a cave which symbolises that our higher cosmic consciousness emerges from these ancient levels of our being. A cave is a woman's receptive affections, but may also represent her grasping possessive emotions, as well as her sexual desires and feelings. It may also express ancient memories, racial or individual.

Apart from the spring, there may be early man, or a snake in the cave. The ancient man is our earliest levels of consciousness. But the spring and snake can bring healing and peace, for we may have tapped the deep sources of spirit in such dreams.

CEILING   Protection, security, against the elements. Something above our head, or comprehension.

CELIBACY   Refraining from desires for worldly pleasure. Concentration on inner values.

CELLAR   See *Basement* and *Cave.*

CENTRE   The spirit. The unseen power behind life. The basic energy behind growth. Our central and innermost self. The point from which our self emerges; the level of being from which our present experience arises. A beginning, a seed, birth, pregnancy, may be symbolised by a dot in the middle of a circle. The centre also represents the point from which the transmuting power arises (see *Alchemist*). The circle may represent earth or mother, or outer self; the dot or centre spirit, power, father or inner life.

CEREMONY   An outer expression of inner values.

CESSPOOL   All those parts of self, such as values, emotions, desires, ideas, hopes, that do not connect with our spirit, or source of life energy. The spirit represents our roots, and if something is cut off from its roots it decays. Thus, cess is all the parts of self that have no connection with the roots within, and are therefore liable to decay and corruption.

CHAFF   The unimportant things in life.

CHAIN   Bondage, strength. Imprisonment or anchorage. The feelings or links that bind you to others, or to work, or a religion, or set of ideas.

CHAIR   Your position or status in life. Your attitudes.

CHAMELEON   Changing emotions, instability, lack of stability or sense of duty. Will change values to suit outer events, rather than be true to promises or duty, or adaptability.

CHAMPAGNE   Luxury, richness, worldly success. See *Alcohol*.

CHAPEL   Inner, sacred feelings. Religious feelings, sense of God.

CHARIOT   See *Car*. The difference between this and car lies in it being drawn by horses. See *Horse*.

CHASM   See *Valley*.

CHEAT   Being dishonest with self. Not living up to your real feelings.

CHEQUE   A promise. See also *Bank*.

CHESS   See *Billiards*.

CHEW   To think something over. To analyse or break it down in order to absorb it. To sample something.

CHICKEN   Being scared, henpecked. Sacrifice.

CHILD   Usually refers to youthful memories, or attitudes that still live on in us. If we become a child in a dream, it may be we feel immature in some way. See *Boy, Girl*.

CHILDBIRTH   Bringing to consciousness a new part of the self that has been developing but remained unexpressed in action. Or the desire to have children. Or the memories of your own birth.

CHIMNEY   Female sex organs. The channel of your energies, or libido.

CHIN   Resolve, sternness, obstinacy, character. Your ability to take the blows of life on the chin.

CHINA   The inner self, mysticism, irrational, secret knowledge, intuition, wisdom of life. It may be a fear of the irrational. That is, a fear of believing or being influenced by ideas that are not logically proven, or commonly understood or held by others.

CHOKE   Not to be able to swallow or accept something.

CHOPPER   Male sex organ, expression of hate or destructiveness. See *Arms*.

CHRIST   That which emerges into our human life through surrendering ourselves to the direction of spirit or innermost self. Christ represents our human qualities that have been transmuted by spiritual energy. They are thus eternalised or are expressions of the universal life, love and wisdom, or God. Christ is God expressing through us. In dreams he does not usually represent an historical person, but our own contact with God. Christ is also the symbol through which we may contact all those parts of self that still remain dormant. We glimpse through Him the possibilities of universal love, the healing power of the spirit, the wisdom of the universal rather than individual, mind. Christ is the state of our own possible completeness; an inner potential that can, to some degree at least, flower into outer life. He is like the image of the rose that the rose seed carries within it. It only becomes an outer reality if the rose attains its full outer stature, if it expresses outwardly its deepest tendencies and thus becomes its true self. But Christ also represents our harmony with all life, all men, all social and divine activities. This inner Christ, if we follow His lead, will take us through spiritual birth, growth, baptism, temptation, passion, crucifixion, burial, resurrection, ascension; and will be a redeeming power in our life. See *Guru*.

CHRISTEN   The inner self expressing to consciousness its true characteristics. See *Name*.

CHRYSALIS   An inner and outer inactivity, while the spirit reforms our life into a rebirth. See *Butterfly*.

CHURCH   Religious beliefs, spiritual life, search for God, journey to maturity. It sometimes represents our complete being. The building is the body; doors and windows senses; nave the general experiences and area of our life; the rail is the curtain between our outer and inner life, the altar our will turned to God, and the Holy of Holies, or Host, is our secret spirit, or God, or life in God. Also represents orthodox beliefs, the dogma of religious organisations.

CIGAR   Male sex organ, luxury, masculinity.

CIRCLE   Completeness, wholeness, all of the parts of our being, body, soul, spirit. It also represents the universe as a whole, harmony, symmetry. Sometimes symbolises an enclosure or restraining influence, or protection, and stands for the womb, or female sexual organs. May also represent emptiness, receptiveness, or a fertile condition. Or just yourself.
In dreams one often walks in a circle, or ploughs, or is moved in a circle. This means that one is enclosing, protecting or bringing the enclosed under the influence of the power that caused you to circle. Our circle of friends.

CIRCUMCISION   Cleansing of mortal tendencies.

CIRCUS   All the instinctive, physical, passionate sides of one's nature, in the circle, or under control.

CITY or TOWN   The outer self. Similar to house, but refers more to outer characteristics.

CLAM   Emotional withdrawal. Our feelings are closed up. We hide within an outer hardness or shell.

CLAY   The body; material affairs. Or yourself, shaped by events and impressions. Physical life, materialistic attitudes.

CLIFF   Fear of fall in eyes of others or self. Fall from power achievement. Fear of not being able to achieve. Sense of difficulty.

CLIMB   To rise above difficulties. To climb in social position. To achieve a new viewpoint. To learn or develop understanding.

CLOSE   To shut out, divide, not wish to know, feel or experience. Fear of being entered, fear of sex.

CLOTHES   Our opinion of and the way in which we see ourselves. Also expresses the idea of how we cloak ourselves in various attitudes, affectations, feelings and opinions; and how we disguise our real nature by dressing ourselves up as something else.
Generally a hat represents thoughts, philosophy, opinions, reasoning and logic. Shirt or blouse feelings, emotions, passions. Trousers, pants, panties, skirt, denote sexual feelings, desires. Underclothes, vest, petticoat stand for the inner self, unconscious feelings, astral body. Shoes, the general situation of our life, as I wouldn't like to be in his shoes. Down at heel. Overcoat symbolises the parts of self we show to the world in general. Gloves as protection, preventing direct contact. Raincoat, attitudes protecting us from emotion, worry, outbursts. Cuff links formality, manners, courtesy.

CLOWN   Feelings of being a fool. Readiness to be a fool for the sake of love or beliefs. Christ has thus been called a clown.

COAL   Money, good luck, energy. Ancient unconscious contents of the psyche.

COAT   See *Clothes.*

COBRA   See *Snake.*

COCK   Warning, aggressiveness, masculinity, male organ.

COFFEE   Many drinks represent a stimulus similar to alcohol, with its property of changing consciousness. They release energy, emotions, change feelings, and can thus be associated with spirit, or the power behind human growth, that changes our consciousness of things. May also represent sociability, friendship, the giving of affection. See *Alcohol*.

COFFIN   Death and rebirth. See *Death*.

COIN   See *Bank*. Sometimes a coin has similar symbolism to circle. Other times represents same as badge. Where it is rusty and corroded, some see it as suggestion of past lives, and deeds done, the effects of which now have to be dealt with, where a problem we face may be the consequence of activities not of this life, but a previous one.

COLD   Frozen or withheld emotions.

COLOUR   Shades of feeling, attitudes of mind. Red, is passion, anger, physical desire, energy. Light red, affection, warmth, life. Orange, is enthusiasm, youthfulness, idealism. Dark orange, cynicism, bias, lack of interest. Yellow, wisdom, life energy, thought, justice, balance.
Green, is growth, nature, receptiveness, virginity. Dark green, envy, loathing, degeneracy.
Blue, is religious feelings, healing, spiritual aims, cosmic energy. Indigo, mystical abilities, spiritual insight, maturity. Violet, guru, mastership, the central self.

COMB   See *Hair*.

COMET   Sign of coming inner changes, new influences from within, birth of new self.

COMIC   Sense of humour; to be taken lightly, not serious.

COMPASS   One's sense of true self expression, one's most fulfilling direction in life. The ability to continue in the face of opposition and confusing outer events.

COMPLEXION How you appear to others. A sense of how we look to other people.

COMPOST The irritating useless, outgrown parts of self, the energies of which can be re-used once the habitual methods of expressing them have broken down.

COMRADE See *Friend*.

CONDUCTOR As man, similar to admiral. As electrical conductor, receptive side of self directing energy. Nervous system.

CONFESSION Admitting to self and to God, what we feel is wrong within.

CONJURER Self deceptions, or deception of others.

CONSTIPATION Inner tension, withholding of feelings, lack of self expression or self esteem.

CONTORTIONIST Mental emotional fluidity, wide compass.

CONTRACEPTIVE See *Castrate*.

CONVENT See *Church*.

CONVICT Anti-social desires and energies. Fear of recrimination. Imprisonment of some of our feelings.

COOK The attempt to make life experience palatable. The means of dealing with life, in the sense of adjusting to it. Also, see *Alchemist, Oven*.

COPPER (Metal) Love, enlightenment, promise of life.

CORAL Beautiful inner experience, ideas, inspirations, or intuitions.

CORD   Like chain, but sometimes suggests the weaving together of many smaller interests to one purpose, for strength. When all energies are linked in a common purpose, we express tremendous strength and power not found when interests are scattered and dispersed, or dissipated.

CORE   See *Centre*.

CORK   Confidence, perseverance, high spiritedness, the ability to rise above circumstances, or win through troubles.

CORMORANT   Intellectual ideas that have the power to dig deep and bring up unconscious wisdom. Knowledge of dreams is a conscious thing that can bring to awareness inner truths.

CORN   Material experience that brings spiritual growth or realisation. Trial may develop patience and forbearance for instance. Physical or worldly experience, but full of possible lessons. Can also represent the harvest of activities or efforts. Sustenance or strength in times of need or trial.

CORNER   Change of direction, meeting place, turning point in your attitudes, or approach to something.

CORPSE   Some feeling, such as sympathy, forgiveness, that we have deadened. We may say, Why should I forgive them, they don't deserve it, and this attitude can prevent parts of our inner feelings living or expressing consciously. Fear of death; desire to see someone dead, or out of the way. See *Death*.

CORRIDOR   The general direction of your life. Sexual intercourse; female sex organs.

CORSET   See *Armour*.

COSMETIC   The mask we wear in hiding our true feelings, thoughts, from others. Our attempts not to see ourselves as we are, or not to face facts. Or femininity.

COUSIN   Possibly represents your opinions or feelings about that person.

COW   Femininity, motherhood, female sexual feelings.

CRAB   Fear or strong emotion causing tension within, especially abdominally. This may be due to fear or guilt of sensual pleasure. It may also represent outer hardness or cynicism covering inner softness; or outer hardness and graspingness in life. A desire to cause pain to others.

CRACK   Female organs. Broken resolves; chink in our armour; fear of breaking under stress. Or beginning of recognition of a way to deal with something, to crack the problem.

CRANE   Soul, spiritual wisdom, luck. The ability to deal harmoniously with the libido or energy within.

CRATER   Memory of old hurt, old emotion or pain, or frightening situation. If it is volcanic, a crack in the outer self, through which inner repressed passions are pouring out.

CREAM   Best of life, luxury, special treatment, affection.

CREEPER   Doubts, insinuations, stagnancy, vegetating.

CRESCENT   Symbol of femininity, intuition, female sex organs, receptiveness.

CRICKET   See *Billiards*.

CRIPPLE   See *Leg*, and *Right* or *Left*.

CROCODILE   See *Alligator*.

CROSS   This symbol is so vast, so world wide, so ancient in man's unconscious, that it is difficult to deal with. It has been used by phehistoric man, all religions practically, and in all parts of the world. Starting with its most popular uses, it represents a difficulty

216

or problem we have, The cross we have to bear. In the sense of a problem, having a tick is right, a cross is wrong. The cross in common use also signifies completion or finality, even death; for we cross something off a list when checked or finished.

At a deeper level it signifies the meeting of the negative and positive, the male and female, or God and matter. The vertical stroke stands for the descending or ascending power. The cross beam acts as the plane of limitation, reception. The upright beam is male, the cross beam female. In this way also it is used to symbolise man's nature. The cross beam is the body, the earthly self, mother of God. The upright is the spirit or God, that acts on the body, enters it as a womb, so to speak, and manifests man's consciousness as an individual. This sense of self, or individuality is represented by the point where the two beams meet.

The Rosicrucians, who use the cross with a rose at the centre, speak of it as symbolising the trials and difficulties of life, upon which the soul personality of man opens and blooms like a rose.

In Christianity the cross also has many meanings. It represents the religion as a whole; Christ's suffering; man's suffering in the name of his religious beliefs; the strength of his beliefs; a sign of spiritual goodness and power to ward off evil. It also means the agony faced in surrendering individual will to the will of God.

At a deeper level still, it symbolises the way in which our outer, egoistic self crucifies and murders the beauty, love and wisdom of the spiritual nature within. It represents the gentleness, long suffering, willingness to bear this tragedy and pain, in order to eventually redeem and spiritualise the outer self through its blood, or life. It expresses the way God gives His very being that we may experience life; and our life is His death, for we forget our true self in our sense of individuality and materiality. Thus the cross represents the illusion, the maya, of the worldly; the transgressions due to the ignorance through illusion, upon which the God in us is nailed and killed, to be born again : and because of this the cross represents life as well as death, growth and renewal, as well as degeneration and decomposition. Lastly, it symbolises perfect union, balance, equality and atonement of the different parts of man's being.

CROSSROAD   Decision; convergence of different desires, and the need to choose a direction. A turning point in life. Or it may represent a sense of indecision, a fear of not doing the right thing. See *North, East, South, West*.

CROW   Fear of death, bad luck, or failure. Sometimes interpreted as warning of death, marriage, or important and difficult events.

CROWD   A crowd in a drama usually means it is an important dream, for all the many parts of self are involved in its subject.

CROWN   Initiation, enlightenment, father.

CRUCIBLE   The centre of our turmoil, tension or spiritual life. In it our nature is changed.

CRUCIFIXION   See *Cross*.

CRUTCH   Substitute, sense of incapacity. Something we use or do because the real thing is not functioning. As alcohol which may be a crutch.

CRYING   The release of sorrow, grief, misery, that has been held back, knowingly or unknowingly, during the day. It may be an intuitive knowledge of another leaving us, or dying, or sorrow over something we have done. Or else they may be crocodile tears in an attempt to convince ourselves that we feel badly over an attitude, desire or action.

CRYPT   See *Cave* or *Basement*. But connected more with repressed parts of self, or other incarnations, or unconscious fear of death, or unconscious dreads.

CRYSTAL   A crystalline form is often a symbol of the Self, the whole being, or the basis or spirit of our being. It has connections with the cross symbolism where it represents wholeness, unity and balance. The shape of the dead matter of the crystal, in its beautiful structure, arises through the workings of some inner force, or power, invisible, but evident in the symmetry of the crystal. So it symbolises the hidden inner power active upon our outer, material life. A crystal may also represent realisation, i.e. It became crystal clear. The crystal ball usually stands for prophecy, the future, our hopes and plans, fate, intuition, gazing into self. And can, because of its shape, denote the self, or completeness. See *Jewels*.

CUBE   Matter, physical existence. It is symbolic of the number 4, and thus stands for stability, strength, material expression, the body. The square or cube is an enclosure in three dimensions, like our body, that in its centre hides a fourth dimension, the soul. Can also represent orthodoxy, the establishment. See *Numbers*.

CUCKOO   Sexual promiscuity, the egg laid in another nest or woman.

CUDDLE   Unity, sharing of feelings.

CUL-DE-SAC   This has definite sexual implications, usually representing the inside of a woman's legs. In this dream, one knocks at the door at the far end. But this represents an unlawful, guilt laden, no way through, sexual experience or desire. There is no way out of it. It also represents, on a more general level, a direction leading to barriers, no way of further expression, a pointless effort.

CUP   In Christianity this is the vessel, or receptive womb, that receives the blood of Christ, or life, or spirit. Thus it represents the soul, the world of inner feelings, hopes, desires; especially if the soul is made receptive to the inner self, or life experience. It also represents femininity, or prayer. We see that in the sayings, our cup overflows, or cup of suffering, it represents all the inner contents, held within the self or soul. The latent tendencies within us. Also, Jesus says, Father, if thou be willing, remove this cup from me. Here again it represents experiences, trials, new spiritual consciousness in store.

CURRENT   The outer flow of circumstances or events as they act upon us and influence or pull us along. The inner pressure of desires, the direction of the inner life, or influence of inner tendencies.

CURSE   Autosuggestion. That is, inner results of fears entertained. Also symbolises the inheritance of past actions, past lives, or hereditary traits or taints. It sometimes refers to the power of material values to influence decisions and life.

CUTTING   To sever connections, to cut off sympathy or affections. Also to injure, or desire to injure. It may represent our sexual desires, that through the pain associated with experiences of being let down, scorned, ill treated, the feelings of love only express as the desire to hurt, to cut, to enter through pain. Can also mean reducing in importance or impact.

CYST   A morbid collection of memories, emotions, energies, that are not harmonizing or adding to life in general.

D
Being fourth, D relates to the Hebrew Daleth, 4th in their alphabet. It represents nourishment, from which can spring growth.

DAGGER   Aggressive urges, hatred, expression of force whether intellectual, moral or physical. Can denote male sex organ.

DALAI LAMA   See *Guru*.

DAM   Repression of emotions, damming up of feelings.

DANCE   Spontaneous expression of inner feelings. Also can express, in harmonious movements, contact with the divine.

DARK   Lack of understanding; difficult to grasp, obscure. See *Black*. A woman with dark hair sometimes represents the intuitive function, as she is intellectually dark, or unconscious. Similarly, a dark skinned person in a dream often represents parts of self that are difficult to understand, and are obscure in the way in which they influence our life. See *Aborigine*.

DARN   Healing of parts of your nature symbolised by the object being darned. Also a careful, saving attitude.

DART   Hurtful thought, hatefulness, aggressive sexuality.

DAWN Beginning of understanding, illumination, realisation and spiritual life manifesting consciously.

DAY Consciousness. Period of life that can begin and end.

DEAF Expressive of a desire not to know what is happening within. Or the fear of hearing things we feel would hurt, or to learn things about self we do not wish to face.

DEATH All physical manifestation, as well as parts of our soul experience, go through cycles of change. The beginning of a new physical form, or soul experience, is really due to already existing materials being grouped in a new way. This we call birth. This new order of things then matures in the sense that it expresses the innate qualities and characteristics latent in this new order of being. Maturity lies in the flowering of this expression, and thus the realization of possibilities. But anything that depends upon the grouping of many materials, goes through change, and if these changes become vast, then the thing breaks up into new forms, or breaks down into basic components. This we call death. That is, the death of one mode of expression. But all through nature, the death of one form only leads to the producing of materials ready for new forms. Or else a vital element of the old form, that synthesises within it all the experiences of the old, breaks away as the old form goes through vital change, and builds up a new one, which is modified by the past experience. This we see in the seed, the sperm, social break-down and social development, and in the spirit, carrying vital experience into new life. Thus, death has the outer aspect, the break-down of the matured form, and the inner aspect, the vital seed carrying past experience into a new expression. So death in a dream can apply not only to our personality as a whole, but also to our beliefs, hopes, plans, relationships, past experience, business, creativeness, illness, family and love.

DEBIT Past actions and thoughts that have not harmonised with your spirit. See *Bill*.

DEBT Similar to debit, but can also express the idea of not living up to the mark. Not giving to others what they, in their life, have given to you.

DECAY   Inner rottenness. See *Cesspool*.

DECOY   Means we employ to lead others to believe something we really do not feel, or think. A self deception of what we feel, as a man, because a job offers a high wage, may lead himself to believe he likes the work, but who inwardly hates it.

DEEP   Within ourselves, the unconscious, your past; something deep in you that thereby affects your whole nature. Very wide meaning.

DEER   The soul, the gentle harmless self that is often hurt or wounded by our aggressiveness and cynicism; or by other people's criticism.

DEFORMITY   Part of your nature, that due to fear, repression or ignorance has not been able to grow in its natural beauty.

DELAY   Putting things off. Unwillingness to make a decision, or confront or acknowledge that which is symbolised in dream.

DELL   A quiet retreat within ourselves. Female sexual organs.

DELUGE   An overpowering release of emotions, as experienced in nervous breakdown or shock.

DELVE   To explore memories, past experiences, inner contents, underlying feelings. See *Earth*.

DEMOLISH   The breakdown of ideas, philosophies, emotional attitudes, or ways of life in which we have been established. The threat to hopes we have cherished. The feeling that some other person is undermining us by criticism, arrogance, antagonism or aggressiveness.

DEMON   Expression of things in life and self that threaten to possess us or influence us in a way we believe to be, though it might in fact not be, sinful, awful, hateful or filthy. Thus, a person who has terrible feelings of guilt about sexual feelings, may represent sexual

222

urges as a demon threatening to possess them or destroy their soul. Therefore a demon may represent guilt, hatred, feelings of uncleanness, aggressiveness or desire for love, and so on. See *Devil, Satan*.

DENTIST   May represent fear of pain. Or else the care we must take of that which comes via the mouth, the things we say, opinions expressed, anger. See *Teeth*.

DEPTH   See *Deep*.

DERELICT   Parts of self you have not taken care of, or not used, or have used badly.

DESCENT   To regress into earlier, more youthful ways of looking at things, or behaviour. A period of depression, or feeling low. A fear of falling or descending from favour, power or authority. Coming down to earth from a more idealistic, fanciful, or visionary viewpoint.

DESECRATE   To belittle or scoff at our deepest intuitions about the purpose of our life, our spiritual directions, our deepest feelings and needs. It is to deny ourselves things for which we may deeply hunger in an inner sense.

DESERT   A lack of feeling; intellectual aridity, scepticism, doubts. A lack of certainty about self, life, the future. The wilderness with which outer life seems to present us, creating a terrible thirst and hunger for certainty and real experience of our inner being. In the desert these desires, and the aridity, cause us to see mirages, or illusions. So the desert represents all the so called logical, intellectual, arid opinions, beliefs, speculations and biases men hold on to when they lack true inner knowledge and certainty. It also represents the actions and thoughts that arise in our lives from such beliefs and opinions. These cause nothing living or carrying real satisfaction, to grow in our lives. It may also represent feelings of isolation, of being deserted, of hopelessness and loneliness, of nothing to live for.

DESK   See *Table*.

DETHRONE   To overcome the restraints put on our nature by fear of punishment, or loss of love and respect from mother or father.

DEVIL   All those desires, ideas, habits, that have come into our life, that go against the promptings of our deepest nature. All the aspects of life of which we are not master and which can therefore influence us against our will. For instance, we may not be master of anger, emotions, hungers, ambitions, and these may lead us to do things that deep down we do not wish to do. While the results of these tendencies may seem devilish, at the same time they offer the opportunity of wrestling with them and developing spiritual power and consciousness. See *Demon* and *Satan* and *Obsession*.

DIADEM   Spiritual consciousness.

DIAMOND   See *Jewels*.

DIARY   Memories, the inner self.

DICE   Fate, chance, luck, a gamble.

DIE   See *Death*.

DIG   See *Delve*.

DIGEST   To absorb, to make use of, to understand and incorporate into your way of life. To accept. See *Food*.

DINNER   See *Food*.

DIRT   The sense of what is unclean, or of being unclean in mind or body. We have to realise however that dirt is only misplaced earth, which can form the material for growing vital things. See *Earth*.

DISAPPEAR   To forget, to lose sight of something. Or it may express a hope to be rid of that thing. At another level, as with Jesus disappearing, it can symbolise spiritual power over the body, or material life.

DISINFECTANT This has been used in dreams to represent the power of healing, of cleansing fear, or feelings of filth and guilt. It is sometimes linked with pain, or burning as a cleansing power. That is, the painful experiences of life have a healing power in themselves, due to the way in which they force attention to the cause of pain, and make us adjust, or let go of emotions, desires and attitudes that have caused trouble, but which we would never have let go of otherwise.

DISC See *Circle.*

DISSECTION Intellectual enquiry that lacks feeling and sympathy.

DIVINING ROD Intuitive realisation of inner self. Or intuitive directions.

DIZZY The Sense of balance, of relationship with others, and the world, is out of order. Fear of falling, sense of strain, or being on the edge of falling in love, out of love, or into inner consciousness.

DOCTOR The healing forces of your being. Also inner wisdom, self knowledge. See *Guru.* May also represent fear of illness or death.

DOCUMENT Usually some important idea, or important information about oneself.

DOG Used in a number of ways. May represent faithfulness, doggedness, a dirty dog, or unclean feelings or urges, usually of sexual nature. Is often used to represent a person who threatens us or attacks us emotionally as a father or marriage partner, who shouts, barks and rages, or shows their teeth at us. In this case it refers more to feelings induced by the attack. Or it can symbolise, depending upon the dream content, your own feelings of anger and aggression.
The dog is generally thought of as a male creature, quite different to the femininity of cats. It thus stands for male sexuality and adventurousness or aggressiveness. As it sees in the dark, and has keen ears, it is sometimes used as a symbol of instinctive or intuitive

knowledge. The dog here also represents the instinctive life. That is, the person who lives without much feeling or thought, like an animal. In some dreams, the dog is used in a similar way to the Egyptian symbology, as a guide into the unconscious, or land of the Dead.

DOLPHIN   See *Fish*.

DONKEY   See *Ass*.

DOOR   When one door closes, another opens. Opportunity, the openings life offers. Also represents an inner opening or realisation of new parts of self, new feelings, new ideas. The door can also represent a barrier put between yourself and others, yourself and life, yourself and God. The opening or closing of this door represents the movement of your feelings and attitudes. Death is sometimes spoken of as the other door, birth being the first.

DOT   An end or a beginning. A point or centre of consciousness; as a collection of activities may centre around one desire, or thought, one aim. Also, the Self.

DOUGH   Money. The possibilities in us.

DOVE   Realisation of the internal nature. Peace, love.

DRAGON   Materialism. See *Snake*, *Fish*.

DREAMING   To dream that you are dreaming can mean a lack of attention to everyday affairs. Can symbolise a contact with innermost contents of your being.

DRESS   See *Clothes*.

DRINK   Connected with the feeling of thirsting or longing. It denotes satisfaction of longings, either emotionally, physically or spiritually.

DRUM   Heart, pulse, unifying power. Or masturbation.

DUCK   See *Cormorant*.

DUMB   Inability to express inner feelings.

DUNG   See *Cesspool* and *Faeces*.

DUST   Ideas; thoughts or ideas that can be lifted up by our inner nature. Or ideas without feeling, dried up.

DUSTBIN   Ideas or feelings that things are valueless, without meaning.

DUTCH   Practicality, efficiency, capability.

DWARF   Unconscious forces, or the powers that work on our being to keep it functioning. Snow White meets seven basic forces, or levels of consciousness that work in the mine, transmuting matter to energy, awareness, emotion.
A dwarf may also represent a part of the self that has been held back in development due to fear or guilt. If we dream we are a dwarf it expresses the idea of being small, insignificant, undeveloped.

DYING   See *Death*.

DYNAMITE   See *Bomb*. Material force.

E

The fifth letter of the Hebrew alphabet is He, and stands for the inspiration of breath as a means of maintaining life, breath being the mediator between spirit and body.

EAGLE   The eagle represents the ability of the soul, the inner feelings and thoughts, to fly above the material world from which they were born. It can also symbolise the devouring or terrible power of our inner life to carry us away. This means that urges of an uplifting nature can be terrifying due to the threat of being carried into the unknown, into a new element, into new worlds, which we have no conscious wish to explore. If we relate well and fearlessly to these inner urges, then we can feel protected or uplifted by them instead of threatened. The eagle also represents royalty, power, freedom and farsightedness.

EAR   Receptiveness of your feelings and self.

EARTH   All the things of a material nature that rise from earth. Earth is, by itself, inert and unconscious, and it can therefore represent these parts or tendencies of yourself. But the earth is receptive, nurturing and maternal. It is mother earth, from whose body all living forms have arisen. It constantly gives of its substance to maintain us, and it receives back from us what we do not need, such as our faeces, and our body at death. So the earth also represents the past, the fallen leaves of our experience from which soil, new structures of self are built. Digging into the earth is digging into your history, and in its layers you find the story of the evolution of consciousness and life in matter or mother. To come up out of the earth, or a grave, is to be born out of this mother's womb, into spiritual life. Thus Jesus is buried and resurrected from a tomb. While it is our Father, energy or spirit who gives us fire and drive in life, it is Mother Earth, or experience and physical sensation in the body with all its limitations, who gives us substance, form, direction for our energies. She also gives us humility and humanity, two rare gifts.

EAST   The spiritual quarter of your life where the Sun, symbol of life and spirit rises. It represents all pertaining to the inner self regarding its mystical spiritual nature. Symbolises the mystery of life. The East stands for rebirth due to the Sun rising; resurrection from ignorance or darkness. It is the seat of the spirit and the teachings concerning your immortal self.

EAT   See *Food*.

ECHO   Inner response from outer action. Hate influences glands and functions negatively; the acceptance of ideas makes their influence powerful. If I believe I am a fool, it is difficult not to act like one.

ECSTACY   Reflects a state of being completely in accord and harmony. There are no discords, conflicts, or divisions of self. This is different to elation, which may be experiencing one sphere of the emotions.

EDEN   To be in accordance with the spiritual nature, but unconscious of self as an individual. Can also symbolise purity, simplicity, happiness.

EEL   Male sex organ. See *Fish*.

EGG   Do not put all your eggs in one basket. Eggs are possibilities, things that can develop and grow if nurtured. Latent abilities and tendencies, good and bad. Also represent hopes. Eggs have also been used since ancient times to represent man's complete nature. In this case it is similar to chrysalis as described. The egg of time.

EGYPT   Worldly experience. The Fleshpots, the unconscious or psychic self.

ELASTIC   The ability to adapt.

ELBOW   A support. An idea or hope, giving support or flexibility in expression.

ELECTRICITY   The inner power of spirit. Energy, power.

ELEPHANT   Sexual intercourse, or sex energy under the direction of spirit. Also symbolises our cosmic, eternal nature. The tremendous inner power of the unconscious, with a mahout, or conscious direction or co-operation can achieve wonderful things. Ganesh, the Indian God represents the remover of all obstacles, the power of spirit manifesting.

ELF   A force active in nature. See *Dwarf*.

EMBALM   The attempt to prolong the present form of beliefs and feelings, despite the fact that life has moved on, and is attempting to express in new ways. Fear of death. Desire for physical immortality.

EMBRACE See *Cuddle*.

EMBRYO Something developing in the unconscious. Something growing within which we are not yet aware of and not yet sufficiently developed to express outwardly. Or a regression to early levels of consciousness. A desire to live in womb-consciousness.

EMERALD See *Jewels*.

EMIGRATION The changing of habits, ideas. The search for self. A change of life.

ENCHANT Being under an influence that is not really an expression of self. We may try to emulate another person because they enchant us.

ENCIRCLE See *Circle*.

ENCYCLOPAEDIA Memory, inner knowledge.

ENEMA May be a memory of infant experiences that has left terrors within. Inner cleansing of unnecessary material and outworn habits.

ENGLAND Obstinacy. Earthiness, persistence, outer creativeness. Lacking expression of emotion.

ENVELOPE The body, surroundings, protection.

EPILEPSY Repression of energy or self expression, often of a sexual nature, that is trying to realise itself but is being resisted. Thus, instead of orgasm and rhythmic body movements, there is pain and disordered movement. Inner tension.

ERUPTION A breaking into consciousness of repressed urges, fears, terrors.

EUNUCH Without sexual feelings. Sexuality has been cut off. See *Castration*.

EVE   The power of sensual seduction. Eve stands for the soul or personality. Also feelings, femininity, or the receptiveness of your feelings to sensations and thus to temptations. She can also represent a man's wife; or in another sense his emotional sexual relationships with her. Eve, originally, meant will power within man, which through the ability to choose between an action in harmony or out of harmony with spirit, brought about self consciousness, or individuality. For before Eve, or will power, man lived in harmony with God or Spirit, but did so because he had no will of his own. This is why Eve can represent temptation, and through will you can make a decision. So she also represents decision.

EVERGREEN   Symbolises the eternal as it expresses through matter with its quality of constant change.

EXCRETA   See *Faeces*.

EXECUTION   See *Death*.

EXPLOSION   May represent anger. See *Eruption, Dynamite*.

EXUDE   Sometimes symbolises the emotions we express outwardly to others, often unconsciously.

EYE   Our intelligence and ability to see things. Consciousness and knowledge, curiosity. Sometimes used as word play instead of I. In such cases it often represents your looking at yourself, an eye looking at I. Many eyes is a recognised symbol for greater awareness, intuition, psychic impressions and spiritual consciousness.

F

The sixth Hebrew letter is Vau, which represents the eye, light and brilliancy. It thus symbolises our connection, emotionally, intellectually and sensually, with the world outside us. The Vau is the link between outer and inner, darkness and light, ignorance and understanding.

FACADE   In some house dreams, great stress is given to the front or façade of the house. Sometimes it crumbles away revealing what is within; sometimes it is painted or changed, and so on. The façade thus represents the front shown to the world, the social self that may hide quite a different interior.

FACE   Similar to façade, but in dreams it often symbolises an outer expression of inner feelings, sometimes unconscious. But it usually represents the part seen by others, whether you are aware of it or not. It can also mean that you are faced with something, or some problem, are in confrontation with it.

FACTORY   The habitual, mass produced reactions to life lacking individuality. Productiveness, industry; inner physical activities such as digestion.

FAECES   Children have great interest and satisfaction in their faeces. It is something they have produced and created; something visible that has come out of them. Dreams often use faeces in mysterious ways, and we have to look to folklore and human experience to understand. Apart from the meaning mentioned under Cesspool, that is, the corruptible parts of human nature that become manure for new growth, faeces can also represent money or riches, fertility. Many mystics or philosophers have had monumental visions, realisations or even religious experiences, while in the lavatory. In folklore donkeys pass gold pieces instead of faeces; or to step in faeces means good luck.
In another sense, to pass faeces with feelings of relief means to be rid of worrying burdensome feelings, of tension, or sexual repression. While to be covered in faeces may suggest a fear of being outwardly repulsive. To play with faeces is a return to infantile behaviour; but it may develop in the dream into a question of what to do with them, or how to use them. This is the beginning of using our basic, earthly nature, to creative ends and the shaping of self.

FAINT   See *Dizzy*.

FAIR (Hair)   Your conscious thoughts. See *Hair*.

FAIRY   Nature spirit, or nature forces, such as electricity, gravity, cohesion, magnetism. The unconscious tends to express such forces pictorially as ideas are portrayed in most dreams.

FAKIR   The irrational rather than reasonable self. The part of you that does things for no logical reason. See *Guru*.

FALL   To fall from certainty about things, fall in your own opinion of self, fall in faith, in power, in favour. Falling in love. Fear of not being in control.

FARM   The cultivation of self, of the personality. The turning from man made laws, society, opinions, ways of life, to a natural inner conditioned growth or relationship with self. Being in a farmyard usually represents efforts to deal with the sensual, aggressive, or animalistic urges. Or it shows your relationship with these parts of your nature.

FAST   To refrain from eating is to refrain from taking into yourself material opinions, ideas, ways of life. It is to concentrate your attention upon your own personal inner life and its growth. To refrain from acting from your desires, hungers, greed, ambition, sensuousness, and to allow the spirit to direct these faculties and harmonise your energies and cleanse you of error and sickness.

FAT   Too much emphasis on material values. Weighted down by cares. Or jollity, sensuality.

FATE   Results of your forgotten actions, or unconscious nature.

FATHER   Either represents your relationship with your father, or the characteristics in your nature that have arisen from this relationship; or can represent God in the positive, energetic, constructive and creative aspect. (See *Mother*.) Can also stand for a teacher, or person by whom we are much influenced. Or else your own positive, protective qualities. Spirit.

FAUN   See *Fairy*.

FEAR   To feel fear in a dream means that you have not yet

233

developed abilities to cope with what is symbolised as causing the fear. One of the wonderful things about dreams is that they gradually show us how to deal with these parts of our nature, how to release the love or courage or wisdom that enables us to face the fear and in fact, gain power and instruction from it.

FEAST   See *Food.*

FEATHER   A thought, an aspiration or ideal. Or an incrimination, white feather. Sometimes a symbol of achievement as a feather in your cap, or as used by Indian chiefs to represent courageous deeds or help given to the tribe.

FEE   The price to be paid. For instance, the price of maturity is greater responsibility. Or the price we have to pay for living inharmoniously with our innate nature is sickness or unhappiness. There is a Spanish saying, Take what you want in life, and pay for it. The fee can therefore symbolise what you will have to pay for your desires, aims and activities.

FELLOWSHIP   Unity between varying parts of yourself such as intellect, emotions, senses, sex. For often our reason does not agree with our passions, and our emotions lead us differently to our spirit.

FEMALE   Anything receptive, that can be entered, that receives, gives of itself in the union, allows the relationship to take of its substance. Or that which nurtures and encourages growth through surrender of its substance, self interest, feelings or even life. A female in dreams usually represents the more emotional, intuitive, irrational part of self. If it is someone you know, she probably symbolises your opinion and feelings about her, or what she has made you feel.

FEMUR   Strength, support, power.

FENCE   A barrier. Difficulty in self. It is either something which bars your progress or expression, or is used as a protection from things outside the self, from things getting at you. Or you can sit on the fence, in an attempt to avoid decision or action.

FERRET Inquisitiveness, sexual forcefulness that can injure another person's feelings. The ability to ferret out things from the unconscious, but usually through force or fear or by denying other feelings.

FERRY Often connected with death or a new spiritual life. The means of crossing over emotions that barred progress or development, such as a child's feeling of being dependant on its parents.

FEVER May be a sign of bad health, or symbol of great stress and emotion that in its intensity is burning out its own causes, and thus ridding you of the worries or insecurities that produced it.

FIDDLE You can fiddle about and so do nothing constructive; be on the fiddle and so be attempting to cheat; play second fiddle or first fiddle and thus realise how we feel about a relationship. Can also represent sexual intercourse, or even masturbation.

FIELD Particular area of your life, particular interests, in your own field. Activities in which one is most capable.

FIG Uncaring, I don't give a fig. Also, as a deeper symbol, Jesus cursed the fig tree, and it is said that when it buds it will foretell the end; when it bears fruit it will be the time for the second advent. The fig tree here represents feminine, intuitive faculty, the soul, that has turned to the world instead of to spirit. Thus is it cursed and does not bear fruit, it is barren as our life and society must be. Anna Kingsford says 'The fig is the similitude of the matrix, containing inward buds, bearing blossoms on its placenta, and bringing forth fruit in darkness. It is the cup of life, and its flesh is the seed-ground of new births. The stems of the fig tree run like milk; her leaves are as human hands. Like the leaves of her brother the vine.'

FIGHT Inner conflict. Disagreement between parts of self.

FILTH See *Cesspool* and *Faeces*.

FINGER Fingers can be expressive of your feelings. It can be the

235

finger of scorn; accusing finger; finger of suspicion; beckoning finger, or to put your finger on it. Fingers represent your grasp on things, your method of materialising yourself, or leaving your mark upon matter. The finger print also denotes your uniqueness. The finger can represent the penis, as is common use in sexplay : or your means of sensing, or fingering things.

FIRE   Can represent burning love, fiery passion, emotional fever, pain or purification. Fire is a tremendous energy that man learnt to use in his infancy. But like all energies, it can warm, produce power, purify, bring about chemical change; or it can consume, destroy, injure, run amuck. It is therefore often used as a symbol for our relationship with our internal energy, of libido or spirit. Also can stand for suffering of a mental or spiritual nature, that purifies one. Or signifies the destruction released spirit creates on barriers opposing it. But when all evil, sin or materiality is consumed, the fire, or suffering dies out. Therefore, to throw yourself, or something, into the fire, is to expose it to this transmuting influence. Thus Hell is pictured as with flames, purifying error and sin which are the actions or attitudes inharmonious to your innate nature.
To use this fire for man's own ends, in mythology, has often produced terrible guilt or reactions probably because it shows a selfish expression of the life-giving energy. Can also be warning of illness.

FIREMAN   Represents those qualities capable of dealing with your energies or burning desires.

FISH   One can fish for compliments or information, or something can be fishy, not quite right. Fish have a sexual significance also, and may represent fertility, pre-natal experience, or life in the waters of the womb. In the Christian mysteries the fish signifies Christ or spiritual truths. Fishes symbolise the ideas, feelings, treasures or sustenance of our inner, unconscious life. They represent the living processes of thought and feeling that go on under the surface. To fish is therefore to seek and bring to light, our inner feelings, or spiritual realisation. To be swallowed by a fish, as was Jonah, and other legendary heroes, represents a period of terrific, and sometimes terrifying, introversion. At such times we see under the waters of the unconscious, and know what it is like to go mad, but if the quest is spiritual with surrender to God's will, or the direction of your spirit, then you survive this irrational state, as Jonah did, and are vomited up on dry land, or conscious rationalism again. The difference is that you have seen the inner world, and felt the power of the Lord to lead you through terror and trial.

FIST   Graspingness, selfishness, anger, arrogance, aggressiveness, tension.

FIT   See *Epileptic.*

FIVE   See *Numbers.*

FLESH   See *Meat.*

FLOAT   To be moved by passing feelings instead of by inner purpose. To be hopeful and buoyant.

FLOCKS   Aspects of self gathered and cared for by spirit. Or to follow blindly.

FLOOD   See *Deluge.*

FLOOR   Your support, your physical life. You can be floored or overcome, lying on the floor representing being overpowered by gravity and the material life. Basic things. Humility.

FLOWER   Growing or growth, the opening out of abilities or feelings, as in flowering. Can stand for a centre of consciousness, or faculty of consciousness, like the Chakras of Indian philosophy. Also beauty, love, emotions. Flowers are used to express your feelings, as in giving red roses. And to lose virginity is called defloration.

FLUID   See *Water.*

FLUTE   Harmony of the soul, harmony of our feelings. The expression of spirit upon the faculties of our soul. This is symbolised by the wind or spirit, creating sound or feelings, through the flute or self. Some folklore and mystics say that God plays us like a flute. It can also, due to its shape, have a sexual significance.

FLYING This has many levels of significance, depending on the dream. It can mean we are flying or fleeing, from something we wish to avoid. This is usually something in our life we try to get away from by becoming over idealistic, religious, or living in the clouds of fantasy. In flight we do not have our feet on the ground and so must be careful not to fall. The climbing of a mountain in a dream provides the middle way between rising, yet keeping our feet on the ground. Flying suggests the desire to rise above things, to attain greater heights, to reach the realm of the spirit. Freud explained all flying dreams as expressive of sexual desires, intercourse, or life in the womb, which in some cases is true. But flying also represents ambition, abstract thought, and rising above our fears. Flying, in a plane, or without it, can also symbolise attempts to gain a view of what lies ahead of us in our development in life and spirit. From the air we can see ahead, and back. We quickly review where we are heading, and the possibilities of our earthly journey. Thus we may fly and see the mountain top to which we aspire. Then, knowing its view and wonder, we can ascend from the valley more certain that it can be attained.

FOG Uncertainty, mental ignorance, inability to see ahead, or understand. It also represents an inner condition of mental stagnation. Befogged by too many intellectual queries, doubts or objections. May also show your desire to hide your real motives behind a fog of self deceit.

FOLIAGE Ideas.

FOOD This can symbolise anything upon which we depend to sustain or strengthen us. Thus it can represent the food of love, religious faith, assurance, or security. To eat excessively may represent a hunger for affection, self confidence, sex, recognition. It may hide a fear or feeling of loneliness and emptiness. It can also denote the things we have to experience. One man's meat, food or life, is another man's poison. Therefore it can symbolise a need for satisfaction in some sphere, or the realisation that something sickens us. Food is the building material of the body, and can be the symbol for experience, which is the building material of our soul. Food or eating thus plays a large part in the ceremonies of many religions.

FOOT   The foundation upon which your life is built. The foot can symbolise beliefs, upon which your actions are built; your basic feelings, upon which your love rests, and so on. Also your direction, the way you are going. Kissing the foot shows it as a symbol of lowliness, earthiness. Putting your feet up gives the foot the meaning of labour, of work. See *Left* and *Right*.

FORCE   To use force in a dream usually means we are trying so to direct ourselves that much of our nature cannot naturally comply. Also an expression of hate, aggressiveness, energy, etc.

FORD   A practical way through emotions.

FOREST   See *Tree*.

FORGE   See *Blacksmith*.

FORGERY   A lie. Deceit.

FOX   Cunning wisdom. Instinctive knowledge.

FRANCE   Pleasure loving, exuberant, emotional, changeable.

FREEZE   To repress emotions. To become cold emotionally. To need affection or warmth. To be unfeeling, but sometimes painfully unfeeling.

FRIEND   Your feelings about this friend. If the dream friend is no one you know then usually represents the inner intuitive feelings that encourage and advise you. Or relates to your contact with friends.

FROG   In folklore the frog has been a bewitched prince or princess. It also is often the carrier of unusual knowledge. It symbolises unconscious knowledge, the power of transmutation or change, like the tadpole which only lives in water, or emotion and the unconscious, and changes to a frog; ancient mysteries, strange inner power, cold bloodedness, and evil caused by the latter.

FRONT   Conscious, known, as seen by world.

FUEL   Experiences you have not yet understood or made use. Knowledge you have not applied. Energy, resources.

FUNERAL   See *Death*.

FUNGUS   Disease. Sick ideas, emotions.

FUR   Animalistic, instinctive, sexual.

FURNITURE   Your inner contents, beliefs, opinions, attitudes.

FUSE   Uniting of different ideas, directions. An electrical fuse represents that part of your ideas, resolves or confidence that may break down if pressure is brought to bear. Or it can be a word play to indicate unity.

G
This is the seventh letter, and relates to Zain in the Hebrew. It represents an arrow, weapon or rod, which is used to administrate, to rule, or as a tool, to conquer.

GALE   See *Air*.

GANG   A group of fears, aggressive tendencies, or parts of self.

GAOL   Feelings of being restrained by your environment, morals, philosophy.

GARBAGE   Ideas, opinions, emotions we have discarded. We must realise, however, that all thought and feeling are expressions of our inner energy. As such, while we discard an expression of the energy, we must not discard the energy lest it leave us empty and unsatisfied. This is why garbage, or cess, must be thought of as material capable of being used in a new form.

GARDEN This symbol often appears in dreams, and can usually be easily identified as representing the way we cultivate or neglect the possibilities of life. Eden was also a garden, but in this case it was not what man had cultivated in his life, but what God had done for him. A garden is also often the place of love in a dream. In which case it can denote what is growing or blossoming in our life. In some cases it may be a walled or secret garden, which refers to the sacredness of our own inner experiences as they develop, a place within us of quiet and contact with our spiritual growth.

GARRET See *Attic*.

GAS Harmful thoughts, insinuated evil masquerading as spirituality.

GASOLINE Emotional or sexual energy. See *Petrol*.

GASPING See *Asthma*.

GATE Opportunity or barrier, depending on use in dream. It represents entrance to a field of endeavour, or new way of life. See *Garden* or *Field* if in dream.

GAZE Concentration, attempt to influence.

GEM See *Jewel*.

GENITALS Usually directly refers to sexual feelings, fears, desires, plans, hopes, of a sexual nature. Sometimes refers to your sex as a whole either man or woman.

GENIUS May represent feelings of inferiority or superiority, or even be similar to Guru, depending on dream.

GERM The very beginning, in material or inner manifestation, of a good or bad growth, direction, or idea.

GERMAN Intellectual, mechanical, worldly, harsh. Or in some cases, intellectual wisdom pertaining to inner things.

GERMINATION A part of self that has been quickened to life and growth by some influence, such as love, interest, change of heart, understanding.

GESTURE Most gestures we make in dreams symbolise some inner state of being. To understand them it is best to imitate the gesture and thereby see what it expresses. For instance, there are the typical gestures of fear, anger, tenderness.

GEYSER Expression of emotions under pressure.

GHOST An old memory, an old fear, or the past, that haunts you or comes back to you. May represent a guilt, fear of death, intuitive knowledge, dread of the unknown, or things you have done that you have tried to bury and forget.

GHOUL This is usually some repressed part of your life that haunts and terrifies you.

GIANT If you are the giant, then it means you have excessive feelings of power over others, and being a big person. If someone else is the giant, then it may symbolise your relationship with them, such as feelings of inferiority, powerlessness, fear. If you take the trouble to understand what the other person signifies, apart from their size, it is often found that they represent one of your emotions, fears, or ambitions, that have become too big for you to handle and has grown to giant proportions.

GILD or GILT Outer show.

GIPSY Intuition, psychic faculties, shifty, rootless.

GIRDLE or CORSET Sexual restraint, or the restraint of pride or vanity that shows only as an outer façade, and does not bring about inner changes.

GIRL   Affection, intuition, maturing female sexuality. Immature emotions, love, motherhood or womanhood. If the girl is known, she represents our opinion or feelings about her.

GLACIER   Emotional tension, repression. Fear of living or expressing your feelings or emotions.

GLAND   Often represents something to do with a state of mind, nervous, relaxed, energetic, ambitious. Or else symbolises levels of consciousness, or gateways to initiation. They represent latent possibilities in your nature, the opening of new doors of under-standing, ability or insight.

GLASS   One speaks of someone's stupidity or evil being trans-parently obvious. Or we say, I can see through you. Glass is some-times used to represent similar ideas. Or barriers in self, fears, weaknesses, we can now see through but have not yet been able to get through.

GLISTEN   See *Glow*.

GLOBE   Wholeness, your complete nature, symmetry or propor-tion. Usually refers to the soul or spirit, in the same way as a square or cube often represents the physical in a dream. Or it may repre-sent the world. Sometimes the globe is in divisions denoting the different faculties or aspects of your nature. See *Numbers*.

GLOOM   See *Dark*.

GLORY   When in glory in a dream, it is a reflection of your whole nature coming under the effulgence of the inmost spirit.

GLOVE   Insularity against the world. It may also be an invitation, like a dropped glove, or handkerchief. Can stand for a hand with-out any life in it. Protection, lack of contact, or something that does or does not fit in some way.

GLOW   When something glows with an inner light, it means that it is expressing the inner energies, spirit or self. The actual form will probably symbolise some personal or soul quality, through which the spirit expresses. It is the inner light, not the form, that expresses the spirit, or God. But from the form we can understand which part of us is relaying direct spiritual influence or guidance. See *Dark* and *Light*.

GLUE   One can be glued to the television, or a book. It can therefore symbolise emotional and intellectual involvement, empathy, or sympathy, love.

GNARLED   Worn by time and work. The difficulties and harshness of life.

GNAW   Something may be eating us, conscience, worry. What is gnawing represents the source of worry.

GNOME   See *Fairy*.

GOAL   Your aims, ambitions.

GOAT   A sacrifice you have made. Or the sacrifice you make of someone else, a scapegoat. Goats are sometimes used as a mascot or emblem, signifying hardiness, ability to accept, digest, almost anything, and climb difficult terrain. Or resistance to God, that has to be sacrificed.

GOD   To dream of God, on a superficial level is to desire to be better, holy, or sinless. Or may suggest guilt about your actions or morality. On a deeper level, to dream of God is to touch the centre of your being. The fact that one is asleep does not invalidate the contact, in this book God is a word, symbolising the source, or central self, the energy of life. This basic part of self existed in God before birth, and death is a return. To be advised by that part of self that takes into consideration the lives of all other things, and directs your activities to harmonise with all life, and thus find your own greatest good. God seldom takes form in a dream, but remains unseen and known only through the impact

244

upon you. Thus you may be moved by God in a dream, may speak from this influence, or may undertake activities. In many dreams, God is not something, some being, apart from man, but that influence, which itself is inactive, formless, desireless, that is forever within us, beyond your personal desires. Drop these personal desires, and there God is. Such dreams are usually of supreme importance, as you truly live and have your being within God. See *Name*.

GOLD   Power, authority, riches. Gold represents spiritual riches, for it does not tarnish, even if burnt or buried; that is, despite suffering or materialism, these qualities cannot be taken from us. Gold may also represent desires for wealth, but strangely enough, is seldom used this way in dreams, as the unconscious has certain universal symbols. The Golden Calf in the Bible represents the intellectual ideas of a spiritual nature that we have raised up, and we now worship as God or spirit. Our ideas, emotions, states of being, while they may be golden, in the sense of expressing spiritual qualities, are not the spirit itself, and must not be worshipped as such. The sun has often been symbolised by a gold disc. Gold here symbolises the earthly aspects of life that reflect the light of spirit.

GOLF   See *Billiards*.

GORILLA   See *Ape*.

GOURD   Female sex organ. See *Cup*.

GOVERNMENT   Either the rules by which you govern your life, or by which it is governed, or the inner forces that govern your health, well being.

GOWN   See *Clothes*.

GRAMOPHONE   May symbolise memory, due to it being a record-player, and replays or records the past.

GRAPE   The grape and its juice, before being fermented, represent physical life without the influence of spirit. The vine also symbolises masculinity, intellect, logic. Can also mean fruitfulness of intellect or ideas. While fermentation means fruitfulness of spirit, or intellect illuminated by spirit. See *Alcohol, Coffee.*

GRASS   Growth. The transmutation of material values into inner, or soul ones. Sometimes can mean overgrown thoughts and feelings that need cutting. Multiplicity, countlessness. The innumerable thoughts that can spring up.

GRAVE   Materiality, death. See *Burial.*

GRAVITY   Being held down by physical appetites, material ambitions, worldly philosophy. Weighted down by worldly experience.

GREY   Unhappy, colourless existence. Morbid or serious thoughts. Officiousness.

GREEK   Past glory, philosophy. Intellectuality under influence of emotion, instead of being influenced by spirit.

GREEN   See *Colour.*

GRENADE   Anger, violence, explosive emotions.

GROTTO   See *Cave.*

GROUND   See *Earth.*

GROVE   Similar to *Garden,* but being trees, specifies the growth or area of your ideas and habitual emotions.

GUARD   We guard our language, our thoughts, our actions. The guard can symbolise the morals, social pressures, fears, used in this way. It may also represent a fear of losing something, such as respect, love, social standing, virginity. Can symbolise protection also, such as in the form of a guardian. See *Police.*

GUIDE   The principles that guide your direction in life. They may be a worthy or unworthy guide, depending on the principles or

246

desires by which you are directed. The guide may also be an animal, in which case see it under its heading.

GUILLOTINE Removal of intellectualism, logic. This often occurs where the dreamer is being led from within to slow down the process of rational thought and consider intuitive, irrational processes as a necessary part of life.

GUITAR See *Fiddle*.

GULF Separatedness. Sense of isolation.

GULL Mentality or ideas that look to the unconscious.

GUN Penis. Hatred or violent urges, often covering a sense of weakness, inferiority, or fear of being attacked and hurt by others. The gun thereby strengthens ability to stand alone against such attacks, and expresses the feeling that violence is the only defence. This applies to sexual feelings also. If the gun is in someone else's hands, it symbolises fear of their violence, or fear of attack from the aspect symbolised.

GUNPOWDER See *Dynamite*.

GURU Represents God's wisdom or spiritual wisdom, as it relates to our life. The guru is not so concerned with physical welfare, as to the realisation of our eternal nature and life in God. Thus the guru in dreams will usually guide us towards greater self understanding, deeper relationships with himself, and instruct us in any necessary disciplines of mind and body, unfolding to us the inner meanings, where necessary, of ancient scriptures. He really represents our own awareness in God; our own spiritual awareness. Thus, as a dream series develops, if we reach the stage of illumination, we will wake up as the guru, or merge into him, or be absorbed in his consciousness. This may be frightening, due to fear of losing individuality or ego. But in fact, the guru is our own true eternal self.

H
The eighth letter of the Hebrew alphabet is Heth, and symbolises a field. It stands for the labours, trouble and efforts, necessary to cultivate self in any way. It also represents the balance between creativeness and destruction.

HADES   The land of death, or the unconscious. It is that part of the unconscious self in which ego urges, sin, self will, are acting against the universal aims of spirit. Thus a condition of torment is set up, between self will and universal will, which is called Hell. See *Hell*.

HAG   Sometimes represents grasping, evil emotional tendencies; or can hide the old wise woman of instinctive or natural wisdom.

HAIR   This symbol is used a great deal in dreams, either as head, face or body hair. It is obvious that as a child's genital hair grows its sexuality develops also. Thus, genital, armpit, chest or face hair are usually direct representations of sexual feelings and urges. But they can represent different aspects. Genital hair can be taken to represent intimate, personal sexual feelings. Chest hair for men would be more suggestive of feelings of masculinity and confidence in relations with women. Women's armpit or leg hair, depending upon dreamer, would represent their social sexuality, their outer relationships with others. Similarly a man's facial hair may have the same significance. See *Beard*. Head hair is more complicated. It too has sexual symbolism, socially and in the unconscious. The teachings of Paul that a woman's hair must be covered in church, is an expression of covering sensuality.
Many orders of different religions shave off their hair as a sign of renouncing material life, sexuality included. The loss of Sampson's hair took his physical and spiritual strength, so some psychiatrists say that cropped hair represents sexual restraints, the denying of sexual feelings. Bound or tightly held hair stands for sexual discipline but not complete restraint, long hair illustrates sexual activity and freedom; but long, matted hair represents the life of the ascetic, who is completely unconcerned about sex.
Hair can also represent your thoughts and intellectual life. Or it can

248

symbolise the spiritualisation of sexual feelings. That is, the development of sexuality into sympathy, fraternal love, protectiveness, union with God. Hairsplitting is an example of the association of hair with intellectuality.

HALL   A point of unity.

HALO   Expressive of the inner light. See *Glow*.

HAMMER   Power, of a material physical nature. May refer to male sex organ, or sexuality in its physically forceful, unsympathetic aspect. Or can express your desires to hammer something home or make yourself felt.

HAND   Your deeds, outer creativeness and power in the material world. What you do outwardly. Thus you can have a helping hand; grasping, wringing, heavy.

HANGING   Anything that hangs depends upon the thing it is hanging by, or from. So hanging in a dream shows a dangerous inner state of depending for support on one thing, as symbolised. Dependence, fear of falling, lacking support.

HARBOUR   Emotional security, protection, resting place.

HARD   Unsympathetic, unfeeling, unresponding. Difficulty.

HARE   Intuition, hardiness, irrationality.

HASHISH   Either the release of intuitive information and experience of inner self, or it can represent artificial insight. That is, insight that has been brought about by outside influences, the individual not having developed the powers within enabling them to achieve the insight themselves. See *Addicted*.

HAT   Your mental attitude or opinions.

HAUNTED   See *Ghost*.

HAWK   See *Eagle*.

HEAD   You can lose your head, have a head for heights, figures, or use your head. Usually relates to your mental cleverness or intellect. Or you can get ahead. Apart from this it represents consciousness, awareness of self or controlling factor.

HEALER   Parts of the self that can channel life force or spiritual consciousness, and thus bring the rest of the being into harmony or health.

HEAR   See *Ear.*

HEART   Emotions, sympathy, tenderness, love, affection. Also inner feelings, secret thoughts, conscience. You can take heart, and thus carry on through difficulties, or lose heart and give up. The heart has also been used as a symbol for the dwelling place of the spirit or eternal nature. It is through the heart that you have links of love with others, living or dead.

HEAT   Strong feelings, release of feelings or exuberance. Sexual passion or excitement as being on heat. Uncontrolled desires.

HEAVEN   Opposite to Earth. Idealism, land of death. The immaterial aspect of self and forces behind nature. Your consciousness freed from the materialism that limits growth, and existing in harmony with spirit. Joy, love, pleasure, hence the saying I'm in heaven. See *Hell.*

HEDGE   See *Fence.*

HEIGHT   Often refers to a level of consciousness, expansion of awareness due to the ability to see further at a higher stage. Or else impressiveness; inability to reach up to this height, emotionally or self confidently.

HEIRLOOM   Good or bad tendencies that have been passed on from family, past lives, or acquired from society.

HELL   Symbolises inner torment, guilt, fear, pain, usually of a purifying nature, resulting from being out of harmony with the innate nature. For instance, part of the innate physical nature is the need to drink water. If you refuse to comply, you suffer hell. You also have innate emotional, mental and spiritual needs, which if not attended to, cause suffering. Hell also represents the projection of your own inner state on to the world. If you are hateful, then the world also seems hateful; if you are depressed, the world appears depressing. After death, or in the unconscious, where the state of mind actually produces the surroundings, as in dreams, you literally, through your state of mind and feeling, create your own heaven or hell.

HELM   As on ship. Will power, the efforts made to direct your life. Whoever is at the helm would symbolise the directing influence of your life. Business man would represent ambition or money, a priest would denote religion; an artist stands for creativeness and beauty.

HERB   Healing, or some particular influence such as drowsiness, stimulation, cleansing.

HERMIT   Sometimes symbolises a desire to escape the demands of the world. Or a hermit is the representative of your inner feelings. See *Guru*.

HERO   The courage to face up to self and wrestle with problems or trials, as represented by the twelve labours of Hercules.

HEW   See *Carve*.

HILL   Difficulty, obstacle, something needing energy with which to deal with it. A hill also symbolises the climb to higher attainment, wider view of life or opportunities. You climb to success, or go down hill to failure, illness, death. You can see further from above, or be overshadowed at the foot. See *Mountain*.

HINDU   See *Indian*.

HIPPOPOTAMUS   Weight, power through physical weight and size.

HISS   Escape of repressed or pressurised ideas or feelings.

HIT   Apart from aggressiveness, you may hit on an idea, hit on the answer.

HIVE   See *Bees*.

HOE   See *Garden*. Efforts of self cultivation, and weeding out faults.

HOLE   An error you may fall into, a fall, a descent into the unconscious, memories, materiality, or female sex organs. See *Cave* and *Fall*.

HOLINESS   Expression of innate self, or spirit. See *Glow*.

HOME   See *House*.

HONEY   Sweetness, healing, results of labour. Its mystical symbolism, arising from its use as a promise in the Bible, the land of milk and honey, suggests the reward of spiritual labours, or facing self and dealing with inharmonious conditions. Anna Kingsford describes its symbolism as 'uniting sweetness of taste with the colour of gold, and contained in the six sided cell or cup of the comb, typifying the six acts of the Mysteries, is the familiar emblem of the land of promise'.

HOOK   Something with a catch in it. You can be hooked on drugs, drink or love for someone, hook on to an idea, opportunity. Questioning.

HORIZON   The limit of your present perceptions.

HOROSCOPE   Inner characteristics; the tendencies to be dealt with in this life. Irrational or intuitive knowledge that can instruct you concerning your inner nature.

HORSE   The horse is a beautiful symbol found throughout human history, in all arts, and unconscious experiences. Basically the horse represents instincts, energy, sexual desires. If the horse is wild and riderless it shows that these energies are strong enough to express themselves despite the anxiety of our thoughts or moral conscience. If the horse is ridden, then it means such energies are being directed. But sometimes dreams suggest that although a horse is being ridden, it ought to be given the rein, which indicates excessive conscious control of your feelings, and the need to slacken your hold on self. In folklore and religion we also find mention of the winged horse. This symbolises the sexual or instinctive drives that have not been repressed, but allowed, in conjunction with consciousness and reason, to develop the higher possibilities latent in them. Physical passion and love can transmute into spiritual or fraternal love and passion. This lifts consciousness, the rider, into higher realms of experience.

The horse is an emblem of the energies arising from the unconscious and as it contacts the spirit, it can also be a symbol of healing, or the release of energies that harmonise and heal the conscious self. However, Anna Kingsford sees the horse as a symbol of intellect, or physical consciousness. This may apply in some cases, as we see Paul falling from his horse, blinded by his spiritual illumination. This seems to suggest a fall from usual attitudes, due to a sudden vision of wider awareness. Finally, the Mare represents the earth, femininity, receptiveness, fertility, peace. The Stallion represents fieriness, masculinity, power, virility, war.

HOT   See *Heat.*

HOTEL   New areas of self. Attitudes in self that may not be permanent. States of mind or being in which you are lodging, holidaying, or passing through on your way to somewhere else. Luxury and ease.

HOUND   Something that persists, or hunts out your attention or fear. See *Haunt.*

HOUSE   Usually represents the dreamer, and his different activities or departments in life. Our speech expresses these unconscious associations when we say, like a house on fire, he was floored, I raised the roof, he's getting a bay window. Because of this a cellar represents the unconscious; kitchen ability to make life palatable;

sitting room relaxation and leisure activities; library the intellect or wisdom; bedroom our sexual life, or state of being awake or asleep to something; attic, our idealism and high mindedness; lavatory, our relief from tension or parts of self unnecessary to us, bathroom, our attempts to come clean with self, or the removal of grime and dirt acquired from our mental emotional contacts with life and people. The roof depicts protection, security, shelter, or the family atmosphere of love and security under which we find shelter and comfort. To take someone under one's roof is to share with them the family atmosphere and goods. The foundations symbolise the basis upon which life is built. See *Basement, Stairs, Window, Glass, Door, Furniture.*

HUNGER   Need of being sustained. We sometimes lose hope, faith or strength, and this hunger represents the inner need felt at such times. See *Food.*

HURT   Wounded by what other people have said or done. Hurt by your own actions.

HUSK   The face value, the outer quality under which may hide beauty, nutrition, wisdom. First impressions.

HYMN   See *Proverb.*

HYPNOSIS   Being influenced by the suggestions of who or what hypnotises in the dream. Becoming receptive and surrendering to the hypnotic symbol. Whether this is good or bad must depend upon who or what it is in the dream to which one surrenders control. In a symbolical sense generally wrong unless consciousness is maintained during the hypnosis, but must depend on the dream contents.

HYSTERICAL   Controlled by fears and emotions.

I

The ninth letter of Hebrew alphabet is Teth, signifying a roof. This is protection, safety.

ICE See *Cold*.

ICEBERG Often used in literature, and sometimes in dreams, as a symbol of consciousness. A little of our being we are aware of, like the ice above the surface. But the enormous bulk of self is invisible to view, beneath consciousness. See *Glacier*.

ICICLE Repressed sexuality.

IDIOT Lacking control of reason. Without development of logical mind. Stupidity.

IDOL Some material thing, money, women, work, pleasure, that directs your energy and actions. Something, somebody you worship. False basis from which to direct life.

ILLUSION Wrong idea, false opinion, deception, wrong conclusion.

IMMACULATE CONCEPTION The dream of becoming pregnant from a light, glowing bolt, or spirit, often occurs. This symbolises the reception within our soul of a spiritual impulse, spiritual wisdom or love. What we do with this is shown in later dreams. Sometimes we nurture it and it is later born. Sometimes we deny or neglect it and it miscarries or passes away. But such a child is often miraculously tenacious.

IMMERSED See *Baptism*, or *Earth*, depending upon what you are immersed in.

IMPOTENCE Fear of sexual incapacity. Loss of manhood or womanhood, masculinity or femininity. Feeling of being weak, unable to express yourself, or to impress others with feelings or ideas.

INARTICULATE Feeling of inferiority when confronted by opinions of others. Inability to express yourself, or inability to define ideas. Fear of saying something stupid, or being thought a fool for your opinions. Indecision, conflicting ideas.

INCENSE Prayer, aspiration due to beautiful feelings. The cleansing or purifying of self. Atmosphere.

INCEST Usually reappearance of infantile urges which have not yet developed, due to a fear or guilt, into more expansive expressions of sexuality. If these urges can be accepted in the dream, they usually begin to mature into adult sexuality.

INCRUST Things, ideas, habits, that have collected around, or overlaid whatever the symbol represents. A dirt incrusted mirror would represent the lack of ability to look at self, or to see yourself as you are, due to material or earthly desires and values.

INDIA, INDIAN Spiritual values, knowledge and capability in dealing with the irrational, unconscious, inner life; but little ability to cope with the outer, mechanical, materialistic life. An Indian in a dream may frequently represent an emergence of the irrational; that is, urges we do not understand, and so may fear or repress. But as he often represents the mystical, inner nature, he may speak in our dream with much knowledge of the inner and spiritual life. Occasionally he takes the form of a trickster, who is at home in incredulity and ignorance of irrational or unconscious abilities; but generally as the guru, spiritual teacher. See *Guru, Christ.* India is the womb in which the Spirit incarnates. She is thus Mother India.

INDIGESTION An accepted idea or attitude that does not agree with you. The inability to stomach something. Or may be actual indigestion.

INDUSTRIES Creative or constructive energies.

INFANCY Parts of self that still reflect infantile behaviour, of being controlled by mother's will. Or else the feeling of being a baby, or desire to be a baby to escape adult responsibilities.

INFECTION The influence of other people's fears, worries, or cynicism upon you.

INFINITE Usually pertains to the spirit.

INFLATE To fill up or be carried away by a sense of your own cleverness, superior abilities, knowledge and power.

INHALE   To take into your thoughts or experience, to consider, to accept mentally.

INITIATION   Discovery of new levels of consciousness, opening at the unconscious level, of new power, wisdom or love.

INJECT   Often sexual meaning.

INK   Something that may leave a mark upon you, such as a blot on your character. Sometimes represents some unconscious content you are dealing with.

INQUEST   Attempt to understand.

INSECT   Actions controlled by habit. Sometimes, as in spiders, has special meanings.

INSIDE   An inside pocket, inside a house, tree, car, most often represents your own inner self, or soul, your inner feelings.

INSIGNIA   Ideas of special importance to you. They usually synthesise a great deal of knowledge or information in the symbol.

INSPIRATION   Intuitive knowledge. See *Breath*.

INTUITION   Information that rises to consciousness either from a summary of our complete memory or experience, possibly including past lives; or is an unconscious contact with the mind of another person, living or dead, or arises from a contact with the universal mind, or memory of nature, which summarises all experience and knowledge, all peoples' and creatures' aims, and the way we can best relate to them, and all future possibilities.

INVENT   Some dreams use the word in a strange way, suggesting that man *invents* nothing, except perhaps falsehood and misunderstanding. But man can *discover* a great deal, either about himself, the universe, or how to apply natural laws in machines. All possibilities are man's to explore.

INVOICE   See *Bill*.

IRISH   Emotions, knowledge of psychic or subtle impressions, contact with nature, irrational, ruled by passions.

IRON   Material force. Strength of will. Brutality. Will that does not allow any partnership with the emotions. Hardness and unfeelingness.

IRRIGATE   To allow emotions, or feeling values, to come into our life.

ISLAND   Something that has come from the depths of the unconscious, but is now established in consciousness. A part of self cut off by emotions. We may like to talk about a husband who is dead, but cannot do so due to our emotions. Our attempt to cut ourselves off from others due to our feelings about them. Loneliness or isolation.

ISRAEL   Unity of will with God. Spiritual consciousness. The struggle to establish life in accordance with our innate nature, or spirit. The difficulties we face in self, in doing so. Coming out of bondage to Egypt is to come out of bondage to material values and unconscious fears. Wandering in the wilderness after crossing the Red Sea is to be lost in intellectual speculation and aridity after overcoming the power over self of the emotions.

ITALIAN   Artistic, pleasure loving, emotional love of religion due to love of beauty, rather than love of God. Sensuality under control of emotion rather than Spirit.

IVORY   The Soul. Black ivory is the unconscious aspects of the soul or personality.

J
Yod is the tenth Hebrew letter, and is symbolised by the finger extended as a command. It represents power emerging or directed from within, eternity.

JACKET Feelings with which we clothe ourselves.

JAIL See *Gaol.*

JAM In a mess, a sticky situation. Conserved ideas, fruits of labour.

JAPAN Inner self, unconscious, that is influenced by intellect, material values. Practical inner issues, outer abilities stemming from within. Beauty or outer things arising from the unconscious.

JAR See *Cup.*

JAW See *Chin.*

JESUS Human nature under direction of spirit. Human qualities that have been transmuted by God. See *Christ.*

JEWEL In general, a jewel is the emblem of eternity, our innermost self. However each jewel has slightly different significance.
Diamond: This is the hardest known material. It lasts forever, so the advertisements tell us. It represents the eternity of spirit, the gem or jewel at the centre of being. Spiritual consciousness. It can also represent human greed, hardness, cold as ice, anything for power. But is not often used as such in dreams.
Ruby: The feelings, sympathies, love, arising from the spirit, rather than material values. The ability to reach out and contact others.
Emerald: The growth principle, growth of consciousness, growth of spiritual awareness, harmony with life.
Pearl: Value, beauty, from the depths of our being. The fact that a pearl arises from irritation makes it the symbol of that beauty or inner wholeness that has arisen from the trials of life.
Sapphire: Religious feelings, devotion, quieting of material consciousness, peace of mind, protection from evil.
Opal: The inner world of your dreams, fantasies, psychic impressions. Protection against anger. Purification.
Amethyst: Bringer of dreams and visions. Protection against being carried away by spiritual elation or inner influences. Healing.
Lapis Lazuli: Sensitivity to inner impressions. Vitality.

JEWELLERY   Usually love given or received. The desire to be loved or noticed. Relations with others or spiritual abilities you have, or can, develop.

JOCKEY   Ability to direct energy and instincts. See *Horse*.

JOKER   See *Clown*. Joker in cards represents the irrational inner self, that can take on any quality, and in itself is neither good nor bad, wise nor foolish, high nor low.

JOURNEY   Undertakings we embark on. New experiences or ways of life we are entering. We can go on the journey of life, spiritual journey, and so on. It means the attitude of mind necessary before we become open to new things. The journey cannot be undertaken unless we are willing to travel, to move from one experience, one attitude or way of life to another. The inner journey, to discover the self, has many landmarks, and the legends attempt to define these in the Quest for the Holy Grail, the Odyssey, the Labours of Hercules. Also the lives of Avatars such as Jesus, Buddha, Mohammed, show the experiences met with on the journey of life.

JUDAS   Lack of faith in the spirit surviving and being untouched by all experience. Judas directs energy or activities of the outer world due to holding the money bag, but although having glimpsed spirit, cannot commit self to its influence, and decides physical means are safest. In a lack of faith, or a conviction that logic, material values and physical means, are the best we lead the inner Christ to crucifixion.

JUDGE   Your sense of whether you have acted in harmony with your innate self, or people.

JUMP   To take a risk, a leap into a situation that is uncertain. Taking a chance.

JURY   Conscience, ideas of right and wrong, attempts to decide. Vengeance is mine saith the Lord.

K

The eleventh Hebraic letter is Kaph. This is similar to Gimel, the hand of man grasping. But here it grasps strongly, is closed and firm. Strength and vitality.

KAABA   This cube, holy to Islam, represents an expression of the divine will in material affairs. See *Cube*.

KEEL   Similar to foundation, or basis upon which your life is built, but also represents that which holds you steady against opposing conditions.

KENNEL   Aggressiveness, passions. See *Dog*.

KERNEL   The inner truth, inner value, innermost self.

KEY   Idea or state of mind that opens up further realisations or experiences. Also a symbol of male sex organ.

KILL   To suppress, kill feelings, deny parts of our nature conscious expression. See *Death*.

KING   Your father. Feelings of being inferior or superior, depending on whether king or subject. The material values in life, and how they may control you, or swallow you up, or rule you. What you are ruled by may be suggested by what or who is king in the dream. If it is an ape or animal, it would be the animal instincts.

KISS   Expression of love, passion, sympathy, union, becoming closer in sympathies or understanding.

KITCHEN   The workshop of the inner self. See *House, Oven*. The place in which we make life experience palatable and sustaining.

KNAPSACK   Often represents karma, the load of the past we carry about with us. All the errors, encumbrances, illusions, false attitudes, we bring from past experiences, past decisions. Bunyan uses it as a symbol of sin, past actions and living out of harmony with God, that falls away as Christian begins to face himself as repre-

261

sented by his journey, and aligns his will with God.

KNEEL   Humbleness, a receptive condition of mind; a state of awe, or acknowledgement of dependence or humility.

KNIFE   Aggressiveness, male organ. See *Arms*.

KNITTING   See *Darn*.

KNOT   A problem, relational tie. A tangle of feelings. In Buddhism, there are three inner knots that have to be untied, before Nirvana or Liberation can be reached. They are the knots of passion, emotion and intellect that bind us to limited and illusory awareness of self. We may be tied to our work, wife or husband, to mother's apron strings.

KORAN   Expression of spiritual insight. See *Bible*.

KRISHNA   The Indian Christ. See *Christ*.

L
The twelfth letter of the Hebrew alphabet is Lamed. Its sign is the arm, signifying anything that stretches and reaches. Thus it includes ideas such as occupation, extension, possession.

LABEL   An outer description supposed to signify inner contents. But you can be labelled in the sense of being called crude, stupid, wise. You may also have unconsciously labelled somebody and be doing them an injustice.

LADDER   A means of climbing, of rising, of reaching heights previously unattainable. In this it is similar to *Hill*. But climbing a ladder is a succession of separate rungs, and so it signifies rising by means of separate events, realisations, efforts. Freud also shows it as a symbol of sexual intercourse, the rungs representing the physical movements of sex and the mounting orgasmic feeling represented by the climb.

LAGOON   Often symbolises the unconscious or unconscious feelings.

LAMA   See *Guru*.

LAMB   Innocence, purity, harmlessness and gentleness. Thus Jesus is called the lamb of God.

LAME   The difficulty of making our way through the events of life. It can represent any impediment in our being that makes going difficult. The symbolism of Jesus healing the lame man, Math. 11:5, is the power of the spirit healing the difficulty in us, that we may face life with the energy and capacity each event demands.

LAMP   Focusing of attention or understanding. See *Light*.

LANGUAGE   The ability to communicate with others and make ourselves understood.

LANTERN   Unlike lamp, the lantern is usually significant of the inner light or spirit. Also, it is the wisdom or understanding that we use to guide us in our life's journey.

LARDER   See *Food*.

LATHER   Cleansing, or fuss, working ourselves up into a lather.

LAUGH   Release of tension, effort to sympathise or calm, ridicule of another or self, taking things lightly, misunderstanding, depending on dream.

LAUNCH   The committing of self. Launching of new venture, a new interest.

LAUNDRY   Attitudes that need to be, or have been, cleansed.

LAVA   Unconscious contents that have emerged under pressure and heat of emotion.

LAVATORY See *Faeces*.

LAWN Parts of self that need frequent attention lest they become out of hand, overgrown. See *Grass*.

LAXATIVE Something you are doing to loosen up tension, and release undesired feelings, memories.

LEAD Material qualities that weigh you down, material values or energies that can be transmuted to Gold. See *Alchemist*.

LEADER May be the part of us from which we presently take our lead. Or parts of us we should take direction from, depending on dream.

LEAF Some living, growing, or outworn (depending on colour of leaf) part of your thinking or feeling. You can also be blown like a leaf, suggesting separation from your roots and main growth; or you can take a leaf from someone's notebook, thus following their example or idea.

LEATHER Animal urges, instinctive drives, or toughness.

LEECH See *Blood*.

LEFT In nearly every case left is used to denote unconscious parts of self; things outside the conscious ego, darkness, ignorance, devolution, the forces of destruction, the earth. To explain this a little more, there is the ancient description in magic of the Right hand path of White or spiritual magic; and the Left hand path of Black or destructive, evil magic. Hitler used the swastika turning to the left. This has always symbolised the forces of destruction, or break-down. These forces are ever at work in us, and are absolutely necessary to life, and can be seen at work on a dead body, returning it to earth. It represents therefore the force that breaks down unity to its basic components. It also symbolises the void, or chaos of materials that are in the irrational unconscious part of our nature, from which our conscious self grows. Thus, the earth, which is disassociated matter, is necessary for the plant, as it supplies all its materials. The living growth principle, or Spirit of the plant, unifies these in a meaningful way. Thus the unconscious, dark, sometimes threatening and irrational side of self, is as necessary to us as the earth is to the plant. But we can only deal with it properly if we are led by the spirit, which enables us to create out of the chaos. If we descend into the unconscious with only our egoic sense of cleverness, inflated self importance and capability, we are in danger of being overcome by the power of disintegration, break down, non centredness, diffusion and irrationalism that are its characteristics. This we call madness; but a descent under the auspices of spirit we call genius or sainthood. The left represents also the mother, the darkness of the womb, or the earth. It may sometimes represent underhandedness, or unconsciousness of what we are doing. However, typically, we may find ourselves either turning to the left, representing a growing awareness of inner contents, or being lame in the left leg, symbolising an over conscious, logical, unfeeling attitude of being. See *Right*.

LEG   Our support in life. This may be parents, job, religion, friends, or anything upon which we depend. Sometimes an event occurs, or we receive news, that knocks away our support or self confidence, and dreams represent this by our legs. They can also be the ability to get about in life. Ambition for instance, may give us drive. If our business fails, ambition may crumble, represented by our legs being kicked away from us. See *Left* and *Right*.

LEMON   Possibly symbolises for us feelings of bitterness, sourness. Can obviously be a part of a health instruction in a body dream.

LENGTH   The length of something in a dream usually signifies its duration. The size symbolises its impact upon you.

LENS   Concentration, focusing of attention or understanding. May also represent something becoming bigger, or more important.

LEOPARD   Sometimes represents libido or sexual drives that appear as threatening.

LEPER   Uncleanness, disease, decay, loss of social acceptance, or feelings of being unloved and unacceptable. Mystically this symbolises a misdirection of life and feelings that have put you out of harmony with life as a whole. Ego has denied the spirit and become diseased. Jesus healing the lepers symbolises the power of the spirit to bring you back into harmony with all life, and return you to health.

LEPRECHAUN See *Fairy.*

LETTER A realisation, usually about someone else, or news about yourself. It can sometimes be a symbol used to express telepathic contact with another. See *Mail.*

LEVIATHAN See *Fish.*

LEVITATION See *Flying.*

LIBRARIAN Faculty of memory or contact with universal mind.

LIBRARY Acquired wisdom or life experience. Sometimes the books are very old, suggesting wisdom antedating this present life and experience. This is the meaning of Jung's theory of the racial unconscious, and equally that of reincarnation.

LIFEGUARD Ability to cope with emotional storms, fears of being drowned or submerged by your problems.

LIFT The ups and downs of life. See *Climb.*

LIGHT In a Masonic initiation, the candidate is led about in the dark, bumping into unseen obstacles, and is eventually asked what he most desires. The answer is Light. It symbolises our ability to see, to understand, to know where we are going, and the nature of what surrounds and confronts us. A noise in the dark can be terrifying because we cannot see its source, but light helps dispel fears and ignorance. This is why, when we enter into darkness in a dream, it symbolises an exploration of things we do not yet understand, or are not aware of. Similarly, the dawning of light is the growing of realisation, experience and understanding. Light therefore represents our consciousness, ego, awareness of individuality and personal realisation. But as far as the unconscious is concerned, the light of consciousness or self awareness, is due to the Invisible or Latent Light realising itself in matter. This is important, so I will attempt to explain.

Light is here used as a symbol of an inner process. It is invisible to us personally until it contacts matter. The sun's light is invisible until it contacts the moon. Thus, although space is flooded with light, our night sky can be black without a moon. Also, colours are latent in this invisible light, only to be displayed or manifest as the right matter or surface is held in the light. Similarly, our consciousness of self, has always been latent in the invisible or latent consciousness throughout the universe. This latent consciousness is God, or Spirit, which has infinite colours, or consciousness latent in it. Our body, and the bodies of animals and plants, are like the particles of matter, or different surfaces, that enable this latent light to manifest some of its characteristics. This is why the body, or matter, is necessary for the realisation of an individual soul or personality. So the invisible, unmanifest light represents God or Spirit, while the visible light represents those qualities of the inner, latent light, that have been made manifest within us through our material experience. This is why a glow, or inner light represents the expression of spirit in us. Therefore, in man's complete being, there is a succession of lights. First there is the Darkness or Invisible Light, which is our spirit. Then there is the duality of matter and force, light and darkness, knowledge and ignorance as in the book of Genesis. Thirdly the consciousness or realisation of self that arises from the dual aspects of self, or spirit and matter, light and darkness, energy and inertia, contacting each other in opposition. Fourth, the expression of the seven basic colours manifesting, or seven levels of consciousness, seven expressions of energy. See *Dark, Glow, Dim, Left, Right.*

LIGHTHOUSE   Danger of unconscious elements that may wreck your life unless avoided.

LIGHTNING   Sudden discharge of tension in a possibly destructive manner. Sudden enlightenment or realisation. Fear of fate or punishment from conscience or spirit. Revenge.

LILY   Has the same significance as the Indian Lotus. Its roots are in mud, it reaches up through water, and opens in air to the sun. This symbolises the roots of our consciousness in the deeps of the unconscious and material experience. This unfolds into feeling values, emotions, the psychic realm, and eventually blossoms into intellect, self realisation that realises the Sun, or spirit. In the Indian scriptures the petals of the mythical lotus unfold to reveal a jewel at the centre. This represents the unfolding of human consciousness to a realisation of the eternal nature underlying all its activities. See *Jewels.*

LIMP   See *Lame.*

LINK   See *Chain.*

LION   Appears in many dreams, and usually signifies anger, desire to hurt, aggressiveness; or fear of these feelings in others or ourselves. We may feel fear of our own anger due to it threatening injury to others in a way that would reflect upon self, and devour our other feelings and desires. The lion can often express feelings of love that cannot express normally, and become aggressive instead. If we see someone we love showing interest in another, or if we feel ousted by brother or sister for parents' love, our feelings may seem to us like a terrible lion. Daniel in the lions' den is a beautiful symbol representing how these feelings may be calmed and changed if our life is given to the influence of the spirit.

LIQUID   The heart, or courage, can turn to water, meaning that resolves have become soft. Or the heart can melt, suggesting a change of heart, opening to sympathy. To become liquid is usually to change, to become soft, formless, flowing. If your legs turn to water, then your motives have let you down. See *Water.*

LITHE   Emotional or mental adaptability, lack of bigotry or obstinacy.

LITTLE   Does not impress our conscious self. To feel small or insignificant.

LIVER Apart from a body dream, often symbolises a state of irritability or long suffering.

LOAF Could suggest laziness. See *Bread*.

LOBSTER See *Crab*.

LOCK A problem, often of a logical nature, that can be unlocked, if we have the key. Also the female sex organs. See *Key*.

LOCOMOTIVE See *Railway*.

LOFT See *Attic*.

LOG Interpretations vary. It can either be old opinions, or old habits of feeling. It is something that grew at one time, and has now become dead wood, fixed opinion.

LONG See *Length*.

LOOK Concentrate on.

LORRY Difficult to define. Like a car, it is your means of getting about in life, i.e. vehicle of expression such as music, drives, longings, ambitions, but the lorry is a means of moving heavy goods, moving house would be a change of self, moving furniture change of opinions.

LOTUS See *Lily*.

LOUSE Thoughts that sap resolves, energy, ambition, and that detract from your sociability.

LOW Beneath us, morally unsound, cheap, vulgar, depressed, little awareness or understanding.

LUCIFER See *Devil*.

LUMBER See *Log*.

LUMINOUS   See *Glow, Light.*

M

Often signifies mother. The thirteenth letter of the Hebrew alphabet is Mem. It symbolises woman. Can therefore be associated with motherhood, fertility and formative powers.

MA   Mother, receptiveness of soul, change, fertility.

MACHINE   Things that are mechanical, habits, some forms of reason or activity as when we say, He is like a machine.

MACKINTOSH   A protection used against emotions. As when someone tells us we are hateful or a liar. Some people get terribly upset or drenched, it rolls off others like water off a duck's back.

MAD   See *Idiot.*

MADONNA   There are several levels of meaning. We can gain an idea of this from Mary's prayer, My soul doth magnify the Lord. Mary is at one level the soul of each man, when it has become fertile and receptive to the direction and influence of the spirit. Previous to this it is symbolised by Eve, who is the soul or will turned to egoistic activities. In the soul as Mary, new consciousness can be conceived and born of the spirit. This can develop and mature into a consciousness of eternal life and being in God. It is God individualised in us, and thus magnified. At another level the Madonna is the Earth, mother and womb of all living, that has received God's life-giving forces, and brought forth all creatures. But can also destroy.
At a deeper level still, the Madonna is the Matter, Mater or Martre of the whole universe, the stuff the worlds are born or made of. She is thus God's wife at all levels of being. She is the soul of all mankind, our Fairy Godmother, who is our inner mother, lying behind and beyond our physical mother. All that is gentle and lovely in us is of this part of our soul. In Buddhism we see the same symbols used, Maya being the virgin mother of Buddha. In Egypt she was Isis,

and most faiths have this Divine Mother. Islam has Fatima; China, Kwan Yin; and India, Shakti Parvati. See *Virgin, Immaculate Conception, Eve.*

MAGGOT   Life or effects in your life, that have sprung from putrefactive or evil parts of self. The effects however, are usually efforts on the part of nature to cleanse or heal or deal with the situation.

MAGI   See *Guru, Wise Men.*

MAGIC   Conscious attempts to direct or control the unconscious, underlying, or even spiritual forces of your being. See *Left.*

MAGNET   Attractiveness. Repulsiveness. Likes and dislikes, physical or personality charms, and the way in which they are used. The power resident in the body, that can be used for healing, or emotional psychic impact upon others; as in hypnosis, where one being has such an impact upon another that his suggestions are carried out to a greater or lesser degree. This is why hypnosis was often called magnetism. Christ is spoken of as the magnet that attracts and redeems. Our Spirit also gradually attracts us, and orders the confusion of our outer life as the magnet does iron filings.

MAGNIFY   See *Lens.*

MAGPIE   Desires caused by material possessiveness.

MAHOUT   The conscious self directing the mighty cosmic forces within.

MAIL   See *Letter.* Can represent the ideas and opinions you radiate to others.

MAKE-UP   See *Cosmetic.*

MALE   The positive, creative, constructive energies that shape matter or the feminine attributes, and expressed innate qualities. It also represents consciousness, intellect, spirit, will, aggressiveness, light. While the female is unconscious, intuition, body and receptive aspect of soul, feeling rather than will, relatedness rather than aggressiveness. See *Female, Mother, Madonna, Christ, Vagina, Light.*

MALFORMATION Whatever is symbolised is not expressing its true characteristics.

MANE See *Hair.*

MANHOOD Expression of innate qualities.

MANSION Too big an opinion of self.

MANURE See *Faeces.*

MAP Clarifying ideas of direction in life. Understanding of what one has or wishes to do, and how to do it.

MARE See *Horse.*

MARKET Our contact with the world in general, the hustle and bustle, the commerce of life, the commercial instincts, the unsympathetic mob.

MARKSMAN The ability to aim at the inner being and hit the Self, or contact or express the Self.

MARRIAGE Desire for, or problems in, marriage. Used a great deal to symbolise the uniting of various parts of our being. For instance men often neglect their feeling values and live in their intellect, while for women vice versa is often the case. Thus, if a woman dreams of marrying a man it may represent the uniting of these two parts. Also signifies marriage of ego to spirit, consciousness to unconscious contents. It epitomises a growth of sympathy and relationship between parts of us that were previously not well related. Naturally it also occurs in many dreams of people about to marry, and clarifies their feelings, difficulties, unconscious attitudes to each other.

MARSH   Your underlying attitudes will not support your activities safely. Symbolises any feelings of being bogged down, held back, retarded. Stuck in material emotional values that are not helping your progress. Sometimes is used to represent the relationship existing between mother and child, or sometimes, though not so often, between father and child. The marsh here represents the difficulty felt in breaking away from parental control, the emotional hold over you, and the ties of security and protection. Or the difficulties faced in becoming real individuals.

MARTYR   May suggest a holier than thou attitude, a reluctance to change opinions in the face of criticism or condemnation, rightly or wrongly. Willingness to suffer for convictions. The sacrifice of part of the being because of convictions. As a dream symbol this is not really healthy, in that all aspects of the nature come alive and are useful under direction of spirit. There is, in fact, when spirit touches us, a resurrection of the dead or repressed parts of self, but made clean and holy or harmonious.

MARY   See *Madonna*.

MASK   Hiding your real self.

MASS in church.   The unification due to spirit influence, of all aspects of your nature. The surrender of self to the will of God, and the commending of our soul, and the souls of others, to God.

MASSEUR   Healing influence, loosening up of rigid attitudes, tensions, preconceptions, repressions.

MATADOR   Conflict with sexual drives. See *Bull*.

MAYPOLE   Phallic symbol, but not necessarily directly sexual. It represents the positive, dynamic, creative forces of growth and fructification in nature and man, that cause the growth of crops in the spring.

MAZE   The confusion we experience in trying to understand, or

273

find our way about, our unconscious contents. This area of self is an area of seeming chaos. It needs some other level of our being, the intuitive faculty, to guide us through.

MEAT   We often say, one man's meat is another man's poison. Here it represents your likes and dislikes, the characteristics, the experiences of life. Meat also represents sexual or physical experience, physical strength, prowess. To partake of meat is to partake of experience of the body, or material values.

MECHANIC   Our means of dealing with habitual reactions to life. If we habitually shout at our children every time they start playing, and wish to mend the fault, our effort to do so may be symbolised by the mechanic.

MEDICINE   Sometimes it means we have to take something we do not wish to. Take your medicine like a man. It also represents healing energies that can be released into our conscious life.

MEDICINE MAN   See *Guru*.

MEDITATION   The search for understanding and spirit. Cayce has described prayer as a talking to God, and meditation as a listening for the answer. It is a means of becoming acquainted with the unconscious areas of self.

MEDIUM   A medium may represent the intuitive function, acquaintance or contact with the psychic rather than the spiritual; the knowledge of unconscious impressions, or of the dead.

MEDUSA   Vanity, self love.

MEGALITH   Forces of the spirit emerging out of the unconscious or affairs of life. See *Rock*.

MELT   To change hardness of nature giving way to feelings of softness.

MERCHANT   The business, commercial side of self. Desires for profit in some area of your life.

MERCURY   Intuition; changeability. Difficulty to grasp.

MERLIN   See *Magic* and *Guru*.

MERMAID   Love arising from the unconscious. The inner image of womanhood, still held in the waters of the unconscious.

METAL   See *Iron*.

MEW   Loneliness, a call from the soul, a longing for comfort, friendship or love.

MICROBE   See *Germ*.

MICROSCOPE   The ability to perceive the subliminal and usually imperceptible parts of our nature, and sensations.

MILK   Due to it being a product of a mother, it usually represents the milk of human kindness, the giving of sustenance, self sacrifice, nurturing the young or needy parts of self or others. Also motherhood, infantile sustenance, sympathy. It can be the symbol of something bland, harmless, mild, lacking the stimulus of alcohol, tea, coffee. Thus one can be called a milksop, which is another name for childlike, unmanly, cowardly.

MILL   Trying times or feelings. Suggests the breaking down of old attitudes and beliefs.

MINE   The seven dwarfs of Snow White worked in a mine. It represents the unconscious physical activities. Some dreams suggest that consciousness is due to spirit, or cosmic energy, acting upon matter, and gradually transmuting it, releasing various potentials, until it manifests as consciousness, and eventually as spirit. Thus the mine might be taken as these activities; or at least your digging within material experiences, memories, deeper levels of consciousness, to bring up the treasure and valuable resources buried within.

MINK   Status, material values, animal or sexual desires.

MINOTAUR   The intellect dominated by sexual desires.

MIRAGE   See *Desert.*

MIRROR   This has a great many levels of meaning. Basically it is a looking at self, a self examination; and the face in the mirror may not match our own. It may be better or worse. That is, in self examination we may come across, or see, parts of the nature that are the worst side of self, the things we have hidden from self. Or we may see innate possibilities as they would be seen in full bloom, which is a reflection of our spiritual possibilities.

The mirror appears in many religious symbols and in much folklore. Water was probably the first mirror, and as such represents man's consciousness, soul, or self awareness, with which he suddenly becomes aware as 'I', a distinct individual. His awareness is thus a mirror in which he sees self. It is also a looking within, as Narcissus did losing self awareness, as we do in sleep. Alice goes through the mirror to enter Wonderland, which is again symbolical of looking within self, and exploring unconscious contents. Indian and Buddhist philosophy use it in a slightly different way, as also Yoga teachings. It is explained that when we look at a mirror we do not see its actual surface. We do not see the actual mirror, only the images reflected on its surface, which appear as reality. Likewise, the spirit or true nature, is like a mirror. In it we see the images of physical existence and life experience, which we take to be the only reality. But the Yogi asks himself, what is this that is conscious of all these images? What is this mirror we call consciousness? If all the images were removed, what remains? Where do these images, concepts, sense impressions, emotions, arise from; where will they subside to? Who am *I*?

Lastly, the mirror can sometimes symbolise the earth, or our physical nature. This is Hermetic philosophy, as above, so below. This sees the earth as a mirror, or reflection, of unseen forces, which in expressing through, or on to matter, realise their innate qualities. This is similar to the ideas underlying the symbolism of light. See *Light.*

MISCARRIAGE   See *Abortion*.

MISER   As money can symbolise power, authority, sexual potency, material security, a miser would represent the fear of losing or using abilities, insecurity, impotence, or of spending or giving feelings to others. Scrooge is an excellent example of this, miserly with worldly effectiveness, affection, sympathy and so on, thus the constant counting of money for reassurance in face of insecurity and fear.

MIST   See *Fog*.

MISTRESS   In the Jungian sense it would represent an anima projection. That is, being dominated or influenced by the projection of all our fantastic longings, imaginings, desires, hopes and hungerings for ideal love, on to a physical and ordinary woman who is not such a wonderful creature, but as we long for her to be such, we project these qualities on to her. It may in fact be that the woman wishes to be regarded in this light, as a goddess, and so encourages these feelings. In legend, before Eve, a being called Lilith was created by Adam's longings. But she was really only a phantom. Nevertheless, when Eve arrived, Adam's attention was still much turned to Lilith. The same problem still haunts men and women.

MOAT   An emotional defence used against others. A woman, being aproached by her husband for affection, and finding none within her, instead of admitting this unfeelingness, may instead say, I have a headache, or I feel ill, thus playing on his emotions.

MOHAMMED   Human expression of contact with God. The voice of the spirit.

MONGOOSE   Attacks we make on our sexual feelings, or on the strivings towards growth of inner energies.

MONK   Spiritual wisdom. Desires to leave the world. Influences of religious teachings in the unconscious. Some people may have been taught a dread of hell and perpetual burning, and similar terrors, is a typical example. The monk or priest may therefore symbolise the influences of the church teachings.

MONKEY   Sometimes a monkey has the face of a man, or talks. In these dreams tremendous power seems to accompany the monkey. This is probably emblematical of the union of our instincts and intellect, which releases tremendous energies due to the removal of conflict in our being. See *Ape*. One also hears the saying, being made a monkey of or made a fool of.

MONOGRAM   Usually a symbol of the whole self, direction of inner possibilities.

MONSTER   Fear, dread, terror of death, failure, impotence and weakness in the face of outer circumstances or inner urges. An epitome of attitudes, hates, fears, that have become monstrous, and turned against you. You can have harboured a monstrous lie, a monstrous deceit, hate, or fear. These can then rise up in this symbol, and threaten your whole existence.

MOON   Another symbol with many levels of meaning. The most obvious being love, romance, the sentimental balmy experiences of life. Youthful love and affection, the welling up of sentiments and longing for the beloved. The moon also symbolises the irrational, the deep inner movements and urges within us, the tides of feeling, desire, madness; the pull and attraction of mysterious, dark, impelling desires, of women's strange, sensual, magical and overpowering attraction, or vice versa. All the unseen influence represented by the moon's effect on the tides. The new or old moon also symbolises the woman's sexual organs, due to its shape. It thus represents femininity, irrational feelings, intuition, lunacy. The moon is also the heavenly companion of the earth, and reflects the light of the sun at night. This has enabled it to be used as a symbol of intuition as a reflector of spiritual consciousness. Or as a man's daemon, or genius, reflecting the inner light.

MOSAIC   The countless fragments of experience and thought, seemingly meaningless, but when seen from higher consciousness become a pattern or design of beauty that represents life as a whole.

MOSQUE   See *Church.*

MOTHER   To dream of your mother usually signifies the relationship with her, and deals with or symbolises hatred, respect, love, misunderstanding. The point being that whatever the outward relationship to motner or father, it is extremely likely that these attitudes also condition the relationship to the inner or heavenly mother and father. That is, masculine creative forces, and feminine receptive and formative forces, spirit and body, may be approached in the same way. Before we can relate fully to God and our unconscious or soul, we have to sort out our relationships with mother and father with respect to our inner feelings; we do not necessarily have to reconcile physically. To dream of one's mother not only signifies the relationship with our physical mother, but it may also be a message from, or about, our own inner mother, the receptive aspect of our soul, and the experience of life represented by Mother Nature, whose wisdom is as the stars. See *Father.*

MOUNTAIN   To fly in a dream is to rise to heights of consciousness which give a view of great expanse. Climbing a mountain achieves the same thing, but we keep our feet on the ground. Flying nearly always denotes becoming too idealistic, too wrapped up in the clouds of philosophy and speculation, not aware enough in the affairs of everyday life. On the mountain, however, we have achieved higher consciousness *through* facing the difficulties and perplexities of material experience, as represented by the climb up the steep slope. The mountain top touches the heavens, and on its tip we touch both worlds, the earth or body, and the sky or spirit. We do so without sacrificing one or the other, without neglecting our daily affairs, or being entirely wrapped up in them. In many religious teachings, and in mythology, the mountain is mentioned. The Gods live on Olympus, and on Meru in India. Moses climbed the mountain to receive the ten commandments. Jesus climbed the mount to preach. This all symbolises the reaching of a higher state of awareness, a realisation of our spirit.

MOUSE   The activities within our house, soul, or unconscious, seldom seen, and if noticed, thought to be too small or insignificant to matter. Feelings that gnaw away at us. The sexual organs. Timidity.

MOUTH   Expression of love or hatred. The entrance or exit to our inner self. We can eat, take in self, or vomit, emit from self, through the mouth. We can also bite off more than we can chew, be mouthy, have a big mouth, or have a mouth like a sewer.

MUD   In some dreams, as in a muddy road, or swamp, the mud is simply the retarding aspect of our hesitations and fears. In other dreams, people search through, or dig in the mud, which represents the cleansing of emotions caused by outer circumstances, the looking through the muck of our life for its treasure, for often a flower or jewel may be found in the mud. This is spiritual growth or wisdom arising from materialistic sensual experiences, or memories of a distressing nature, and sense of uncleanness, unworthiness, or earthiness. Mud is like clay, it is a substance that can be moulded, and so presents the idea of the basic memories and emotions of being that can be shaped. Mud may also symbolise healing, as it contains all the elements of past, which we need for completeness.

MUEZZIN   The call of the spirit of God, in the midst of everyday affairs; in our very forgetfulness, He has not forgotten us.

MULE   Stubbornness. See *Ass*.

MUMMY   The attempt to preserve ourselves as we are, instead of opening ourselves to the constant change, death and rebirth, that life brings. This only results in mummification or dessication.

MURDER   The repression of feelings or departments of our life. A man may kili his love for a girl because she does not come from a wealthy family. Or we may kill our feelings because we are ashamed of them or guilty about them. We may kill a creative streak in self due to feelings of incapability, unworthiness. See *Death*.

MURDERER   Representation of a fear or anxiety that is threatening to, or is killing feelings, energy.

MUSCLE   Physical strength, sense of being outwardly forceful and impressive, masculinity in its physical aspect.

MUSIC   Harmony in the self. Spiritual feelings, beautiful and harmonious emotions that heal and soothe our being.

MUSTANG   Youthful sexuality, aggressiveness, noncomformity. See *Horse*.

MYSTIC   See *Guru*.

N

Nun is the fourteenth letter of the Hebrew alphabet. It symbolises the child or offspring of the female.

NAIL   Binding power, strength to hold together, as a common belief will bind people together of opposite temperaments. A nail may also represent, as in Christ being nailed to the cross, the painful links that bind us to our body, our earthly experience, our pains and trials.

NAKED   To be stripped of the façade, mask, or attitudes we adopt in meeting the world, to hide or clothe our real self. We may hide dislike with a smile, if we are not pleased to meet someone, we may hide our feelings with courteous behaviour, shaking hands, but a child will usually refuse to talk to, shake hands, associate with, someone they dislike. Their real feelings are therefore naked to view. To be naked in a dream may thus express a desire for people to know our real feelings; fear of being disclosed or revealed; or discovery of our real self. See *Clothes*. Due to our social conventions, to appear naked has become a symbol of revealing our innermost self and behaviour, our secrets, our privacy, shortcomings, and our malformation. Christ stripped of his garments before crucifixion, symbolises the spirit stripped of its outer expressions, the seamless robe meaning the personality made whole through the spirit. These aspects of self are divided among the soldiers. Through its very long suffering, the spirit has revealed itself to us. But all we do is to place value upon its outer manifestations, our ego and the world, while we crucify the life within.

NAME   Symbolically, one's name is a secret description of self. It is a sort of formula describing one's being. Not merely a sound, but an expression of make-up, function and personality. Just as a crow sings differently to a lark, due to its shape, throat, character, and its sound is an expression of what it *IS*, so our name is symbolically an outflowing of what we *ARE*. Today we use names just because we like them, they are merely sounds, but the unconscious is far more direct, it uses names because they fit, as ancient man did. We see this in our use of the word GOD. It describes nothing, it is only a sound, a name, as meaningless as our own. But in older cultures, the names of God, such as Jehovah, Zeus, El Shaddai, Mazda, all described something in people or nature that could be seen. The name described a principle that was experienced, thus understood. Names in dreams are used in the same way. They represent us as a unique quality and being, distinct from all else. Some dreams give us another name, a secret name. This second name represents our spiritual nature as distinct from our outer self. A daffodil bulb grows new leaves and flowers each year. Each year these leaves and flowers die and disintegrate, but the bulb remains, and can bloom again above the soil. Likewise the spirit ever remains, and can put forth, or incarnate into, a new body, and then when the body dies, the spirit yet continues and can bloom into physical existence again. Our usual name symbolises the present self flowering in this body. The secret dream name signifies our spirit, or bulb, which is the root, the synthesis, of all our existences.

NAMELESS   No real quality, without a formulated or distinct being, without a soul.

NARROW   Limited movement in any but one direction. Limitation of choice. Narrow minded.

NATION Characteristic symbolised by the people as a whole. See country in question.

NATURE Those parts of your being that have arisen with little or no interference. Not moulded by conscious ambitions, desires.

NAVEL A symbol of an outer connection with our innermost feelings and being. It also represents a sign of dependancy, of our dependance upon mother, upon God, upon earth.

NECK You can stick your neck out, which means to take a risk; have a lot of neck, or nerve or audacity. These meanings have arisen possibly from the head being severed in execution, or hanging, or strangulation. The neck is a weak point, and to offer it suggests confidence, fearlessness. To be strangled in a dream may be due to difficulty in breathing, feelings of being strangled in life. That is, a feeling of life being cut off; cut off from self. To have your head cut off, is to have thinking divorced from feeling.

NECKLACE Power, authority, augmentation of personality, social attractiveness, charm or amulet. May also represent the things you hang round your neck, as a millstone round his neck. That is, obligations, difficulties, set backs. May associate with person who gave it, and the relationship with them. See *Jewellery.*

NEEDLE Sharp pain. Penetrating insight, self searching. Male sex organ. The power of mending ills, fears.

NEGRO Depends upon which race one belongs to. A white man dreaming is different to a black man. See *Aborigine.*

NEIGHBOUR Probably a symbol of their qualities. They may be helpful or grumpy. Or may be used as a male or female symbol. See *Male, Female.*

NEST Female sex organs. The womb or womb consciousness. Protection, relaxation, warmth. Home, or homemaking. Parenthood. or nest egg.

NETTLE   Some irritating factor in life. To be nettled.

NEWSPAPER   Something that is commonly known. Thoughts or memories you are well aware of. Consciousness as distinct from unconsciousness. Something that is news to you, or you have just become conscious of.

NICKNAME   See *Name.*

NIGHT   See *Light* and *Black.*

NINE   See *Numbers.*

NIPPLE   See *Breast.*

NIRVANA   Spiritual consciousness.

NOON   Height of consciousness, ego, rationalism.

NOOSE   Fear of death, of being caught or trapped; desire to catch or trap.

NORTH   Ignorance, mental and emotional darkness and aridity. It is the place from whence we seek the light, or spiritual or inner wisdom. Evil, death, stagnation.

NORTH STAR   The spirit's destined home. Man's eventual state of awareness; his goal, his guiding star, his spirit or guardian angel. That which guides him through his life's journey.

NOSE   Curiosity; sensitivity as when you have a nose for danger or news. Anna Kingsford says it represents 'Individuality, the divine Ego, the I AM, of the man.' Also may symbolise your direction, as when you follow your nose.

NOSTRIL   Half of your being. See *Left, Right, Breath.*

NOTICE   Literally means to notice, to be conscious of.

NUCLEUS See *Centre*.

NUDE See *Naked*.

NUMBERS These are difficult to define, and are very often only connected with personal associations. They may refer to a particular year of your life, number of a house you lived in, date that something happened, and thus draw our attention to these events and emotions surrounding them. They may also refer simply to multiplicity or size, as a crowd of events, a big experience, a many faceted realisation. However, since man could first count, numbers have had a fascinating, mysterious and even magical significance. In this way, early man found in numbers realisations of inner qualities, spiritual understanding, unconscious wisdom. Dreams often use numbers in the same way.

1 One is the first number and is indivisible. It symbolises a beginning, the first manifestation, something that is so basic and fundamental it cannot be divided. It represents the heavenly Father, the male, masculinity, power. One can divide into any number leaving that number unchanged. It therefore symbolises the power of spirit to enter into all things and yet not change their outer manifestation, as all manifestation has arisen from the one. That is, although each manifestation may be different in outer form yet one can enter each and not change it. Thus a hundred divided by one is still a hundred. One stands for the astrological sign Aries, and represents personality, ego or sense of individuality, pioneering abilities, and the head. It can also mean length or height. Although it is an odd number, and therefore masculine, it is sometimes shown as hermaphroditic due to its ability to go into all.

2 When anything is divided by two it falls into exact halves. Two represents duality, negative and positive, male and female. It represents the one quality dividing into negative and positive, matter and energy, light and darkness, consciousness and unconsciousness, good and evil, inner and outer. On the other hand, two, being even, symbolises femininity, receptiveness, the womb, passivity, the formative power, the earth or basic matter. Astrologically this is Taurus the Bull, the builder or farmer governing the throat. So basically it represents division, decision, choice, femininity, formative power, receptiveness, motherhood, breadth.

3 Dividing a number by three brings it to equal thirds. It is symbolised by the triangle, and represents a unity of the positive and negative to create a new condition. Thus we see it as mother and father bringing forth child, which is a mixture of both but different from either. It is the spirit and body manifesting individual consciousness. Three represents the three great processes by which God manifests being or physical life. One is the undivided, preconscious stage. Two is division into opposites contacting each other. Also Creation, Preservation, Dissolution. Matter and energy have arisen from the same source, meet in opposition, and manifest qualities. Three therefore represents affinity that unites opposites; that which springs from, or is born from opposites; fruition, reaction. Its Zodiacal symbol is Gemini, the artist and inventor, the creator or created. It also rules close relationships and their results; and the arms and lungs.

4 The symbol of four is the square or cube, representing stability, materialisation, earthiness, strength of a physical nature, permanency. It is the symbol of the four points of the compass; four elements, earth, air, fire and water; four functions, sensation, feeling, thinking, intuition; the four aspects of self, physical body, astral body, soul, spirit; four aspects of body, gaseous, mineral, vegetable, animal; the four aspects of activity. In other words the physical action, which has been caused by the astral or transitional, or mediumship which has been set in motion by a thought, desire, or feeling. Whereas *one* may represent intuition, *two* thinking, *three* feeling, *four* represents sensation. Astrologically it is Cancer, the prophet or teacher, realisation at a physical level, home and background, and the breasts.

5 The alchemists called this quintessence, because it arises from the other four elements. It symbolises man, due to his two arms, two legs and head, as in a five pointed star. It is the unity that arises from the four elements, or aspects of self. Five may also represent your hand or foot. Is sometimes called the sign of marriage, but is mostly the symbol of man incarnated in a physical body, and functioning therein. Here, all four aspects of being are expressing in a fifth quality, physical life and consciousness. Astrological sign is Leo, the king. The fifth house of the horoscope relates to children or offspring, and Leo rules the heart.

6 The symbol of this is the double triangle, or circle divided in six. It represents symmetry, unity of spirit and body, the visible and invisible. It is the harmonious relationship between man and God, spirit and body, the eternal and the transitory. Its sign is Virgo which expresses as craftsman or critic. It is a sign of service and rules the ·intestines. The sixth house rules health.

7 The symbol of seven is the Triangle above the square. It relates to the cyclic expressions of time in the cosmos and in man's life. It is an outer expression of an inner spiritual principle. Thus at seven a child loses its milk teeth, at fourteen develops sexuality, at twenty-one enlarges the faculties unfolded in the teens, at twenty-eight stabilises them etc. There are said to be seven chakras, or centres within man's body, which are foci of the spiritual forces acting on his body and soul. These are expressions of different levels of consciousness, and different forces or principles, such as growth, reproduction, and sensation. Thus it represents the influence upon the physical, of the invisible rhythms within man, the cosmic keyboard of harmonic vibrations or energies. The zodiacal sign is Libra the manager. It rules the kidneys, and the seventh house rules marriage. Seven is the number of initiation, and there are seven colours in the spectrum, seven notes in music.

8 Usually associated with generation, degeneration and regeneration. In the growth of a seed, we can take the seed to represent number one, its relationship with the soil or opposite as two; the budding of seed into shoot as three or the point of growth: then the reaching above ground and rooting as four. The opening of leaves five; the development of stem six, the formation of bud seven, the opening of bud and fertilisation eight, the forming of seed nine. Thus eight can be seen as a climax where the old self opens to the development of the seeds of the new. It is a sort of death or degeneration into matter, that yet develops the seeds of the future, of spiritual consciousness. It is thus the sign of death and rebirth. Also of Justice. In the symbol of the figure eight, we see that the down-

287

ward loop drops and then doubles back to rise again. The Zodiacal sign of Scorpio, the governor or inspector. It governs the generative organs, and the eighth house governs legacies, death, the occult.

9 The fact that all numbers rise in series of nines and then begin again, and that babies are born in the ninth month, lends itself to nine symbolising the completion of a process, or stage of growth. There are also, in some mythologies and religions, nine orders of angels or forces. At the ninth hour, the veil is rent between spirit and matter. The astrological sign is Saggitarius, the sage or counsellor. It rules the thighs, and the ninth house rules travel and dreams.

0 Zero is taken as complete negation and meaninglessness, yet it is the very substance upon which all the other numbers, all the rest of manifestation, rests. When we see, sense, know or realise anything we do it against the background of space, of absence, the void. Things are distinct because they appear in this void. A tree only has being because it is surrounded, even if only slightly, by space. It is said that we can lose ourselves in a crowd, but not in a space. Thoughts also are only coherent because of the absence of other thoughts, because we are not overwhelmed with thought, because there is a mental space into which this thought can materialise and be recognised. Everywhere we see that this void is absolutely necessary for individual realisation, as a background to all life, and all its processes. From this void we emerge, into it we withdraw again. It is the chaos or unconditioned state prior to the emergence of One. It is the Ain Soph, or Unknown God of the Kabbalah, that is beyond all manifestation. It is the void of Zen Buddhism. In it all opposites are lost, there is neither movement or non-movement, good or bad, up or down, creativeness or destructiveness, love or hate. It is beyond the opposites. Yet it is the very source of all that arises, beginning with one, and yet itself never moving.

10 From nine onwards one must start from the beginning. Although one divides into all things without changing their nature, when it is added it makes a definite change. But zero can be added to all things without changing their nature, proving that it is symbolically representative of the void, or spirit in its unmanifest aspect, or nirvana. Eleven is two ones. One plus one equals two. Twelve is three, One plus two equals three. Thirteen is One plus three equals four and so on. After nine, the series starts again on a higher octave. So ten represents a new beginning on a higher octave. We start afresh, almost as if from scratch, but all the past experience lies behind us. The seed, falling from the pod, and growing, carries with it the essence of the old plant. So it symbolises reincarnation, the starting again, under the influence of past experience and karma.

The astrological sign is Capricorn, the priest or ambassador. It rules the knees and circulation, and the tenth house governs careers and notoriety.

11 The eleventh hour has represented last minute activity, last desperate efforts. It also represents strength to face and control animal nature or instincts, which gives us liberty from them. It is two on a higher level, or another level, symbolising a reflex of number ten, which is the dynamic directive to reincarnate, or re-express. Eleven is the matrix, or mould, within us, that receives and restores form after the pattern we have already created in the past; or on the basis of what we have experienced in the past. The astrological sign is Aquarius, the seeker or scientist. It governs ankles and nervous system, and the eleventh house rules long friendships.

12 A remarkable number as far as the unconscious, and symbolism is concerned. It is cosmic in its significance. We have the twelve Zodiacal signs, twelve disciples, twelve knights of King Arthur, the Druids had twelve helpers, twelve labours of Hercules, twelve tribes of Israel, twelve brain nerves. It is possible that the same unconscious wisdom that painted the stars into the Zodiac with its giant grasp of inner truth, also projected a similar correspondence upon these other twelves. It is an important number to be projected upon so many aspects of life, the cosmic and the human. It represents at one moment the pathway of experience confronting the human soul in its search for completeness, at another the faculties within the spirit that can express into life. There is not sufficient space to explain the pathway of experience symbolised by the Zodiac, but we can see part of the zodiacal wisdom used as symbols in the twelve disciples of Jesus. These disciples represent qualities we have to develop within self to be whole. Peter is Aries, the impulsive, instinctive. But his lower instinctive forces are redeemed by Christ, and he becomes the rock of faith. Andrew is Cancer, strength of mind, that can be servility to the world, or awe in the face of God. James, Saggitarius. Hope or aspiration, faculty of judgement, or discrimination. John, Leo. This is the ability to love. He and Mary are united as Mother and son by Jesus, representing the unity of masculine and feminine love within us under spirit. Philip, Virgo. The personal power, calculating, precise use of energy in life. It represents control of our enormous energies to do ill or good. Power over actions, speech, thoughts, all of which, under direction of spirit can become a huge force. Mathew, Capricorn. The will power, and intellectual discernment, or worldly wisdom. Outer abilities in the world.

Thomas, Scorpio. Inner understanding, intellectual curiosity investigating the inner self. Doubt, which can destroy inner truth, or if it is a doubt that is unbiased and seeks truth, can define inner experience, and can express wisdom boldly and surely.

Bartholomew-Nathaniel, Libra. Imagination, creativity of thoughts and feelings. An open mind.

Thaddeus Jude, Aquarius. The power to eliminate the unnecessary or outgrown. The ability to put aside outworn conventions, ideas, feelings, to look through to the spirit underlying them.

Simon Zelotes, Taurus. Physical and emotional substance, background, past, habits and memories.

James the Lesser, Gemini. Sense of order, or symmetry. Ability to place ideas, experiences into meaning and a fitting place in life.

Judas Iscariot, Pisces. Remaining doubts, the unredeemed part of self that is never quite sure of inner experience. The twelfth sign of the Zodiac is Pisces, the poet or interpreter, ruling his unconscious, and the feet. All else rests upon the feet, or unconscious, the root of our awareness, but if they are made of clay, we may stumble.

13 This represents the twelve aspects of man's soul under direction of spirit. If an aspect is still unredeemed, then pain and misfortune attend us. If the spirit is made conscious in God, then there is nothing but completion and wholeness associated with this number.

NUN   The part of your feelings turned to spirit. Receptivity to spiritual wisdom. See *Monk*.

NURSE   Healing, fears of health, desire to be nursed or cared for. Desire to be loved as a child.

NUT   A fool. Also symbol of the inner self, the kernel of truth.

NYMPH   See *Fairy*.

O

The fifteenth letter of the Hebrew alphabet is Samech, the symbol of which is an encircling arrow, the limits of which one cannot pass. Thus it represents fate, the circumscriptions of destiny. See also *Circle*.

OAK   Strength, perseverance, mightiness, sheltering, protection, hardiness, fruitlessness. Many people translate or understand the cross of Jesus to be a tree. Artists have often depicted Jesus nailed to a tree. Often, this is the oak, which symbolises the power of the earth's foundations in spirit; the power behind material creation. See *Acorn, Cross, Tree*.

OAR   Means of directing life through its course. May also have a phallic significance due to its in and out motion. Could also be used as word play for whore.

OASIS   Feeling values, sympathies, growth of living emotions, within the aridity of materialism and dry intellectualism. See *Desert*.

OATS   Sexual energy. Wild oats being the expression of youthful sexuality and sensuality. See *Corn*.

OBESITY   See *Fat*.

OBLATION   The offering or surrender, of some part of self to whatever is symbolised as the point of the oblation. Offering an animal to God would be surrender of instinctive or sexual urges to spiritual direction: offering of a human head to an idol of a woman might mean that one has sacrificed reason to sexual desire.

OBSCENE   Some obscene dreams represent desires in the self which we may be horrified of, but which are natural in their place. Being horrified of them, we repress them, and so they are only capable of releasing themselves in dreams, and then often only symbolically. But our repression or disgust has not removed them. Far from it, they are now active within us, influencing our unconscious behaviour towards others and self. Far better to admit them and enable them to express in constructive ways.

OBSESSION   We are all obsessed or possessed in various ways until we find liberation in spiritual consciousness. For instance, we may not be able to walk down the street without shoes, or be unable to appear in public without a collar and tie, or properly shaved, or with the wrong people, we are thus literally possessed by social codes, fear of looking a fool, and so on. Being possessed by such things our actions are controlled by such fears. These are demons that rule our life and enslave us, and that Jesus, or spirit, casts out. These factors are often symbolised in dreams as an obsessing agent.

OCCIDENT   See *West*.

OCEAN   See *Sea, Water*.

OCTOPUS   Depending upon whether we are the octopus, it may symbolise the desire to ravenously seize another in our emotions and possess them. Or it may represent fear of being possessed by these emotions, either in self or in another. Hadfield points out that a baby at its mother's breast often seizes upon her in this way while suckling. The octopus can of course also symbolise any unconscious fear that may drag us into its realm of irrational terror or loathing.

OCULIST   The aspect of self that attempts to improve our view of things, or gives us a false view of things. See *Spectacles*.

ODOUR Depends entirely upon what is smelt, what emotions surround it. For instance, one can say I smell a rat, or something smells fishy or the whole situation stinks to high heaven. A perfume can remind us of a particular person, and therefore symbolise them, or a particular memory or events in life. Odours often represent feelings, attractions, repulsion, fresh or stale, living or dying. They can also represent feelings emanating from us, or the symbol.

ODYSSEY Usually symbolizes the problems, of a personal and inner nature, that we have to deal with in order to find happiness, self, God, success.

OFFERING See *Oblation*.

OFFICER or OFFICIAL Mostly symbolises the part of us in control of a particular area of self. Love for a husband and children may act as a controlling factor on desires to have a good time with others, or over innate laziness. Or fear of being a nobody may direct ambitions and plans. Sometimes represents the action of the spirit upon the soul, and its authority to guide and direct.

OGRE Generally, temper, anger, lack of sympathy or understanding, that devours or crushes others. Or a symbol of the same thing in others and how we relate to it.

OIL We can pour oil on troubled waters; be an oily or slippery sort of person, or be well oiled. The word is sometimes used to mean flattery, unctuousness, cunningness, working well, removal of friction or argument and disagreement. In the parables it is referred to as resourcefulness, forethought, and as a symbol for the soul. The lamp is the body, the oil the soul, the wick our self surrender to spirit. The flame then transmutes the oil into light, or spiritual consciousness. To be anointed with oil is to receive an outpouring of spiritual power or blessing.

OLD See *Ancient*.

OLIVE   Peace. It also represents love and kindness, because the oil from the olive is rich and soothing.

OM or AUM or OMNE   A representation of the Word, or whole cosmos, or whole being, body, soul and spirit, or the complete range of forces within self and the universe. Completeness, harmony.

ONE   See *Numbers*.

ONION   May represent crying, or tears, or something we find it difficult to face. The Egyptians and Druids also used it as a symbol of God, and it was used as a means of divining. Its symbolism possibly arises from its layer upon layer going into the centre. Onions have been used as a symbol to ward off the devil, as is garlic. Also the thick outer skin is said to be thicker if a bad winter is coming.

OOZE   See *Mud*.

OPAL   See *Jewels*.

OPERA   Sometimes symbolises either the dramatisation of inner feelings, or the stage of life, or development reached. See *Stage*.

OPERATION   Some inner attitude is sick, and is being removed. Fear of illness.

OPIUM   Is often used to describe an attempt to hide weaknesses by idealism, romanticism, religion. It can symbolise any means by which we hide fears, failings, inability to face life, inability to come to terms with life.

ORACLE   Intuition.

ORANGE   See *Colour*. A thirst quencher, satisfaction, fruitlessness. May also symbolise the Self or whole being, or aspects of self under the one skin. Due to its colour it has been used as a sun symbol, and so a sign of the spirit.

ORCHARD   Fruitfulness, the results of labours. See *Garden*.

ORB   See *Circle*.

ORCHESTRA   The harmonious union of different desires, ambitions, emotions, thoughts.

ORE   See *Mine*.

ORGAN   The different areas of your life, different ideas, capabilities, feelings, sympathies, weaknesses, strengths, that can be played upon.

ORGY   The release of repressed desires, glutting themselves.

ORIENT   See *East*.

ORPHAN   Fear of being unloved. Feeling of being misunderstood, insecure or homeless, either in mind or body. May represent the feeling of being lost, or parentless in the midst of material life, of not knowing your origins, or spiritual parentage.

OSSIFICATION   Becoming too fixed in your habits, your mental and emotional outlook.

OSTRICH   Generally used as a symbol for not wanting to see what is going on by sticking its head in the sand.

OUR LADY   See *Madonna*.

OVAL   Is a symbol of the egg, or being circumscribed or limited, or in the throes of time. It can therefore be a symbol of material existence, and time. See *Circle*.

OVEN   In common speech is used as a symbol of the womb, one in the oven. Also as a symbol of the crucible or melting pot, where changes in life are made. The oven is a magical instrument, because we put in one substance, that may be inedible and taste-less, and out comes something quite different. It therefore represents transformation. See *Alchemist*.

OWL   Intuition and spiritual wisdom, due to its ability to see in the dark, and turn its gaze in any direction. Sometimes represents a fear of the dark, or inner contents of self, or of death or the unconscious, the latter being synonymous.

OX   See *Bull*. Represents the earthy part of human nature.

OXYGEN   Energy, life giving forces.

OYSTER   Silence, tight lipped, secretive, hiding a secret beauty. It may also represent the body, or material existence, in which our soul develops as does the pearl, through irritation, and is trapped by its restrictions. May also represent outer hardness to others, the shell closed around our inner feelings. Eating oysters is thought by some to stimulate sexuality, and so it could be a symbol of this. And there is the saying, the world is my oyster, suggesting we can find riches and beauty in life once we open the shell. See *Pod*.

P
Ayin is the seventeenth Hebrew letter. It represents all that is crooked, debased, wrong, disillusionment.

PADDLE   See *Oar*.

PADLOCK   See *Lock*.

PAINT   There are many sayings that illustrate how paint can be used in dreams. We can paint the town red, paint too rosy a picture, whitewash everything, paint too clear a picture.
These suggest letting loose pent up high spirits; being too optimistic; trying to cover up mistakes; being too honest. Painting can also symbolise self expression, realisation of inner contents, hiding the real condition of things with a veneer of paint, or to put a new appearance on things.

PALACE   A sense of importance, or desire to be important.

296

PALMIST Intuition; or inner feelings about how life should be used, or where we wish to go.

PANTHEON Consciousness or contact with the gods. That is, awareness of the prime moving forces of the universe.

PAPER Valuelessness. Not worth the paper it is written on. Or we can have a clean sheet, or a receptive state ready to receive words or ideas. See *Newspaper*.

PARACHUTE A symbol the unconscious would use to represent overcoming the fear of falling. See *Fall*.

PARADISE In harmony with one's innate nature.

PARALYSIS An expression of how fear paralyses control of self, or conscious control.
Sometimes we become paralysed because unconscious fears attempt to become expressed; or urges we fear attempt expression. We can also be paralysed by sense of guilt, sense of inadequacy, or ignorance. When Jesus healed the paralysed man he said Thy sins are forgiven thee. This symbolises paralysis through sense of guilt or sinfulness, of being outside God.
As soon as the guilt is removed, as it can be by our spirit, then we are no longer paralysed.

PARASITE A case is known to the author, where while relaxing, a man saw a dark and frightening shape leave the region of his heart. The man had suffered an illness, and now felt a fear of weakness concerning the heart. The dark shape was an embodiment of this fear, which sapped his energies as a parasite. These can appear in dreams as a demon or incubus, and represent our own terrors, fears, thoughts and desires out of harmony with our spiritual energy.

PARCEL Usually a memory or experience we have not explored, investigated or cared to open to consciousness. Talents we have not used, ideas we have not applied, loving words we have not uttered.

PARIAH Parts of our felings we have repressed or refused to allow expression in our life. They now become dependant and parasitic like beggars, because we have not allowed them to develop their innate possibilities and spiritual qualities. See *Tramp*.

PARLIAMENT   Your sense of social unity. The point of decision, of whether the issue is needed by enough aspects of self to make it necessary or rightful.

PARROT   Copying, without judgement, what others do or say.

PARTHENON   The temple of Athena. The sacred place where intuition communes with God.

PARTY   Gaiety, frivolity, usually symbolises lack of depth, of satisfaction, wisdom or meaning. Light heartedness.

PASSENGER   If in a car, it suggests we are being driven by something or someone. Dependence on other people's decisions, energy or drive.

PASSPORT   Symbol of travel, of change, of one's own integrity.

PATH   One's direction in life; the ideas or aspirations that govern direction. If we love caring for others, these feelings may direct us along the path of healing, nursing, medical practice. The path therefore symbolises the direction indicated by the innermost feelings, or innermost self. To lose the way, or go off the path, is to lose contact with, become confused over, or ignore this inner tendency. The path has been used as a religious symbol for thousands of years, and here means the direction in which spirit seeks self realisation. It is the path of experience we tread from unconsciousness, or preconsciousness, lost in the forces of nature and instinct, to liberation and individualisation of self in a conscious realisation of the innate being, at all its levels. The path is a natural outflowering, or becoming conscious of, and expressive of, all that is latent in our being. The plant, as it grows, treads the path of self realisation in giving expression to all that is latent in the seed.

PEACOCK   Pride, outer show, attempt to impress. Due to the beauty of its tail, and the iridescent eyes thereon, it is sometimes also a symbol of the opening in the soul of beautiful spiritual qualities, and a realisation of the eye of God watching us, directing us.

PEARL   The soul. See *Jewels*.

PEDESTAL   To place apart, to separate, to place above other things, to idolise or worship.

PEGASUS   See *Horse*.

PENDANT   See *Necklace*.

PENGUIN   At home in cold and water, not in air. That is, at home within self, emotions and introverted feelings, but not in thought. Clumsy on land, or in everyday life.

PENTACLE   See *Five* in *Numbers*.

PEOPLE   Several people in a dream usually represent social contact with others or with various parts of the self that are involved in the dream issue.

PEPPER   Stimulant, hot tempered, heated feelings, desires to hot up the affair.

PERFUME   See *Odour*.

PERSIA   Beautiful feelings of the soul, but swayed by emotion and love of finery. The discriminating between the real and the unreal, eternal and transitory.

PERSPIRE   Strong emotion, deeply moved, fear, intense feeling.

PESTILENCE   Unable to stop our thoughts and worries when we wish to sleep, is to be plagued by the negative side of our nature. The plagues of Egypt represent the troubles that come to the outer life when the inner life is in bondage to material values. If Israel, our soul, is set free to follow its quest for the promised land of self realisation and spiritual consciousness, these plagues will not be sent upon us.

PESTLE Masculine force, or drive, used to break down problems. Also phallus, when thinking of the sexual use of the words pound or grind.

PETAL Sensitive and gentle parts of your nature, that may be crushed or destroyed.

PETER Faith. See *Numbers* (12).

PETRIFY The normal expression of self is blocked through fear. As an example, I loved my father, but was petrified of showing it due to his cynicism.

PETROL Emotional energy and drive. Potentially explosive emotions. Liquid fire.

PETTICOAT Inner feelings that few see. Sometimes symbolises sexual feelings, or even psychic body or aura.

PHANTOM See *Ghost* or *Demon*.

PHLEGM Rubbish, blocked emotions, fears about health, poisons in system of body, or mind. Sluggish, stagnation.

PHOENIX Death and Rebirth. See *Death*.

PHOTOGRAPH A memory, an impression one may have forgotten, or occurred subliminally. In some people's dreams the photograph comes to life, suggesting a memory, hope, or impression that is now coming into activity.

PHYSICIAN See *Doctor*.

PIANO Expression of self in some way.

PICTURES—PAINTINGS Your works, the things you have done, the picture you have painted of self through your actions in life. See *Photograph*.

PIE   See *Cook* and *Oven*.

PIG   Low, greedy, having no refinement. But due to the sow's ability to suckle enormous numbers, may also symbolise sustenance of a material sort. Pig headed is stubbornness. Generally represents sensuality, lost in material vices. Can sometimes mean the power of material experience.

PIGEON   Thoughts, aspirations. Also see *Dove*.

PILGRIM   Symbolises the quest for self realisation, or understanding of self.

PILL   A bitter pill to swallow, a sugar coated pill, meaning a hard experience to accept and an experience that is difficult but has benefits, as when someone we like dies but leaves us a fortune. Frequently symbolises our experiences, our attempt to deal with things, and our outer methods of coping with inner situations.
If we dream of a particular pill, one we have just been taking, it naturally associates with the events or reason for taking the pill.

PILLOW   Restful, relaxing thoughts and feelings. The softer parts of self.

PIMPLE   Irritating inner feeling that has risen to consciousness.

PIN   Connections with things, as you can't pin that on me. Good luck.

PINCH   Hard times, painful circumstances, miserliness, stealing. Test of reality.

PINEAL   Spiritual consciousness as sight.

PINEAPPLE   Fruitfulness of soul. Quality or royalty. Self confidence. See *Apple*.

PIPE or PIPE SMOKING   Masculinity, adulthood, assurance, calmness, patient and peaceful.
Crawling through a pipe suggests feelings or fears of being hemmed in, trapped, or in the narrow straits, or difficult circumstances within or in outer life. May also represent birth, either symbolically, or as memories of birth.

PISTON   Force, energy. Phallus.

PIT   Trapped by events or outer circumstances, but due to attitudes and desires, that have led you to the pit. Problems, feelings of being imprisoned and buried by your life.

PITUITARY   Intellectual realisation of spiritual values.

PLACENTA   Aftermath of dependences. Our dependence on others, or theirs on us.

PLAGUE   See *Pestilence*.

PLAIT   The inner strength that comes from uniting parts of the being into one aim, one direction, one leadership. Thus Jesus speaks of having a single eye. That is, all the faculties are directed from one source, the spirit.

PLANET   In a general sense, the planets symbolise a desire to rise above difficulties, to discover strange marvels, unique joys and adventures, to be different, or may link with something we have just read. But for thousands of years the planets have had a particular meaning, and often the unconscious uses the planet to symbolise this.

Sun   Centre of being, the source of vital energy and life. The emanator of light, intelligence or wisdom, heat, feelings and emotions and power, life. It thus represents the Spirit or Self. Masculine.

Moon   Receives and reflects power, influences the tides of man's

302

affairs, loves, hates. Acts on emotions and inner life and mind. See *Moon*.

Mercury Intuition. The patron of thieves because intuition is not only nearest the Sun, or Spirit, but also has information, or takes wisdom or secrets, from all sources.
It thus represents universal mind, or knowledge of all things. Also changeability, or a reflection of change, as with mercury in a thermometer. Hermes, or Mercury, intuition is thus not only the rock upon which one's church, or religion should be built, but also the star or guide of the Magi, and the cloud from whence the Holy voice speaks, by day the pillar of vapour, by night the pillar of fire. (Kingsford).

Venus Love, motherhood, receptivity, feminine loveliness and gentleness to which a man can turn and find strength and inspiration. Wife and Mother of God. Man's wife. Eve and Mary. Emotions, feelings, sympathy; beauty, harmony and love.

Mars Expression of energy through activities. Can be destructive or warlike, or add vigour and fire to creativeness. Masculine; energy ruled by passions, desire, greed. Aggressiveness.

Jupiter Growth, expansion, increase and preservation. A huge influence of a benevolent, generous nature. The soul becoming free of material values. Wealth, prosperity, good fortune.

Saturn Slowness, retarding influence. Emotional coldness. Ruler of time.

Uranus Change, fluctuation, sudden reverses.

Neptune Psychic; emotions, inner self, death and the unconscious.

PLATE In having a lot on one's plate, it means a lot to cope with or deal with, or get through. A plate symbolises tasks, duties, the things we are tackling, hopes and plans, ability to receive.

May also symbolise needs, hungers, appetites. At one time a symbol of status, when only the rich afforded china or silver.

PLOUGH   To break and change habits, opinions and attitudes of the past. To prepare for change or the reception and growth of new ideas. To make past experiences fertile.

PLUMBING   The way in which emotions or feelings are directed. If we believe in free love, this belief directs the emotions differently to those of one who feels that sex is a sin, or one who surrenders to the spirit. Each of these attitudes is a different plumbing system. A burst water pipe would therefore represent a breaking out of controlled emotions.

PLUMB-LINE   A sense of rightness, of living according to what we know, deep within, to be the true upright.

PLUNDER   To abuse someone's rights and feelings against their real wishes. If a man forces himself upon a girl, and despite her requests for him to leave her alone, uses her body for his own ends, then he has plundered. In lesser, or other ways, we are often plundered by others who disregard our real feelings, or vice versa.

PLUNGE   To press into something that is unknown, untried.

POACH   Unconscious inner events that kill or influence instincts or sexual feelings. A hypnotic suggestion that we fall in love with a person would be poaching on our feelings.

POCKET   Memory; inner reserves of vitality, money, capabilities, tools, pen, etc.; possession, ownership.

POD   Restrictive and protective influence you break out of. Somebody is said to come out of their shell when they break free of reserve or restraining influences.
Parental influence could be symbolised as a pod.

POEM   See *Proverb*.

POET   Imaginative faculty that may, through inspiration or intuition, express our deepest feelings that are hidden to the more conservative, conscious, self.

POINT   Meaning: meeting or unity; direction. See *Dot*.

POLE   See *Maypole*, *Oar*.

POLE STAR   Self or Spirit. See *North Star*.

POLICEMAN   Social code; sense of right and wrong, or how we wish to appear in the eyes of others. Conscience, rules of conduct. Our morals, or ideas and feelings as to how we should react to others. The policeman does not necessarily represent innermost or spiritual directions, but only social or more conscious codes. These, like the country's laws, can change, arbitrarily, and be replaced by other laws or moral codes. The policeman is therefore most often a symbol of outer and social relationships, and how we feel about them. Often represents a sense of guilt and shame, behaviour influenced by the need to conform to orthodoxy or uniformity.

POLICEWOMAN   As policeman, but moral issues that have arisen more from sympathies and feeling values than from accepted or unconscious conscience or sense of sin and guilt.

POLITICAL   Sometimes symbolises interests in the government of outer life as distinct to inner life. Naturally, if one has strong political feelings, it would symbolise the underlying attitudes that produce these feelings or ideas.

POLLEN   Sperm, fruition, fertility as from new ideas.

POOL   Inner feelings.

POPE   Spiritual values, depending on associations. See *Christ* and *Guru*.

POSTER   See *Newspaper*.

305

POSTMAN   Some part of self, or a realisation that has brought something to our notice. An experience that has made us realise something. Hopes.

POSTURE   Expressive of how you feel or think.

POT   (See *Hashish*) A cooking pot is similar to an oven. A receptive part of us which, because it receives the new things of life, opens us to change. See also *Cook, Oven, Circle, Oval, Food*.

POTATO   Depends more than usual on the dreamer's own associations. Do we regard it as fattening, starchy, forbidden, enjoyable, messy, or what?

POTTER   We can potter around, which suggests doing nothing in particular. Objectively, it may symbolise an attempt to shape and make something of life. Subjectively it suggests being affected by outside influences.

POUND   See *Pestle*. Weight may suggest gravity or seriousness. See *Fat*.

POVERTY   May either be representative of ideas of being worthless, or of inability; or if one is very proud, or haughty, it may symbolise being poor in spirit, lacking in human qualities. Sometimes an expression of insecurity.

PRAY   Expressive of an inner desire, fear or need. Also an alignment of self with God. See *Meditation*.
May present information about the inner self of which we are unaware.

PRECIPICE   Fear of falling. See *Cliff* and *Fall*.
Fear of failure. Difficulty in attaining our goal.

PREGNANCY   If physically pregnant, then it most often refers to this, and the fears, hopes, attitudes, desires, ideas and physical condition regarding it. It can also symbolise the development of some new approach to life, new outlet of expression, or new faculty.

PREMONITION When we have a premonition in a dream, it may not necessarily materialise. Sometimes it must be taken symbolically. To fear a fall down a ladder may easily symbolise apprehension with regard to the loss of one's job, failure in marriage, or losing the esteem of others. A premonition of a drowning son may symbolise the feeling that hopes in life are being drowned by emotions of inferiority. But of course, many such dreams do prophesy actual events, although once again, such prophetic dreams may themselves be symbolic, and not set in a dream of premonition. There is usually a particular tone about such dreams that one can learn to notice.

PRESCRIPTION Usually a suggestion from the inner self, to the outer, conscious self, to be taken seriously. Suggests being out of harmony, or diseased with the inner self.

PRESENT Depends very much on who or what gives the present. May symbolise the giving or receiving of love, recognition, depending on the context.

PRESS See *Newspaper.*

PREY Either the victim or others' desires, or victimising others. The fear of being hurt or destroyed in some way.

PRIEST Depends on the attitude to priests, and experiences of them. May represent religious or spiritual aspirations. Sense of sin.

PRIMEVAL Deep levels of consciousness, instinctive feelings, unconscious powers and activities. Levels of being that developed in us in ages past, and are given to us as a physical and mental heritage. We are usually not aware of these parts of self.

PRINCE Conscious (or in a woman may be unconscious) intellectual, masculine qualities. Sometimes the search for truth, or attempts to direct or use the physical and mental heritage.

PRINCESS Conscious (or in a man may be unconscious) emotional, feminine qualities. Sometimes represents the inner self, receptive, gentle, sympathetic nature. A sense of beauty and love in alignment with life.

PRISON   Most often feelings of being imprisoned by the inability to cope with circumstances, moods, relatives. Trapped by inadequacies, fears, moral codes, ambitions, sense of superiority. Any limiting influence within, or outside of us. We have to realise, however, that if the influence seems to be from outside, it is only because we have not yet discovered our own inner attitude that makes us subject to that limitation. One child may easily becomes independent of home and parents, another may never do so, because they are inwardly different. The prison doesn't exist if the inner condition changes. Stone walls do not a prison make, nor iron bars a cage.

PRIZE   Some gain in self understanding or insight found through your endeavours. A desire to win, or be superior. Fear of losing.

PROP   Some idea, belief, or outer influence, like alcohol, or drugs, which we may need at a particular time to keep us from falling in some way. We may take a particular medicine due to a fear of illness. Although we may not be ill at all, the medicine helps to suppress the fear. Dreams often aim at removing the prop and facing up to the fear which caused us to lean upon it.

PROPELLER   The driving energy behind emotions. May be ambition, will, desire to be somebody, or to get somewhere, or just energy.

PROPHESY   See *Premonition.*

PROSECUTION   Either a fear of having done wrong, a desire to do so, or guilt. Or the feeling that someone else has wronged us.

PROSTITUTE   May symbolise the misdirection of love and affection for financial ends, or selfish motives. Or feelings of sexual inadequacy. Needing to resort to buying a prostitute's services. Or wallowing in material values, cynicism, hopelessness, bitterness or sensuality, as, there is no God, or spiritual future, so why not have a good time in the only way I know. The whore is also a symbol of the earth in its destructive mother aspect. The swallower of souls, of masculinity and attempts to mature. It is the whore, or mother, from whose emotional or sensual hold on us we have not found a way to break free.

PROVERB   Many people dream of a popular proverb, or sentence from a poem, hymn or song. This is because it summarises their feelings, desires, or inner realisation as depicted in the dream.

PSYCHO-ANALYSIS   Often used as a dream symbol of attempts to understand self, to release self from problems, to find one's true being. It may also be used as a symbol of a fear of mental illness. The psycho-analyst represents the part of self effecting change, mental and emotional growth, insight. See *Guru*.

PUBIC   See *Genitals* or *Hair. Vagina.*

PUBLIC HOUSE   Social enjoyments, sense of pleasure, pleasure loving or social side of self. If you are a rigid teetotaller it may symbolise the feelings that have led to this code of living.

PULLEY   The philosophy or ideas governing your actions.

PULSE   State of your life or energy.

PUPPET   To be controlled by another's whims. Or to control in the same way. You can likewise be a puppet of a love for whisky, religious ideas, betting, and so be a puppet of your own desires; we do not control them, they control us.

PUPPY   Youth, heedlessness, spontaneous affection.

PURGATORY   See *Hell.*

PURIFICATION   See *Baptism.*

PURPLE   See *Colour.*

PUS   Malfunction, stagnation or lifelessness or area in which pus is seen. Pus in mouth would symbolise inadequacy or degeneration of ways of communicating with others. Feelings of repulsion.

PYJAMAS   Sleepiness, unwillingness to face the day; doing something in sleep; suitable only during sleep. Suggestive of sleeping, unconsciousness, or sex.

PYRAMID   In popular association, the dead, mysteries. Its shape, however, would speak to the unconscious in another way. Having a square base it represents physical stability, while its triangular sides symbolise the material connections with creative processes, or the hidden side of life. A perfect expression in matter of invisible, or creative, forces. The point denotes God, where all things meet. The top stone stands for Christ, or Krishna, or Osiris, or Buddha; the link between our human qualities and spirit or God.

Power flows down from God to the base, and up from the base to God. Anna Kingsford says 'Thus, from God proceed the gods, the Elohim, or divine powers, who are the active agents of creation. From the gods proceed all the hierarchy of heaven, with the various orders from highest to lowest.' The rising power represents evolution of form and consciousness, from the lowest to the highest. Therefore, the inside of the pyramid represents initiation. It is the descent of divine power resulting in the growth of expanding consciousness and faculty in man. The stages of this unfolding are the stages of initiation. Man is therefore, as an initiate, the descent and ascent of divine creative power. The descent is the spirit's incarnation into matter; the ascent is the realisation of one's divine potentials. The Queen's chamber represents Baptism, the King's chamber rebirth or spiritual consciousness and the pit the soul lost in material values. See *Baptism*, *Death*.

Q
The seventeenth Hebraic letter is Phe.
It represents speech, or the outcome of our actions. The results of our activities in the world.

QUADRANGLE   The area of your life experience. The garden of your soul. Material experience.

QUARTZ Sometimes represents the innermost self. See *Crystal, Rock.*

QUAY See *Harbour.*

QUEEN Your mother. Ruling passions. A desire to rule over others emotionally, or to be respected.

QUICKSAND Feelings of hopelessness that swallow up all plans, hopes, efforts. Fear of losing ground in competition with others. Emotions that engulf us.

R

Tzaddi is the eighteenth Hebraic letter. It means an aim or goal. The letter R has a strongly masculine influence, in the same way as M has strong feminine or mother associations.
Such strong, energetic words as regal, royal, rich, ripping, rousting, rumpus, race, ram, all come under this R sound.

RABBI Symbol of your attitude to your religious tendencies, or to Jewish religious ideas.

RABBIT Sometimes used as a sex symbol due to its sexuality and rapid breeding. Also used in dreams to denote softness, idealism, emotions, or a sense of beauty, that rises in the conscious self from the unconscious. These emotions stem from fears and insecurities, so that if I have as an ideal the desire to better the world, or help others, it may arise from my fear of being a nobody, or fear of failure. While a desire to be in the public eye might arise from feelings of inferiority, a desire to prove oneself or fear of being lonely and unwanted. Sometimes the rabbit is killed or sacrificed in dreams, symbolising the sacrificing of such unconscious ideals to the spirit or growth of self. The rabbit is used as such a symbol because it lives and breeds underground, is easily hurt, is soft and preyed upon by many predators, yet is quite lovely to see.

RACE Feelings of competitiveness, questions of capability, worthiness, or fear of losing or being inferior. Your self respect is bound up in the symbol.

RADAR   Intuition.

RADIANT   See *Light* and *Glow*.

RADIO   Entertainment, news of others, communication with others. May symbolise telepathy, or contact with God.

RADIOACTIVE   Powerful energies arising from within, that seem to threaten the conscious self. Contamination, harm through unconscious influences, such as emotions picked up from others, attitudes radiated from others that we have not noticed, but have been influenced by.

RAFT   A flimsy philosophy, or inadequate motives or ideas, with which we hope to deal with life. For instance, a person who knows nothing of large cities, setting off to a big town to seek independence and security, without any particular job, home, or ability, is setting sail on a raft.

RAGGED   Without neatly defined morals, philosophy, etc.

RAILWAY   Several ideas are expressed symbolically by railways. The rails themselves represent orthodoxy, the accepted way of going about things, moral values. Thus one can say someone has gone off the rails. The engine stands for the often tremendous energy which takes us through life. The carriages represent the events or influences or things brought about, the train of experiences or events that follow in the wake of our actions.
A train or railway station also symbolise our efforts or desires to get somewhere, to go on a journey, to find fresh territory, new friendships, opportunities, understanding; to travel to new experiences or parts of self. Self analysis is often symbolised as a journey. Someone preventing us getting to the station or train denotes fear or attitudes holding us back in life. To miss the train is like missing the boat, we have missed the opportunity, lost the chance. To be run over by a train is to be threatened by the things we have set in motion, or by the orthodox on the rails beliefs or attitudes of self or others. Thus the train can symbolise success or failure to get on in life.

RAIN George Fox states, in his Journal, that in Wales during a drought, wherever he preached rain fell. He likens it to the release of spiritual feelings, a release of spirit from materialism and ignorance.

Generally rain symbolises emotions, release of feelings, usually of a moral or spiritual nature, though not always.

If the rain is gentle it is usually a relaxing experience and a release from ideas and intellect. If it is a downpour and storm, it is feelings which may drench us, as in sadness or grief about a friend passing. If the land is inundated, then our commonsense is lost to sight in the emotions released, and danger may threaten.

RAINBOW A promise, an agreement, a harmony between self and spirit.

RAM Tenacity, masculine strength, toughness and power. A man's strength. The sacrifice of the ram is a surrender of this strength to the spirit that it may be directed by God.

RAT One can be a rat, or smell a rat, or rat on someone. In this sense it means to be skulking, or underhand, a person who fails others through fear or trying to be better, or who deserts his party, especially during stress; as a rat leaving a sinking ship. Underhand activities carried out without admitting the real motives, such as sex without love, or for material gain, as a man marrying a rich woman. Is also said to represent time gnawing away unknown at our life, and we may turn to find it empty.

RAVEN Death, fear, the unknown. The dark intelligence. Forces in life that seem to have intelligent direction, yet are not outwardly visible. Bad luck.

RAZOR Intellectual acuteness. The ability to cut through the useless or misleading to the real issue. But such cleverness may be dangerous if we are not very humble, for you can also cut away feelings and pleasure in living. It symbolises the thin dividing line between wisdom and folly, life and death, genius and insanity, self and spirit.

READING Realisation, thinking, looking at self, reviewing ideas, considering something, or memorising.

REAP Experiencing the results of our actions.

RECIPE The way to use self, or the right proportion of things, all work and no play makes Jack a dull boy.

RECLUSE See *Hermit*.

RECORD See *Gramophone*.

RED See *Colours*.

RED INDIAN The psychic, inner life. The part of us that is at home in the irrational or unconscious, and relates to the spirit through this.

REED Humility, flexibility. In religion and mythology the reed represents the human will that has been surrendered to God or the spirit, and is thus directed by God's will. It does not represent weakness, for it takes a strong will not to be moved by worldly ambitions or sensuality, but to surrender or sink personal interests into those of the universal.

REFRIGERATE To cool off emotionally.

REGENERATION See *Death*.

RENT The demands life makes upon us in particular situations. If we want a big garden the rent is the work it takes to look after it.

REPTILE May symbolise a snake, or have similar meaning to snake. Cold bloodedness, the ever open eye. See *Snake, Alligator, Frog*.

RESTAURANT Sociability, relaxation, friendship. Search for sustenance or strength, or ways of directing your life. See *Food*.

REVOLUTION Major changes in self, in viewpoint, understanding, activities, in governing desires.

RHEUMATISM   Repression of anger or bitterness. See *Ossification*.

RHINOCEROS   Throwing your weight about. Using your influence. The same thing applies sexually. The old business of I'll get you in films if.... ?

RICH   See *Bank*.

RIFLE   Aggressiveness; to plunder.

RIGHT   The right foot, arm, leg, eye, ear, all symbolise conscious attributes as opposed to unconscious. May also suggest right as opposed to wrong. For those who are right handed, the right hand is the active, creative, dynamic hand. The left is the passive, supporting, or female helping hand. When we knock a nail in, the right hand does the work while the left holds the nail, and so on. So it suggests, in the right side of our body, the active, conscious, extroverted and male aspect of self. See *Left*.

RIGID   Maleness; unbending emotions, dogmatism.

RING   Probably represents our relationship with the person who gave it to us. Or the reason it was given. Thus it can symbolise marriage, engagement, or can represent wholeness if it is not one which has been given us. The feelings we associate with the ring. See *Circle*.

RIOT   See *Revolution*.

RITUAL   See *Ceremony*.

RIVER   Most rivers are associated with a male quality or fatherhood. We thus have Father Thames or Father Rhine. Rivers have often symbolised a source of fertility, in that the *Mother* Earth was made fertile from the waters of the *Father* River.
A river stands for the current of our energies that carry us along, or can sweep us away, or in which we can drown. Being water it is basically emotional or feeling energies. It is also similar to a snake

in its curving and so can be associated with this. Also represents the passage of time.

The meaning of the Hebrew word nahar or river, is the movement of life forces. Basically, life energy. Crossing it means a change. Going against the current is to go against your inner flow or may be an effort to find the source, or get back to the womb.

In the Bible, the river that flows out of Eden to water the Garden thus represents the basic flow of life forces at the primal level of consciousness, or Eden. This energy or prana flows to the Garden, or becomes materialised to create forms and life, thus manifesting its latent qualities. This one great stream of energy is split into four basic manifestations symbolised by the names Pishon, Gihon, Hiddekel and Euphrates. Pishon means the force in nature that brings to material reality the ideas latent in God, and is the physical plane of existence, and all in it. Havilah, the land it encompasses is the material or physical expression of anything. Gold is therein reflecting the light, consciousness or intelligence of Self or Spirit. Gihon means the astral, magnetic, or chemical forces at work on matter. Magnetism shapes iron filings, giving body. Gihon is the formative powers, impulses, the fire or drive. Hiddekel is will power or force directing the fire or magnetism of Gihon in its activity upon Pishon or matter. It represents conscious decision, thought, consideration, directing the chemical or nervous energies and emotions of our being, which in turn influence the body. Also universal principles. Euphrates or houa phrath, which has nothing to do with Euphrates, means a blessing or power to propagate, to generate or be fruitful.

RIVET   Binding connections or relationships. Sexual organ.

ROAD   The direction you are pursuing. Each such direction cannot help but lead you to a particular point in life. A road is your destiny, much of it self created by your decisions and predispositions. A road can symbolise any direction you have taken, or are thinking of taking. A love affair, marriage, business, where will they lead you? In the dream you try to look at the possibilities of these roads, and where they go. The size, richness, poverty, cleanliness of the dream road comments on how your inner self sees these avenues you have taken. See *Cul-de-sac.*

ROAR   Aggressiveness, warning.

ROCK   Solidity, strength, foundation, steadfastness in the face of storms, problems, emotions. The rock has often symbolised security, refuge and protection on the physical or social level. As a characteristic it represents rigidity or being unmoved in face of opposition. Inwardly it signifies faith that can see you through turmoil. Mentally it represents the ability to understand, and not be moved. To understand life is to be a rock amidst the waves.

Rocks or stones are the nearest material thing we have to eternity. They thrust up from the deeps of the earth. As upright columns they are often used as phallic symbols. They are placed upon graves, symbolical of the spirit outlasting the decaying flesh. As symbols of eternity they are used to mark places where holy experiences have happened, or where a man contacted God. In temples a rock was the original altar, or contact with God, upon which you sacrificed or surrendered yourself.

ROCKET   Your energies seeking release from material boundaries and limitations. The spiritual quest.

ROD   Your will. See *Reed*.

ROOF   See *House*.

ROOT   Your beginnings, basic levels of consciousness, things you are tied to by necessity, love or connections.

ROPE   Strength through unity.

ROSARY   Prayer and its influence. Stages of inner experience.

ROSE   Love; the flowering of spiritual qualities, your soul or self. See *Lily*.

ROUND   See *Circle*.

ROW   See *Oar*.

RUBBER   See *Elastic*.

RUBY   See *Jewels*.

RUDDER   The principles you hold to guide your actions.

RUNNING   Trying to escape from some emotion, some fear, or hastening to something. A sense of hurry.

RUSSIA   Material power; the denial of spiritual values; the futility of life cut off from its roots. Force, aggression, might is right attitude. Communal living.

RUST   Negligence. The transitoriness of material things.

S

The nineteenth Hebrew letter is Quoph, symbolising any tool, weapon or machine that works for man.

SACK   May suggest unemployment, ruin, plunder. Acquisitiveness on a mundane, earthy level. Poverty.

SACRIFICE   The surrendering or giving up of some part of self; or sacrificing the wishes of others for your own purposes. See *Bull*.

SADDLE   To impose your will on something. To be imposed on, or saddled with, something.

SAFARI   Coming face to face with the instincts.

SAFFRON ROBE   Spiritual wisdom, renunciation. Loss of material values.

SAILOR   Means of coping with emotions. Desire to change, to move, to see more of life. Ability to cope with life.

SAINT   See *Guru*.

SALAD   Eating of living growing things in self. Meat is always in a state of decay, or death.

SALIVA   Love or hate. It carries your inner feelings or spirit with it.

SALT   Value, goodness, luck, taste, adding spice to life. Salt also preserves. When Lot's wife looked back and was turned into a pillar of salt, it symbolised the desire to stop spiritual or mental progress. Not to look forward to greater unfoldment and the loss of old values, but to look back to the past, even failure, as it is easier than change. Salt here symbolises materialism, stagnation, lack of growth or change, preservation. Also friendship, good or bad luck.

SAND   Time, the incessant wearing away of things, the multitudinous aspects of life governed by time. See *Desert*.

SATAN   The power of material values in life. The things in life we cannot control, such as anger, sex desires, ambitions, fear, worries, etc. Those things that lead us contrary to the innate nature.
Steiner has depicted these forces as dual, calling them Lucifer and Ahriman. Lucifer is the power of egoistic desires, pride, looking after self first. My work, my religion, my beliefs, are better than yours! All these selfish traits lead to inner conflict, conflict in the world, and are the work of Lucifer.
Ahriman is the power of ignorance, of reason without feeling values, of dry intellectualism, the emphasis of materialism and a science that leads to lack of aim, lack of contact with all life; an education that is full of facts, but without any wisdom or insight, that does not develop the power of intuition. The mass media, and dictatorship, making puppets of men to a regime, a man, a fear, a totalitarianism. Christ, or the power of spirit alone puts these forces into their place. Only then do these act as powers of growth, development of understanding, the energy used to rise up. They are then unveiled as evolutionary powers that were threatening only because we could not use them correctly. See *Devil*, *Obsession*, *Demon*.

SATELLITE   Communication with others and with higher self. Link between physical and spiritual nature.

SATURN   See *Planets.*

SAUSAGE   Male sex organ. Material values.

SAVINGS   Sense of security, energy, wealth.

SAW   Criticism, cynicism, a questioning state of mind. Enquiry.

SAXOPHONE   Self expression, spontaneity.

SCABBARD   The body, the sheath of soul.

SCALD   To tell off, or be told off, or criticism.

SCALES   Balance, justice, fair play.
Scales on fish may represent the shining thoughts and feelings that make up the innermost self.

SCAR   Memory of a painful experience, emotional upsets.

SCARAB   Eternity, continuity of life, the soul, the transmuting influence. See *Alchemist.*

SCARECROW   Having no life, no spirit, empty of feelings, of worth. An illusion.

SCENT   See *Odour.*

SCHOOL   Life; the capacity or desire to learn. Something learnt; lessons of life. The need to understand. May represent experiences at school.

SCIENTIST   Analytical nature, an attempt to weigh and measure life, to discover its usefulness and how to apply it. May also symbolise an intellectual unfeeling attitude.

SCISSORS   Cutting remarks, cynicism, sharp tongue, anger or hate, and when we cut someone up. Sometimes appears in dreams of castration, where parental aggressiveness has cut off the development of the child's emerging manhood or womanhood. See *Castration*.

SCORCH   Anger, over-heated remarks or attitudes which may cause mental injury.

SCORPION   Bitterness, the sting of bitter remarks.

SCOTS   Careful, thoughtful, economical, but attempting to be just.

SCRAPE   To scrape something often symbolises the friction between two parts of our nature, or between us and someone else.

SCREW   Sexual intercourse. To make secure, an attempt at security.

SCROLL   Important ideas or realisations.

SCRUB   See *Bathing*.

SCURF   Ideas, opinions, thoughts.

SEA   To be all at sea, or lost. Whereas a river has a male significance, the sea is the mother into which the male enters. It is Mer or mother of consciousness. Life began in the sea, at the depths. Our blood is salt like the sea, and thus we have an inner sea. It represents universal mind or being, the collective unconscious, nature's memory where all experience is stored. The infinite cosmic mind. The surface is conscious life, on which the ship, or idea of self, floats, but is really supported and surrounded by uncharted depths. To dive into it is to dive into self, to look beneath the surface of consciousness, to look back to the source of life, to enter the womb or soul, to reach limitless mind. The sea shore is the point where all our elements meet. The sea holds either in its depths, or floating somewhere, vast treasures, all the things which men have ever made or thought of or done. Thus the sea can wash them ashore and bring them to our notice, or unveil them to us.
Because the sea is Mother and the united consciousness of all

beings, or the unconscious, it is associated with birth and death. To come up out of the sea is to be born, to become conscious. To cast oneself upon, or under the waters, is to die to conscious life, to leave the physical world and the sense of individuality, and return to one's origins.

The sea is also universal substance, the stuff that dreams or thoughts or emotions are made of. It is moved by the moon or the wind, and shaped by the earth. Thus it symbolises an aspect of inner life, the substance of consciousness, that takes form as thought, emotion, revelation, depending upon which circumstances are shaping it, or whether it is the spirit or inner urges that move it. See *Fish, Water*.

SEAL   As in sea, the inner energies, rising within. A seal is a trust, a security or promise, a sign of integrity, which we can abuse or use as a power. It reflects the inner self.

SEAM   Connections with others; the strength of beliefs or convictions; the weak point of attitudes or philosophy.

SEANCE   Attempt to contact the unconscious elements of self. A condition in which intuitive knowledge, repressed desires, or unconscious wishes can express. Ideas of death and after life. The unknown, the irrational, the dead.

SEARCHLIGHT   Focused attention, concentration on a particular issue. Meditation and concentration.

SEAT   See *Chair*.

SEAWEED   Developments, ideas or concepts that have formed in the unconscious, and have come to mind ready made. An intuitive answer to a problem. Inner tangle of feelings.

SECRET   Something known inwardly, but not yet recognised outwardly. We may know at heart that someone does not care for us, but because we so badly want them to, we may refuse to recognise this.

SECRETARY   The other woman, the second interest. The background of activity upon which creative work can take place. The orthodox aspects of self that yet lend a hand in the development of the creative or spiritual aspects.

SEDATIVE   Sleeping pills may represent attempts to cover up worries, fears, anxieties, painful emotions and thoughts. An attempt to push them into the unconscious.

SEED   See *Germ*. The seed carries the stored experience of the past that creates new possibilities in the present, leading to experiences in the future. See *Numbers 8*.

SELF   The way we appear, or do not appear in a dream, represents our relationship to, opinions of, and hopes for self.

SEMEN   Usually symbolises manhood, or potentials, the essence of life or personality. It is stored power.

SEPTIC   Infected by some opinion or fear, as when someone says You'll never get anywhere, you've got to have influence, this can cause us to give up effort and indulge in hopelessness.

SEVEN   See *Numbers*.

SEW   See *Darn*.

SEWAGE   See *Cesspool*.

SEX   Sexual dreams usually express hidden desires; the way we would like to express sexually, or problems in this area.

SHADE   Feelings of being in the shade, or obscured by somebody else. It may be wife, husband, or parents who make us feel inferior, and in their shadow. Usually something is standing in our way, in the sense of not enabling us to see the light, or gain understanding. A shadow is also a symbol for the unconscious activities that sometimes control actions. Someone may say something that seems harmless, but we get terribly upset and angry, or morose. It may be that unconsciously we are terrified of criticism, or feel very guilty about this thing, thus our shadow reacts violently.

Shadow can also be a sign of coming events, the shadows cast from the future. This is because we often see someone's shadow before we see them.

SHADOW   The inner feelings seldom expressed.

SHAMAN   See *Guru*.

SHAMPOO   Wash that man right out of my hair. Get out of my hair. This symbolises the effort to forget, or get over something or some-one. To be rid of longings, ideas or emotions. To cleanse sexual feelings. See *Hair*.

SHARK   A trickster, swindler, or desire to swindle. A threat from within, such as a desire to hit or hurt someone that will or may destroy us, our self respect.

SHARP   See *Razor*.

SHAVE   See *Hair*.

SHEEP   Being easily led. Can be a sign of being abused, or of accepting advice and help. See *Lamb*.

SHELL   Sometimes represents self or inner self. Or the shell we crawl into for protection against the world. See *Oyster*, *Clam*.

SHIELD   Desire for protection, or to protect.

SHINE   See *Glow*.

SHIP   Hopes of change, new things. Also self. It symbolises the personality in which we make the journey of life. See *Boat*.
Ark. A particular religion or general philosophy can be represented as a ship, as it is a means by which large numbers of people face the unknown factors of life.

Shipwreck is personal breakdown, being unable to cope with life.

SHIRT   See *Clothes.*

SHIVER   Conflict, fear, or repression.

SHOE   See *Clothes.*

SHOP   Often represents the possibilities in life, the decisions we can make, the variety of attitudes or activities we can choose from.

SHOT   To be threatened with death. The destruction of one part of self by another which is demanding our energies in an aggressive way.

SHOULDER   Strength; ability to support self or others. To let someone cry on our shoulder is to support or help them to unburden themselves through the strength of sympathy and the ability to help. Shoulder to the wheel also represents putting influence, strength or weight into something. Ability to take the burdens of life.

SHRINK   Losing power and impressiveness, changing relationship with things.

SICK   The feeling of having thought, felt, or expressed things that do not agree with your real feelings. A girl may say, I kissed him, but it made me feel sick. That is, no desire or love was in her heart, and she did it against her deeper feelings.

SIDE   Something on the side is something that is not real pleasure, or real work, not our greatest aim or goal. Some side issue.

SIGHT   See *Eye.*

SILENCE   Lack of egoistic activity, desires, etc. Inner stillness.

SILVER   The soul. See *Moon.*

325

SING   Sense of harmony with others or self. An expression of some inner harmony.

SISTER   Relationships and feelings concerning a sister.

SIX   See *Numbers*.

SKATE   Sense of balance and proportion in life.

SKELETON   Death, fear of, desire for. Hidden fears. The past. Secret annoyance.

SKIN   One's situation, environment, inherited traits or characteristics. Sometimes depicts the essence of the material or outer self, that is cast off as the inner self emerges, like a snakeskin. Here it depicts also the past. One can be thick skinned, and insensitive, or thin skinned and easily hurt. Protection.

SKIRT   See *Clothes*.

SKY   Spirit, heaven, something above one's head. Home of the gods. The invisible forces that shape life.

SLEEP   To dream of being asleep, is to be unaware of something, as one's real nature. See *Awake*.

SMELL   See *Odour*.

SMOKING   Sometimes used to represent the power of habit.

SNAIL   A snail withdraws quickly into its shell, and sometimes represents great sensitivity that makes us withdraw from life.

SNAKE   Male sexual organ. The divine energy or life force in human beings which realises and releases some of its potentials. Also a symbol of inner wisdom, or knowledge of life's secret processes; and of healing, as used by the medical profession. The snake can shed its skin, and so symbolises self transcendence, rebirth. As the power of energy that lies behind all life, it can express in many ways. As attraction and repulsion, sensuality, sexuality, love, sympathy, emotion, thought, higher consciousness. It is like a plant that can express further and further potentials if allowed to grow and develop in the right way. Thus the alchemists put a gold crown on its head, symbolising expanded or spiritual consciousness arising from the same energy as sexuality. Often a diadem, gem, or light is at its brow symbolising the possibility of expanded consciousness, or awareness of the eternal nature, and life in God. Christ is sometimes depicted as a crucified serpent.

The serpent who tempted Eve is called Nahash, meaning blind impulsive urges. But the colour and situation of the dream snake contain much information. A green snake means the life giving, growth principle of inner energy. White or gold symbolises spiritual wisdom and initiation. Blue, religious experience. Red, the sexual aspect of the energy. Orange, a mixture of sexuality, emotions and idealism. Yellow, wisdom, energy, as gold. Indigo or violet, the ranges of spirit energy and inner experience. The snake represents the energy that rises from the unconscious depths of being. It is basically an evolutionary energy moving back to spiritual consciousness. Its roots are in the processes between energy and matter, beginning in universal spiritual consciousness at it contacts matter, and develops into individual self consciousness, which then moves towards universal consciousness again, but now as an individual. In other words, from pure consciousness it creates individuality, then expands the awareness of individuality until it is aware of the whole. Thus the snake is different to the dove, or sun, which is spirit energy in its descending aspect, rather than evolving as an individual. But the snake reaches up to the sun, and the two blend, as sperm with ovum.

SNARE Seemingly appealing idea or plan, which is basically wrong.

SNEEZE Spontaneous cleansing of self, caused by the inner self rather than conscious intention.

SNOW Usually frozen or repressed feelings or emotions. Sometimes purity, dormancy, the stilling of the outer life as in winter, when the seeds and roots rest in the earth, or unconscious, till the new spring. Ideas, morals, or intellect that have frozen our feelings.

SOAP   Cleansing. An attempt to come clean, to be rid of guilt or conscience.

SOCK   The earthy aspect of personality. To pull one's socks up.

SOLAR PLEXUS   Loves and hates, controlling factor of physical life, for when hit in the solar plexus we cannot breathe.

SOLDER   Friendship, unity, strong bonds.

SON   Feelings or worries concerning a son. Growing part of self. Hopes or worries about the future.

SOUL   Individuality; existence as a definite and unique person as distinct from other people. Inner feelings, ideas, beliefs; in fact one's whole experience as an individual. Consciousness of self. To lose one's soul, or to sell one's soul, is to lose self awareness, and slip back into a lower level of consciousness. Soul is distinct from spirit, as spirit is universal consciousness and energy, as opposed to individual consciousness and activity. See *Name*.

SOUP   In the soup means being in a mess, and the dream often uses it as such a symbol. May also be sustenance, sustaining or strengthening emotions. See *Food*.

SOUTH   In some countries, as in USA, may symbolise different attitudes, as to the coloured population, or different ways of life.
The South is the symbol also of our life illuminated by higher consciousness or spirit. Whereas the East is the source of spirit, its rising, the South is our personal experience of it; the way we build it into our lives.

SPACE   The void, the absolute, the unknown God. The level of our being that is beyond opposites, unconditioned, eternal. See *Numbers o*.

SPADE   Attempts to cultivate self, or to discover what lies under the surface of consciousness.

SPEAR   Anger or words, that may impale or wound others, or even

328

self. Attempts to defend yourself from the ideas, influences, criticism of others.

SPECTACLES   Rose tinted glasses symbolise an idealistic view of life. Glasses represent attempts to understand things; the attitudes which colour your view of life.

SPECTRUM   Something showing many possibilities. Thus it can symbolise spirit manifesting its seven basic qualities. The range of your own personal experience, view or emotions. See *Colour*.

SPEECH   To make a long speech possibly symbolises a desire to express yourself, to make yourself understood, to see your inner feelings at work in the world, to be acknowledged. See *Impediment*.

SPEED   Progress, or lack of it. A state of tension, patience, desire to get somewhere.

SPERM   See *Germ*.

SPHERE   See *Circle*.

SPHINX   The riddle of our existence. Why are we here? Where are we going? The process of individualisation or development of consciousness. Can also stand for the whole being.

SPICE   Love of pleasure, of sensations, spice of life.

SPIDER   Any emotion or desire that devours the strength or purpose of your life. The spider is also used as a symbol of sexual orgasm, but only if we are terrified, disgusted or guilty about such feelings. Sometimes symbolises a mother's power, as in the way we are caught in the web of her desires and emotions. Inability to become independent of the mother.

SPIRIT   The level of consciousness that is one with God or universal life, without form, but is potentially all things. It is the centre of our being. But it has three aspects. Firstly, spirit beyond any expression or manifestation. In the church this is God the Father. Secondly, spirit expressing as power and matter. This is the Holy Ghost or the spirit that moves us. Thirdly, there is the result of the action of the spirit, God the Son, or the product. Spirit is that something which underlies manifestation and life. See *Name, Soul.*

SPIRIT-FORM   To see a spirit, a disembodied personality, in a dream may symbolise thoughts or feelings on death. May be a contact with the dead, or those about to be born. In some cases, the spirit comes to the parents and asks them to form a body for it as it wishes to incarnate, and they could provide a suitable body and family environment.

SPIT   See *Saliva.*

SPLINTER   Ideas or opinions that are irritating to your feelings.

SPOTS   See *Acne.*

SPRING   Growing. Time of inner unfoldment. See *River.*

SQUARE   See *Cube,* and 4 in *Numbers.* Also *Garden.*

SQUINT   Difficulty in understanding. See *Eye.*

STAB   Either refers to aggressive activities, hurtful words, or aggressive sexuality.

STAG   Male aspect of the soul.

STAGE   All the world's a stage. Can refer to your life in general; your stage of development; the inner self and what drama is being enacted therein; a desire to be in the limelight; or the centre of present interest or activity. Conscious activities. See *Actor.*

STAGNANT   Blocked emotions or energies. See *River.*

STAIRCASE   Similar to ladder in the symbolism of rising in power, in awareness. But is also used as a symbol of sexual intercourse, or the mounting excitement in sex relations.

STAMMER   See *Inarticulate*.

STAR   A hope, a wish, an ambition. Also the goal of spiritual quest. See *Glow, Numbers 5 & 6, North Star*.

STARVATION   Hungering for something such as love, self expression, recognition, self realisation. See *Fasting*.

STATION   See *Railway*.

STATUE   Unfeeling, like a stone. Unresponsiveness.

STEAM   Emotions expressed under pressure, as words spoken in anger; or things done after a shock or fright.

STEEL   See *Iron*.

STEPS   Usually the different steps taken in any undertaking. The first step towards marriage is courtship, the next engagement, and so on.

STERILISE   May express a fear of illness, of germs. Or an attempt to cleanse self. See *Bathing*.

STEW   We may be in a stew, or in a muddle or confusion. A stew can also represent different parts of self being unified into a homogenous whole, a sustaining power instead of a confusing one.

STIFF   Formality, rigidity, extreme morality.

STILE   See *Gate*.

STING   Hurt by what has been said or done by someone. To be stung to action, means pain has stimulated you to do something about it.

STINK   A fuss or argument. Unpleasant emotions.

STOMACH   Acceptance. It symbolises your ability to deal with events, situations, ideas and people.

STONE   To be unfeeling, heart like a stone, frigid instead of loving. See *Rock*. To throw stones is to give nothing but hate and coldness, to be unsympathetic.

STORK   The soul. Symbol of birth or babyhood.

STORM   Violent emotions, fears and thoughts. Anger, terror, or release of pent up feelings in a dramatic manner.

STRANGLE   Life or energy is being cut off by some attitude, fear or repression.

STREAM   See *River*.

STREET   See *Road*.

STRING   You can string along, be strung up, or be tied up emotionally or in your activities. Or you can feel tied up in knots inside.

STUFF   You can stuff with food or knowledge. You can be stuffy in your attitudes. Usually represents being lifeless and insincere. Also refers to courage or self assurance, as the saying, all the stuffing was knocked out of me. Can suggest sexual intercourse.

SUBMARINE   In some dreams may take the place of the symbol of the whale. See *Fish*.

SUCK   May refer to infantile feelings, as in sucking at the breast. Or may symbolise being a sucker or fool.

SUGAR   Enjoyable things in life, or pleasant things in self or others. Desire to cover up unpleasant things in our experience, or in others.

SUIT   See *Clothes*.

SUMMER   Maturing process, warmth of emotions, energy expressed outwardly, an outgoing personality. The height of your success.

SUN   Symbol of life, energy and spirit. Represents the whole being, or source of consciousness. See *Planet*. To sun-bathe means to expose yourself to life-giving energies from within. To drop away morals, opinions, attitudes, as represented by clothes, and allow your energies natural expression. All energy and health, happiness and success.
Or you can have sunburn, or sunstroke, symbolising an exposure to your inner energies before knowing how to cope with them.

SUNDAY   Relaxation, rest, religious observance.

SURF   Waves of feeling, inspiration, experience.

SURRENDER   To hand over your will. To become open to influence.

SWADDLING CLOTHES   Limitations due to the body, environment and personality.

SWAMP   See *Bog, Marsh*.

SWAN   In folklore and mythology people turn into a swan, or God takes the form of a swan. The swan represents the soul, or sometimes the spirit. It may represent the parts of your inner life that are not understood, or are hurt by your environment or others; the loving parts of the self that are killed or unloved, and turn into a swan leaving us with a sense of terrible loss.

SWASTIKA   See *Cross, Left*.

SWIMMING   Water represents our feelings, a river the flow of our feelings and energies, and the sea the whole personality from outer surface to the depths of the unconscious, so swimming becomes an ability to cope with our inner feelings and energies. Inability to swim in a dream means we have not learnt to launch ourselves upon the waters of our inner self. To swim easily is to have confidence in self, to trust life, to support our activities and efforts. To be at home in the waters is to feel at ease with our sexual urges, ambitions, desires and instincts. To be threatened by the waves or water, is to be afraid of yourself, of your own feelings, to doubt your ability to face life and its experiences. To feel threatened by your desires and energies.

SWING   May have sexual significance.

SWORD   Many meanings. May be your discrimination and search for truth; protective instincts or strength of character, with which you can also help and protect others. May represent the soul within the body, or sheath; willpower as used to defend the truth as you see it, your ideals, or those of others. Sometimes used to symbolise an inner faith, a trust, a heritage from your father or family; a tradition that is passed on; or to denote the cross. See *Cross*.

SYRINGE   Most often a phallic symbol. But may represent energy, emotions, ideas, injected into one, such as schooling, that may be foreign to your real nature, or of only temporary effect.

T

The twentieth letter in the Hebrew alphabet is Resh. It suggests the source or origin of something. The head of man as the governor or source of his activities.
This symbol of T is sometimes used to represent the cross. But where it does so, it stands for the evolutionary forces within, rebelling against the inertia of physical life, traditions, the past, our habits, resentments to change.

TABERNACLE   Man's body as the temporary house of his soul and spirit. Man's being, the open court being his body and outer life. The covered tent represents his intellect and hidden inner thoughts. The Holy of Holies is his inmost soul, the receptacle of his spirit.

TABLE   Outer or material life and affairs. A table is a working surface, and can be a symbol of the things we work on or at, or depend on for sustenance. It also often represents an altar, on which parts of our nature are worked on, changed, blessed, or surrendered to spiritual influence.

TABLET   See *Pill*.

TADPOLE   See *Frog*.

TAIL   May have phallic meaning. Or may denote your past or background, or even backbone, in the sense of strength and purpose. Instinctive urges.

TAILOR   The ability to alter attitudes or opinions. The power to alter your contact with others, or outer self.

TAJ MAHAL   The beautiful aspect of the soul, as a shrine for the spirit.

TALISMAN   Some idea, belief or emotion that helps to ward off fear, or the dominating influence of others.

TALKING   See *Speech*.

TALMUD   The wisdom gathered from life as illuminated by the inner spirit. We may have many experiences in life, but never look within to see what the spirit has to say, or how the inner self may explain them.

TAME   If something is tamed in a dream it means a changed relationship with that part of self symbolised. In the book *The Little Prince* by Antoine de St Exupery, he says that to tame is to establish ties. It is a beautiful book that well explains how we may thus change from distrusting parts of our emotions and energies, to establishing love and sympathy.

TANGLE   An inner confusion. Mixed up desires, ideas, anxieties.

TANK   Aggressiveness.

TAP   To turn on the tap refers to tears, or the emotions that produce tears, but a tap may also refer to emotions of a more satisfying nature.

335

TAPESTRY   See *Carpet*.

TAR   The unconscious. The inner self in its negative aspect. If we have a fear of heights yet have not the slightest idea why, the feelings of fear are emerging from the unconscious. Such fears could be represented by tar or soot sticking to the body, clothes or belongings. Tar on a road will also represent the unconscious, but in a slightly different way. To dig into it, is to attempt to get below the surface of self to find the hidden sources of behaviour and life.

TARGET   Ambitions, hopes, aims.

TARNISH   See *Rust*.

TART   May represent a woman.

TASTE   Usually refers to conscious or unconscious standards; taste in furniture, friends, hobbies. Also relationship to people and events.

TATTOO   An experience that has left an indelible memory or mark. Being bitten by a dog may leave a permanent fear of dogs. Being hurt emotionally by someone may have a similar effect. See *Scar*. A tattoo could also represent the effect on self of personal habits or efforts.

TAVERN   See *Public House*.

TAX   See *Bill*.

TAXI   See *Car*.

TEA   Often represents some stimulating idea, hope, person, or spiritual contact experienced. As with alcohol, it represents the change that can be made on behaviour by inner energies or spirit. Can also represent sociability, encouragement, sympathy, or relaxation. See *Coffee*.

TEAR   An emotion, feeling, sympathy or unhappiness.

TEAR BOMB   An experience that causes unexpected but copious emotion.

TEDDY BEAR   Desire for comfort, sympathy and love, of a nature that cannot hurt or answer back. Childhood traits and emotions.

TEETH   May represent biting remarks, hurtful words, especially if in a dream, the teeth are falling out. Also the maturing process, as when milk teeth fall out and adult teeth grow. Freud says falling teeth represent loss of semen, while Jung says that in a woman, falling teeth may represent childbirth or giving birth.

TEETOTAL   Morals or standards in life. Or may symbolise unwillingness to be influenced by change, stimulating emotions, or spirit. Or fear of doing something foolish if we express ourselves freely. See *Alcohol* and *Tea*.

TELEPATHY   May in a few cases be real telepathy during sleep. But could symbolise sympathy, agreement, understanding, or sudden insight into self or others.

TELEPHONE   Communication with self or others. If we do not answer it, it may suggest we are unwilling to listen to our inner feelings or intuitive advice.

TELESCOPE   Attempts to see the direction of life; or the effects of seemingly small incidents. It may symbolise making something big out of a small experience, as a mountain out of a molehill.

TEMPLE   See *Church* and *Tabernacle*.

TEMPTATION   Decision, or choice of action, and the desires or motives we will act upon.

TENNIS   See *Billiards*.

TENT   A temporary state of being, attitude or experience. Or an attitude of changeability, lack of perseverance, not building a solid life.

TERROR   Inability to face or cope with those emotions, fears, ideas or urges represented in the dream.

TEST   An attempt to deal with difficult questions or problems which life poses. Fear of inadequacy or of being tested. Doubts concerning fitness and capability in life, marriage, or parenthood.

THAW   To forgive, to melt hardness or coldness, to feel sympathy; to relax intellectual rigidity and so allow the inner life to flow, to express, to grow.

THEATRE   See *Stage*.

THERMOMETER   See *Barometer*.

THERMOS FLASK   Keeping alive some feeling, hope, or inspiration received. This can apply to warm or cold feelings.

THIN   Lacking physical power, material force, but may have more inner power.

THIRST   See *Drink*.

THORN   See *Splinter*. Painful experiences, which are difficult to pass through.

THREAD   The thread of thought represents delicate or fine connections or directions, that can be easily lost or broken unless great care is taken. Or can mean a fine or tiny idea, or energy, we may easily lose, as when life hangs by a thread.

THRESHOLD   Beginning of a new experience, idea, of life or decision. To cross the threshold is to begin the new thing. A wife is carried across the threshold to prevent her stumbling, turning back, or escaping.

THROAT   See *Neck*.

THUNDER Warning of stormy emotions, anger.

THYROID Symbolises speech, or the ability to contact the dead, or form delicate influences such as telepathic contact, into words or more defined impressions.

TIARA Spiritual consciousness.

TICKET To get the ticket is to get the idea, method, or capability. A ticket also represents the ability to pass through barriers or difficulties in life, as the price has been paid in life experience.

TICKLE Usually represents sexual stimulation.

TIDE See *Moon, Sea*. The ebb and flow of enthusiasm, desires, cravings, ambition or energy.

TIGER Power, anger, sexual power, inner terrifying urges. Fear of another person's anger or forcefulness.

TIGRESS A woman's anger or sexual craving.

TOAD Parts of the inner self that are cold and ugly. See *Frog*.

TOILET See *Faeces, Cesspool, Urine*.

TOMATO Passions, love, desire. Fruitfulness, ripeness.

TOMCAT Sexuality, aggressiveness and promiscuity. See *Cat*.

TONGUE Inner feelings, ability to communicate, expression of anger or dislike. Also the male sex organ.

TOOL Self expression, capabilities, practicality.

TORCH See *Searchlight*.

TORNADO See *Wind* and *Air*.

TORPEDO   Unconscious desires to injure others. Hitting below the belt. Also phallic symbol.

TORTOISE   Outer hardness or shell, in which we may hide when others try to contact us deeply. Slow but patient efforts. Sensitivity and shyness.

TOTEM   An aspect of self that relates to the spirit or intuition.

TOWN   Outer activities, state of being. The self.

TOY   Childhood habits, desires or attitudes not yet outgrown or changed.

TRAIN   See *Railway*.

TRAMP   Unacceptable parts of self and others, which can be held back and so depicted as a ragged, unsociable person. If an attempt is made to find ways to express or accept these repressed parts of self, then the beggar or tramp changes in subsequent dreams, and develops positive and useful characteristics. See *Aborigine*, *Beggar*.

TRANCE   Depends how the trance is expressed in the dream. It may represent neglect of outer affairs. Or can symbolise a becoming aware of inner levels of consciousness.

TRANSFIGURATION   When we fall in love with someone, the feelings, emotions, ideas, and energies released by the experience of love can change or transfigure our whole life. Similarly, the release of inner feelings, spiritual energies, new ideas, can have a transmuting effect upon us. It thus symbolises outer change through the release of inner forces.

TRANSPARENT   See *Glass*.

TRAP   See *Snare*.

TRAPEZE   Ideas or decisions based only on intellect, that may, unless we are very careful, result in a fall or difficulty. See *Flying*.

TRASH See *Dustbin*.

TREADMILL A feeling that life is nought but work and effort. That you are trapped by duty and work and demands made on you.

TREE Just as the snake or river represents uprising energies, the tree represents the same thing, but symbolises the structures of thought, abilities, characteristics, strength or weakness, developed in life through the expression or suppression of energies. As knowledge, the tree represents ideas or opinions that can be developed into concepts or convictions influencing conduct and relations with others. Sometimes these ideas are outgrown, and they may then be symbolised as dead wood, or a rotting tree trunk. The same applies to emotional or behaviour patterns. In this way a tree can symbolise the whole development and structure of your life. On some old manuscripts, we find this idea illustrated as a tree growing from a man's loins. This occurs in present dreams also. The energy manifested as sexual drive can develop beyond sexuality into sympathy, empathy, insight and spiritual wisdom, flowering into spiritual consciousness. Sometimes the tree represents the spine, its branches the nerve branches. A tree is the materialisation of inner forces acting upon matter, or the affairs of your life. Jesus is often depicted as crucified upon a tree. See *Cross, Wood*.

TRESPASSING When you force your attentions on someone, or vice versa.

TRIANGLE See *Numbers 3*.

TROUSERS See *Clothes*.

TUNNEL If the tunnel is dark, it usually signifies entering into experiences you do not understand and are not fully aware of, usually of an inner nature. Entering into unconscious contents. Reliving the experience of birth.

TURQUOISE See *Jewels*.

U

Shin is the twenty-first letter of the Hebrew alphabet, and symbolises cyclic movement, duration, time. This letter may also symbolise self as you, or even a cup.

UMBILICAL   Ties based on dependance rather than love or mutual interests, etc.

UNCLE   Feelings for, and relationship with an uncle.

UNDERGROUND   Usually symbolises inner feelings, unconscious direction and tendencies.

UNDRESS   To reveal true feelings, cast off restraining or inhibiting attitudes, fears or morals. A desire to display or express ourselves.

UNEARTH   To discover in the memory, or in self.

UNHARNESS   To remove the restrictions or moral restraints from energies and desires. See *Horse*.

UNIFORM   Conformity, orthodoxy. Also, authority, power, an expression of a universal activity. A priest has the power of the church behind him; a policeman has the power of the law.

UNION   Conformity due to outer pressure rather than inner direction. The power of united emotions, energies, ideas.

UNIVERSITY   The higher school of life. Can represent personal experiences at university, but in many dreams is used to denote the lessons learnt about self and life, once an attempt is made to understand self.

UNRAVEL   To understand; to untangle the confusion of anxieties. To heal fears and tensions.

URINE   To urinate is to release tensions, whether they are sexual, emotional, business, or educational. Urine generally symbolises sexual feelings, or experiences in the womb.

V

The twenty-second letter of the Hebrew alphabet is Tau, and represents perfection, worldly and spiritual success. The V also can represent victory, confidence or mockery.

VACCINATION   See *Syringe*.

VAGINA   Represents not only sexual feelings and desires, but is a symbol of complete womanhood and femininity. The vagina and womb, in their shape, represent the human qualities of sympathy, receptivity, loving, acceptance, desire to absorb. The womb is a symbol of fertility, the willing sacrifice of personal resources, life, energies and ideas, so that the new life, new love, new spiritual impulse, can take form. The new idea uses the old parts of self, but reshapes them, adding new features or qualities. The vagina and womb shape the growth of the new impulse or form. Woman, in her relationship with man, is not generally so active in the outer world, but through her sympathy, love, receptiveness and giving of self, shapes the man's actions and creative forces, as depicted by the womb shaping the creative forces of the sperm. On the other hand, a man is not generally so active in his inner, intuitive life, and his outer activity penetrates the woman's inner life, stimulating and directing her intuition and soul. Taken as symbols of the two parts of one person's nature, the penis represents the outer self, creative and active, intellect and reasoning; ability to succeed in business and social activity in its constructive elements. The vagina symbolises emotions, inner feelings, irrational self, intuition, sympathetic and inner contact with people, the ability to produce new ideas, new energies, new concepts. The two working together fulfil and complement each other, outer activity expresses, tests, and brings to realisation the intuition. But this inner receptivity, as it is faced with the problems and difficulties of the outer self and is emotionally and sympathetically linked with both this and with spirit, is stimulated to direct the intuitive and creative function in particular ways. Without this strong intellectual and outwardly expressive side of self, the inner would have no real direction of enquiry, but tend to become diffuse, lost in pointless enquiries, emotions, irrational beliefs or prejudices. The outer self without the inner self would tend to become unfeeling, with rigid and mechanical ideas and concepts, having lost the creative faculty and ability to conceive new ideas and values.

VALLEY   A descent into material values, gloominess, outer activity, practical issues, and sometimes into problems and fears. Can also represent the female sex organs. Cwm in Welsh is a valley between the hills, but also refers to the vagina.

VAMPIRE   Some idea or fear that is draining energy, ambition, resolution.

VASE   See *Cup.*

VAULT   May represent memory.

VD   Feeling of uncleanness in connection with sex.

VEGETARIAN   Restraint from passion, aggressiveness and destruction. The cleansing of self of actions and desires arising from sexual, aggressive urges, and thus a greater realisation of the spirit. It does not, as a symbol, represent the repression of aggressiveness and sexuality, but suggests a search for urges arising from the spirit.

VENEER   The outward self, which is shallow, and may hide desires, longings, reactions, which are quite different, and of a rougher, or coarser quality.

VENUS   See *Planets.*

VET   The healing energies capable of helping the instinctive and unconscious self to become acceptable in conscious life.

VILLAGE   Usually self, or the aspects of self, as is house.

VINE   The rapid growth of parts of self.

344

VIOLET See *Colours*.

VIOLIN See *Fiddle*.

VIRGIN The inner state of being, that has not been influenced by other people's opinions, forcefulness, or worldly values, but has remained true to personal inner standards and values. This state of mind can surrender to the spirit, and thus become conceived of a holy child, or higher consciousness. See *Madonna, Immaculate Conception, Vagina*.

VIVISECTION The unfeeling, ridiculous attitude on the part of intellect and reasoning, that it is quite apart from, and independent of, the instinctive, irrational, sexual aspects of our own nature. Consciousness is the product of unconscious activities. It depends upon the instinctive, biological processes just as the light of a bulb depends upon the wires connected with it. To kill and dissect these parts of self is to begin the process of death of consciousness.

VOID See *Space* and *Numbers* (o).

VOLCANO See *Eruption*.

VOMIT See *Sick*.

VULTURE The tendency on the part of intellect unguided by sympathy, to prey upon the weakness of others.

W
WADE See *Water, River*.

WAITRESS To be a waitress in a dream may suggest feelings of service to others, in providing their needs. To be waited on is the reception of help from others or within self.

WALKING In dreams one often walks along a lane, or up stairs, or through a stream, or across a field. Walking usually symbolises your present activities and experience of life; and the conditions where they are taking place are suggested by surroundings in the dream; the future is represented by where you are going. If you are walking backwards, it suggests a wrong attitude, or going down hill. Also, personal effort and ability.

WALL   A problem; a difficulty; or situations that confine, protect or shelter. The saying to hit your head against a brick wall indicates inability to solve a problem through thought alone.

WALL-PAPER   Often represents a veneer, or surface show, that hides the real person underneath. See *Veneer*.

WAND   See *Rod*. A wand may suggest the power of will backed up or directed by faith or belief.

WAR   Conflicts within self. If you want children, but are terrified of the responsibility, or of not being able to support them, this is a conflict; one feeling wars against the other.

WAREHOUSE   Memories, past experience, inner self, storehouse of thoughts or wisdom.

WARMTH   See *Hot*.

WARP   Inner feelings or energies misdirected by outer beliefs or fears. The wrong idea; misunderstanding.

WASH   See *Baptism, Soap, Water*.

WASP   Irritability, hatefulness, spite, anger, vengeance.

WATER   Water usually denotes the soul. It can thus be feelings, emotions, desires, moods, depending how the water appears in the dream. If it is muddy it means your feelings are influenced by outer circumstances, worries, material problems, or values. If clear and sparkling it symbolises faith, fearlessness, purity of feeling, hope and joy. Water takes the form of any vessel that contains it. So it represents your ability to be influenced either by fears, force, under-standing or ignorance, love or duty, and so on. See *River, Sea,*

Baptism. Or *Colour*, if the water is coloured. You can also be a wet blanket, can pour water on some scheme, or be wet. See *Liquid*.

WAX   See *Clay*, *Candle*.

WEAKNESS   In many dreams we find we are suddenly weak and unable to fight off an opponent, or too weak to run. This represents fears of not being able to deal with the situations that face us in life; of being too weak to say no to someone; of our resolves weakening; of having an inner weakness or fault. Thus we speak of weak kneed, or weak minded.

WEATHER   The weather is used so much in speech to indicate feelings, that in dreams it is almost certainly a symbol of a mood, and emotion. You can have a sunny disposition; be stormy; events, like clouds, can have a silver lining; a person can have a flood of tears; or we say dry up, brighten up, or stop looking so gloomy. Sunshine usually represents happiness, life-giving energies, growth, positiveness. Cloudiness is akin to despair, fear, depression, emotional unhappiness, gloomy attitudes. Raining can be a release of emotion in a pleasant relaxing manner, or a flood of emotion that overcomes you. Storms are anger, violence, release of emotions in a dramatic way. See *Inundation*, *Air*, *Water*, *Sun*, *Rain*, *Storm*.

WEB   See *Spider*.

WEDDING   See *Marriage*.

WEED   See *Garden*.

WEIGHT   See *Fat*, *Slim*.

WEREWOLF   Our own, or somebody else's rapacious desires, animal lusts, urges, hates.

WEST   The west symbolises motherhood, death, union between light and darkness. It represents life in the body, logic, reasoning, activity in material ways. It is union with the unconscious, a return to the womb or primordial consciousness.

347

WHALE   See *Fish*.

WHEAT   See *Corn*.

WHEEL   The ups and downs of life, the wheel of fortune. See *Circle*.

WHIP   Scorn, hatred, pride, feeling of being superior. Also sexual aggressiveness; the conflict between sexual desire and dislike, which resolves itself in whipping, that is, sexual enjoyment and hurting the person at the same time. Or it can symbolise guilt and horror of sex, yet desire for it.

WHITE   Purity, completeness.

WIDOW   May symbolise unconscious desires to be alone. Or can suggest you are not expressing your intellectual abilities and constructive thought, but depend too much on the emotions and irrational nature to guide you.

WIFE   Relationship with your wife. Your feelings for her. May stand for your emotional, irrational nature, or intuition. Or else how you see her. To think in the dream my wife is forever nagging, then it would be symbolising these same qualities in yourself.

WIG   False opinions, false ideas, attitudes. See *Hair*.

WILD   See *Tame*.

WILLOW   Flexibility, adaptability, or growing from the waters, or emotions.

WIND   See *Air*. Changeability, spirit, unseen influences in our life.

WINDOW   Our outlook on life, our contact with other people and outer events. See *Glass*.

WINE   Vitality, Energy. See *Alcohol, Tea*.

WINTER   Death, rest, inner processes that have not shown them-

348

selves in consciousness. Inactivity. See *Cold*, *Ice*. The falling away of outer activity to concentrate on inner consciousness.

WIRELESS   See *Radio*.

WISE MEN   When we start trying to understand self, and give birth within ourselves to an attitude of mind and being that links us with our deepest self, or spirit, the three wise men, or the ancient inner wisdom within us, comes to consciousness and releases its gifts, right aspiration, right perception, right judgement. These come to consciousness via the star over the stable, which is our intuition in our most mundane and instinctive levels of being. Thus the magi represent the wisdom of our past experiences and past lives, that becomes conscious when we give birth to the inner Christ. See *Guru*, *Christ*, *Star*.

WITCH   Inner forces of the unconscious that are being misdirected due to our conscious relationship with them. The desire to influence others via their unconscious fears, weaknesses, superstitions. If she is a wise, kindly witch she represents a mother symbol, inner wisdom, mother nature, intuition, or inner consciousness. See *Madonna*, *Mother*.

WIZARD   Unconscious masculine elements such as reasoning powers, outer activity, organising ability. Can influence our life negatively or positively very forcefully, due to being in touch with hidden powers or our unconscious energies and aspects of self.

WOLF   Ravenous desires, dangerous instinctive energies, anger, etc.

WOMAN   See *Female*, *Vagina*.

WOMB   To return to the womb, while it can represent an infantile event, really symbolises our experience or consciousness at that time. The womb represents a state of mind that is merged with all consciousness, yet undefined, lacking self awareness. To gain understanding of this, one has to realise what has developed in consciousness since birth. Basically we can say we have developed ability to think in words, in pictures, ability to speak, concepts and thought structures such as theories, beliefs, explanations of experience; also

349

our sense of individuality and separate existence. If we remove all these and ask ourselves what is left, this is womb consciousness, or experience of death. The Zen Buddhists call this the Void, and one of their meditations is What was my face, or what was my experience, before I was born? See *Vagina, Madonna, Eve.*

WOOD   In general, wood represents ideas, opinions, habits, that have become a fixed part of the nature. Just as the tree is originally green and supple but becomes hard and fixed as solid wood, so our opinions and philosophies as they develop are first pliable, then often become rigid—in which case, unless these habits and ideas allow for further growth, the life principle which ever seeks further development, is either repressed, or leaves the old wood to rot, and builds a new tree or house, whatever is the symbol we use. Thus, an old dying tree trunk symbolises parts of self no longer capable of adapting to incoming ideas and experiences. Cutting up wood, building new things with it, is to use old ideas in new ways, and so on.
However, a wood, or collection of trees, has quite a different significance. In folklore and myth, the symbol is used a great deal. Dante, at the beginning of his great poem, says he is lost in a wood. Heroes lose their way in woods, or are torn and cut while searching in a wood, and so on. Here it represents all the knowledge, education, facts, information acquired in life, and yet leaving the feeling of being lost amongst them, not understanding why we are here, what life is all about, what is birth or death. See *Tree, Carpenter.*

WOOL   May represent the soft, indulgent things of life, gentle thoughts, and pleasure, as in woolgathering.

WORD   In Indian holy writings, and in the bible, the same idea is expressed, In the beginning was the word. . . . Sometimes in dreams a special word is realised or given. Such words are symbols of creative power and should therefore be used in meditation, to rebuild the emotional and mental attitudes or conditions surrounding the word. See *Name.*

WORLD   Outer life, physical activities. The world of thought and imagination, depending on the dream.

WORM   Lowliness, decay, earthiness.

WORSHIP   To worship something is to allow it to direct personal energies and destiny and even to take on its qualities or weaknesses.

WRECK   See *Boat* and *Car*, etc.

WRITING   Expressing inner self. Clarifying feelings, materialising or recording them and thus making the inner feelings more defined, definite, less vague.

X
See *Cross*. May represent ten, Christ, or an unknown quantity. Sometimes used as X marks the spot, or a sign of error.

X-RAYS   Invisible influences in life. Penetrating insight, fear of being seen through, looking at the inner self. Fear of illness or inner faults.

XYLOPHONE   Playing upon another's feelings, or sympathies.

Y
Also an unknown quantity in mathematics. May symbolise You.

YACHT   See *Boat, Ship*.

YAWN   Tiredness, physical depletion, boredom.

YEAST   The tiny ideas or inner forces, that can ferment in the being, and change the whole life.

YELLOW   See *Colour*.

YOGA   An attempt to unite your conscious limited self with the source of its existence.

YOGI   Your real nature, spirit, intuition, inner consciousness. See *Guru* or *Indian*.

Z

Unknown quantity. Sometimes represents lightning or electricity.

ZEPPELIN   Usually refers to sexual urges that threaten intellectual stability. See *Air Raid, Air.*

ZERO   See *Numbers.*

ZIP   Connections with others; unity in attitudes.

ZODIAC   The whole range of inner possibilities. The course or path of the soul through earthly experiences. See *Numbers* (12).

ZOO   Inner urges and instincts repressed, or caged up. Moral sense.

ZULU   The power of the unconscious self, or instinctive self.